To Maureen

Howdy!

Vivian

Vance

Minnie Pearl
with Joan Dew

minnie Pearl

An Autobiography

Simon and Schuster | New York

Copyright © 1980 by Minnie Pearl
All rights reserved
including the right of reproduction
in whole or in part in any form
Published by Simon and Schuster
A Division of Gulf & Western Corporation
Simon & Schuster Building
Rockefeller Center
1230 Avenue of the Americas
New York, New York 10020
SIMON AND SCHUSTER and colophon
are trademarks of Simon & Schuster
Designed by Irving Perkins
Manufactured in the United States of America
1 2 3 4 5 6 7 8 9 10

Photo editor: Vincent Virga

Life Magazine photo © 1974 Time, Inc.

Library of Congress Cataloging in Publication Data

Cannon, Ophelia Colley.
Minnie Pearl, an autobiography.

1. Cannon, Ophelia Colley.   2. Comedians—United
States—Biography.   I. Dew, Joan, joint author.
II. Title.
PN2287.C25A33   792.7'028'0924 [B]   80-17332
ISBN 0-671-22914-1

To Henry . . .
For the good times

Acknowledgments

It is impossible to thank all the kind people who helped me with this book.

First of all, my friend Joan Dew, who put up with my erratic schedule and mental aberrations, must be the most patient of all writers. She deserves my heartfelt thanks. And, we had *fun!* (We hope you have fun reading it, too.) Let me also thank my family and friends who, along with me, racked their brains to recollect all the little details that bring to life the events of my past. Without their enthusiastic cooperation during its three "birthin'" years, this book would not have been possible.

MINNIE PEARL

Introduction

Excitement was running high at the Grand Ole Opry on the night of October 13, 1975. The Country Music Association's annual televised awards show had built to a peak of anxious anticipation as Tennessee Ernie Ford walked on stage to announce that year's recipient of the highest honor in country music—the CMA Hall of Fame Award. The large bronze plaque, draped in velvet, had been rolled into place on an easel, ready for the unveiling. Ernie began describing the winner, ". . . came to the Opry in 1940. . . ." And then I heard the name . . . *"Minnie Pearl."* The auditorium exploded into screaming, whistling applause as I made it to the stage in a state of joyous hysteria. Ernie unveiled the beautiful plaque and read these words:

> Humor is the least recorded but certainly one of the most important aspects of live country music. No one exemplifies the endearing values of pure country comedy more than Minnie Pearl. Born Sarah Ophelia Colley in Centerville, Tennessee; educated at fashionable Ward-Belmont College; joined the Grand Ole Opry in 1940. Her trademark—the dime-store hat with the dangling price tag and shrill "Howdee! I'm just so proud to be here!" made her the first country music humorist to be known and loved worldwide.

9

Through my tears of happiness, I looked at the etching at the top of the plaque of that silly ole country girl with the price tag dangling from the brim of her hat, and I blew her a kiss. Oh, if my cheering friends in the audience and the millions of television viewers watching only knew! That kiss was my heartfelt salute to her . . . "the first country music humorist to be known and loved worldwide." That wasn't how I had intended it to be. I'd had other plans. The truth is, if Sarah Ophelia Colley had had her way, there never would have been a Minnie Pearl.

Chapter One

I was a mistake from the start.

There was nothing in their ancestry to prepare my parents for the shock of a child who came into the world determined to be in show business. I'm certain my mother and father had never come into close contact with anyone who made their living standing on a stage "cuttin' the fool," much less spending a lifetime as a clown. On the contrary, show people were still considered wild and Bohemian when I was born in 1912.

Someone has said that each time a baby is born on earth, the angels in Heaven smile. When I was born they must have laughed right out loud. I'm sure they felt they had played some wonderful joke on my proud, conventional Southern parents.

Mama did love music and plays—done in good taste, of course. She was an accomplished pianist, and whenever a show was performed locally she played the background music on the old upright piano at the Opera House. These little recitals, plays and musicals were the only entertainment we had in Centerville, Tennessee (my hometown), until the movie house opened in the early twenties.

The Opera House was not exactly a house, nor were operas performed there. Actually it was the top floor above several small businesses located on the town square. But it was our seat of culture and we all loved going to performances there.

When Mama first came to Centerville as a bride in 1897 it was a frontier community as primitive as any log-cabin settlement in the Wild West. The town square was laid out on about two acres of flat ground on the crest of a hill. A brick courthouse had been constructed in the center of the square with a wide dirt street separating it from buildings on all four sides—a hotel, a livery stable, a saloon, a bank, a feed store and a couple of dry-goods stores, where they sold everything from patent medicine to hardware. There were no sidewalks, and when it rained the dirt street turned into a huge, four-block-square mud puddle. Hogs, wandering loose around town, considered it their private playground and congregated there to wallow away the day.

There were no cowboys shooting up the streets, but many of the men did carry guns, and rugged lumberjacks came in from the camps on Saturday night to drink and brawl at the saloon just like the wranglers did out West. There must have been times when my mother wondered if she'd left all semblance of civilization behind her in Franklin, Tennessee, where her life had been so vastly different. As a little girl I loved hearing Mama and Daddy tell about those early days.

Daddy's family, the Colleys, had come from Virginia and settled in Tennessee before he was born. He was the youngest son in a large family of lumbermen. They first moved to Manchester, Tennessee, then on to Franklin, 18 miles south of Nashville.

Franklin was a sophisticated, social little town, and still is. It was settled around 1799, much earlier than Centerville, which made it very different. The lifestyle in Franklin is steeped in old Southern tradition, lovely homes and gracious living. Aristocracy is more important than money, though the latter certainly isn't shunned.

One of the most disastrous battles of the Civil War was fought in Franklin on November 30, 1864. It was the town's blackest day. Five Confederate generals were killed in one afternoon and a sixth died of wounds ten days later. The bodies of the five generals were taken to a beautiful mansion called Carnton and laid on the porch until they could be sent to their homes. At that time Carnton was owned by Col. John McGavock, and it is now being restored and is open to the public. The fighting that day centered on the Carter house, which is also now open to the public. No army had ever lost so many leaders at once, and it left the Confederacy in shock. Franklin hasn't forgotten it to this day. The die-hard Southerners there never refer to the war as the Civil War. They say there was nothing "civil" about it. They call it the War Between the States.

Mama's people had been in Franklin for generations when Daddy's family moved down the street from them. He said he had his eye on her even when she was a teenager, but he was 17 years older, so he had to wait a long time before he could court her. He used to tell us how pretty she was, walking past his house in the summertime, and Mama would say, "I don't know why you noticed me. I looked so stupid in that silly bonnet my mother made me wear to keep the sun off my face." In those days it was important for Southern ladies not to have the slightest hint of a suntan. Only field workers exposed their skin to the sun. Mama was a slender, delicate-featured woman, very graceful and the epitome of a Southern lady. (I obviously did not take after her.) Daddy always said she was "the belle of Franklin and she never quit ringing." Mama didn't protest when he teased her this way because she was somewhat vain about her popularity as a girl. She loved to tell us about Sunday afternoons in Franklin. Parents of young ladies held open house so the boys could come calling on their daughters. A girl's popularity was determined by how many gentlemen callers came to sit in her parlor, and Mama told us often, quite unabashed about saying it, that she always had more callers than anyone.

Mama had a "drawing room" upbringing. Her home was filled with fine furnishings and oriental rugs, and the library shelves were lined with the classics. She played the piano for guests who came to dine at crystal-and-sterling candlelight dinner parties attended by white-coated servants. She and her friends went to romantic formal balls where moonlight mingled with the smell of jasmine and young men lined up to get their names listed on the ladies' dance programs.

Daddy's background was different. He was raised as a gentleman, but a gentleman of the woods. He was a man of the earth, tall and gaunt with big hands and feet, built rather like Gary Cooper, with a similar soft-spoken dignity. Daddy's business took him where he found the best virgin timber and by the time he met Mama he and his brother, Uncle John, and their father already had their lumber business established in Centerville. Uncle John ran the camps, and Daddy was in charge of the sawmill and merchandizing the lumber.

He didn't start courting Mama until after she'd come back from Price's College in Nashville, where she majored in music. After that they dated for a couple of years before he went to her father, William House, to ask for her hand. Grandfather House was a graduate of the University of Virginia and a very popular attorney in Franklin, and had become successful at an early age. He had sent mother to what was then one of the best finishing schools in Tennessee, and I doubt that he much liked the idea of his beautiful, social daughter going off to live in rugged frontier country. He told my father, "Why, Tom, you don't want that frail young thing. She wouldn't last a minute down there in Centerville. She won't know how to make a home for you in that wild country." But Mama and Daddy were so much in love they were able to persuade him to put aside his misgivings and give his consent.

I still have a fragile, yellowed copy of my parents' wedding write-up which appeared in the local newspaper. It says in part:

> Once more has Cupid donned his dress suit, and once more has he led a handsome couple to the altar and to happiness. . . . The Methodist church was crowded with an eager throng to witness the marriage of Miss Fannie Tate House to Mr. Thomas K. Colley. . . . Loving and tasteful hands had decorated the altar and chancel with holly, mistletoe and palms in harmonious profusion, the soft light of many candles, arranged with artistic effect, presenting a beautiful setting for the ceremonial. The audience was representative of prominent families in Williamson and other counties and of Nashville, and utilized every foot of available space. . . . The bride has had a ladyhood of pronounced social success, her charm of person and varied accomplishments rendering her exceedingly popular. The gentleman who won her hand and heart is a son of Mr. T. S. Colley and is prominent in both social and business circles, his genial bearing and business capacity being finely blended. . . . The *News* hopes that no sorrow may ever darken the life of this man who stands so high among his fellow men, and whose life is now rendered thrice happy by the companionship of the woman whose heart he won. . . .

I get such a kick out of the style of journalism that was used in those days. Imagine reading a wedding write-up today where the bride was described as having had a "ladyhood of pronounced social success," or the bridegroom as a man of "genial bearing."

Mama and Daddy moved to Centerville as soon as they were married. While Daddy was building their home they lived at the Dean House, the only hotel in town. That first year must have been difficult for Mama, leaving her lovely home and all her friends in Franklin to live in a hotel where the view looked down on hogs wallowing in the streets. She had a beautiful, elegant trousseau and no place to wear it. She told us she was more or less confined to the hotel until Daddy finished the house because she couldn't walk around the square without passing the livery stable on one side and the saloon on the other. Men ogled ladies who walked by these establishments, and Mama didn't think that was proper. Besides, she didn't want the hems of her pretty, long dresses to get soiled by the dusty street. There wasn't much for her to do at the hotel while Daddy was at work, so she read a lot and wrote letters back home to Franklin.

Her favorite time of the day was late afternoon, when Daddy left the sawmill to walk back to the hotel. She'd meet him halfway down the hill, then they'd stroll back together. They had to pass the site, on a hillside ridge above the river, where Daddy was building their house. They would stop to check the progress, discussing plans for each room down to the smallest detail. Daddy wanted the house perfect for Mama, so he let her help design it, and he personally picked out every piece of lumber that went into it. He used yellow poplar, which you can't get today. It was a white clapboard house with gables and gingerbread work on the front, and it had a wide porch that ran halfway around it. Years later that porch would become the scene of many of my childhood fantasy adventures. The old house is gone now. It burned in 1940, but I can still see it in perfect detail because it was the setting of many of the happiest memories of my life.

Mama named the house the Gables. Daddy had finished it just in time for the arrival of their first baby, Frances, who was born in 1898. Mama said she was almost as excited about the arrival of her furniture from Franklin as she was about the baby. After one entire year in a hotel she was at last going to be in her own home surrounded by her family heirlooms and all the beautiful wedding gifts that had been packed up for so long.

Fifteen months after Frances was born, Mama had Virginia. Three years later Mary was born, and Dixie came along three years after that. By this time Mama was very involved in raising her four little girls, as well as working to spearhead culture in

Centerville. Mama liked to *go*. She and Daddy were both gregarious and social, though I think Daddy went to many of the local soirees more to please her than himself. He gave her everything he could to keep her from missing the life she'd left behind in Franklin, and I think it made him proud to spoil her. She had the best horses, the finest carriage (called a barouche), and later the first bathroom in Centerville, as well as one of the first automobiles. Daddy never liked cars so he never learned to drive. He said, "I'll ride in one of those things, but I won't put my weight down." He preferred his trustworthy horses. But he bought Mama a classy four-door Dodge touring car with isinglass shades.

Every time I think about Daddy's distrust of automobiles I think of the story Minnie Pearl loves to tell on Uncle Nabob:

The first car came through Grinder's Switch on a hot summer morning when Aunt Ambrosy was sitting on the front porch shelling peas. She heard the noise, then looked up and saw this thing coming at her, so she jumped up, flinging peas everywhere, and ran into the house hollering for Uncle Nabob.

"Come quick," she screamed. "There's a varmit—biggest one I ever saw—just a-roarin' down the road."

Uncle Nabob went running out on the porch with his shotgun and fired at the automobile. It terrified the man driving, who jumped out and ran for the woods. When Aunt Ambrosy heard the shot she called out from her hiding place in the parlor, "Did ya kill it?"

"Naw," Uncle Nabob answered. "But I made it turn that fella a-loose."

Mama had begun playing organ at the Methodist church in Centerville even before their house was finished, so by the time my sisters were school age she was active in every group at church that was open to a woman. She had helped organize the Women's Missionary Society, and also the local Eastern Star Chapter, as well as a number of cultural groups. Since she had all the reliable help she needed at home, Mama was pretty much free to come and go as she pleased, and, as one of the social leaders of Centerville, she had become as proud of her new home as she had once been of Franklin.

It never occurred to her then that she might have another child. Her baby, Dixie, was already in the first grade. As far as she was concerned her family was finished, and Daddy had long since resigned himself to the fact that he would never have a son. When she discovered she was pregnant at 37, she was both shocked and thrilled. Daddy was 54, so the idea of siring a child at that age was undoubtedly an extra boost to his ego. It was also one last chance to get that boy he'd always wanted. My sisters say all the girls were excited beyond words about my impending arrival. Dixie was seven and they hadn't had a baby around the house in a long time.

My sisters remember that prior to my birth Mama and Daddy had never told them when a new baby was coming until after it arrived. (No mention was ever made about the "facts of life" in our household, even after I was growing up.) Virginia and Mary and Frances didn't even know Mama was pregnant with Dixie until Daddy came into their room one morning and said, "I've got a surprise for you." They squealed in delight because a surprise always meant a new baby or a new colt. Then he took them into the bedroom where he and Mama slept and showed them the new baby. She had had Dixie the night before right there in the room next to theirs and they'd never heard a sound. Years later when Virginia asked Mama about it, Mama said, "Of course you didn't hear anything. I had my babies like Indian women. I never let out a sound with any of them. Carrying on about it shows a lack of fortitude!"

For some reason, perhaps because she was older and there was a greater possibility of trouble, Mama sent the girls away the night I was born. They slept at the house of one of their best friends, Virginia Arnold, which they thought was a real treat. The next morning Daddy sent for them and they came running, so excited about seeing the new baby. Virginia recalls that I was sleeping in Mama's arms when Daddy took them into the room. She says I looked so tiny, with a fluff of pale reddish hair, and they thought I was the prettiest thing they'd ever seen. Daddy told them they had named me Sarah Ophelia—Sarah after his sister, and Ophelia after Mama's mother. My sisters called me Ophie and Daddy called me Phel, pronounced *feel*. (Later, when I was a little girl, he often called me G.M., for General Manager. He said I ran the house, which, in truth, meant I was spoiled.)

Mama let all of them hold me right away, and Virginia says they argued over whose turn was next and who had held me the longest. Since Frances and Virginia were the oldest, they took me over. They not only paraded me around the town square for everyone to see, they even showed off my layette. My older sisters say they would actually lay out my clothes on the front porch so their friends could look at the little dresses and touch them. I doubt if Mama knew about that. But she did let them dress and undress me 90 times a day. As soon as they got home from school they would rush into my room and wake me. They'd dress me up, then push me around town in my carriage, or Mama would get one of the men to hitch the horses to the barouche and we'd all go riding. The minute I could walk they began teaching me little songs and dances so I could show off in front of their friends.

I dearly loved my older sisters—it was as if I had five Mamas. They were all equally attentive and loving toward me, and still are. I'm sure the fact that I came along so late in Mama and Daddy's life had a lot to do with the way everyone treated me. I was almost like a grandchild, and they spoiled me rotten. I learned to play piano when I was about four, standing up and hitting the keys with two fingers. I could plunk out tunes by ear, sing at the top of my lungs and dance a jig in front of the piano all at the same time. And I was ready to do it *anytime*, with very little encouragement. I must have been insufferable, but my sisters thought I was too cute for words.

Daddy had his own method of showing me off. Since his last chance for a son was gone, he made me into a tomboy. He taught me to whistle before I could talk, and showed me how to do all the bird calls. Even before I could walk he'd sit me on the front of his horse and take me with him when he went riding around to the lumber camps. I can still remember the reaction from those rugged outdoorsmen when Daddy would come riding into the camp with me in front of him in the saddle. These were *rough* men. They had to be to survive their hard life in the wilderness. But I was never touched by gentler hands than when they'd reach up to lift me down from Daddy's horse. Then they'd make over me and pet me and pass me back and forth until it was time to set me up in the saddle again, and Daddy and I would ride off together. Oh, I thought those visits were such exciting adventures!

While Daddy was making me into a tomboy and my sisters were encouraging me to be a show-off, my poor mother was trying to raise a little lady. The fact that my natural inclinations leaned more toward Daddy's and the girls' influences didn't make her job any easier. But I learned very emphatically when I was about four that if I didn't act like a little lady around Mama I'd pay the consequences.

Mama was holding a meeting of the Chautauqua Circle at our house. That was one of the organizations she'd founded in Centerville. It was a ladies' reading group. They ordered books from Chautauqua, New York, a seat of literary culture in the early twenties; then they'd meet monthly to discuss and review what they'd read. Dainty refreshments were served and it was all very proper and dignified. I remember thinking it was like grown-ups having a tea party. I loved it when Mama got out her beautiful Haviland china with the delicate pastel floral motif, and her fragile little Japanese cups in which she served Russian tea. It seemed so exotic!

At this particular meeting, which was held in our library, someone asked me to play the piano. Everyone in town knew I could plunk out those little tunes, and normally I jumped at the chance to perform, often not waiting to be asked at all. But this time I pretended to be shy.

"Oh, I can't play," I said. Mama said, "Don't tell them you can't play. Go over to the piano and show them you can't." But instead I went over and sat down in a little rocker that I loved. Mama thought, "My, she's being sweet and ladylike today." I was wearing a new pair of ruffled panties—we called them underdrawers which I thought were just beautiful. Mama and those lovely ladies proceeded with their meeting, and all of a sudden she noticed a couple of them glancing in my direction with a peculiar expression. She looked over and knew immediately why. There I sat, my dress pulled up to my waist, one leg slung over the arm of the chair, the other one spread out as far as it would go, just rocking and smiling, dying for someone to look over and notice my new drawers. Mama was horrified. In those days ladies of any age did not sit with their legs spread apart. They didn't even sit with their legs crossed. They sat straight with both feet on the floor, or their ankles crossed demurely. I'm sure I knew I was doing wrong, but I was so determined to show off my new underpants, I went right ahead.

Mama stood up quietly and said, "Will you excuse me, please?" Then she took me firmly by the hand and led me from the room, where my underpants were exposed again—this time to a switch!

I can still remember Mama's whippings very clearly. She could make you dance with a peach tree limb! Mama believed in the old adage "Spare the rod and spoil the child," and she always said no child of hers was too old to get spanked. She was our disciplinarian, and she was wise about it. She never said, "Wait until your father hears about this," or threatened us in any way with Daddy. She dished out the punishment at the scene of the crime. I never heard her tell him about having to spank one of us.

Daddy had a different way of controlling us. All he ever had to do was say, "I'm disappointed in you," and it hurt worse than any whipping Mama ever gave. I'll never forget the first time Daddy ever disciplined me. It nearly broke my heart. And it scared me half to death! I was about four or five and I had misbehaved in church, which was nothing unusual since I was so spoiled. But this time Mama told Daddy he ought to whip me for it. When we got home from church he saddled his horse and told me we were going to see the gypsies. I thought that was wonderful. We all knew about the gypsy camp just at the edge of town, but none of us had seen them close up. What I didn't know was that Daddy had been selling them lumber and had gotten to know the fine old gypsy who was the head of the group. We rode into the encampment, where I saw colorful wagons and tents all around and a woman in a long, full skirt stirring something in a big iron pot over an open fire. An old man with a bandana around his head came out to greet us. Daddy didn't let on that he knew him.

"Are you the leader here?" he asked. The man nodded. Then Daddy asked, "Well, how would you like to buy a nice, plump little girl?"

I couldn't believe my ears! My daddy, who loved me so much, whom I *adored*, was offering to sell me to the gypsies! Tears welled up in my eyes and I clung to the saddle horn for dear life.

"Oh, I don't know," the old gypsy answered. "Have you got a little girl for sale?"

"Yessir, right here," Daddy said. "She's been bad in church and we've decided to sell her. I just wanted to know what you thought she might be worth."

The old gypsy went right along with Daddy. He reached up and felt my little legs and pinched my arm. Then he said, "Well, she ain't no *plump* little girl. She's mighty skinny if you ask me. I don't think she'll bring much."

"She'll fatten up if you feed her right," Daddy said.

By this time I was screaming and crying and clinging to Daddy's neck and begging, "Please, Daddy, *please* don't sell me to the gypsies. I'll never be bad again, I promise. *Please* don't sell me!"

After he let me carry on like that for a minute or two, Daddy had a big laugh with the gypsy, and I realized they were friends. Then we rode back into town and he bought me some candy. Is it any wonder I was spoiled?

I'm sure the reason the gypsy experience stands out so clearly in my mind (I can still feel that old man pinching my arm) is because my early days were spent in such a happy, carefree, secure environment. When I look back on my idyllic childhood it saddens me to realize those days are gone forever—not just for me, but for most children growing up now. Television, with all its benefits and potential for education, has stripped us of our innocence, even in rural areas, and children know more now about the seamy side of life than I did when I went away to college.

I grew up totally innocent of evil or wickedness of any kind. I think one of the reasons Minnie Pearl has found so many fans is because she retains some of this guileless, childlike innocence that characterized my formative years. No one locked their doors or feared their neighbors in Centerville. The whole town was my playground. I ran and romped everywhere, investigated everything, visited anyone I chose to visit, and had a wonderful time doing it. It was even better after Monnette moved to town and I had someone to help me create and share the delightful fantasies of my childhood.

Chapter Two

ONE morning on my way to school I saw a cute, dark-haired little girl with a Dutch-boy bob coming out of the house next door to my cousins'.

A new family in town was exciting in itself, but, at eight, I found the possibility of having a new playmate as good as Christmas. I hurried to catch up with her so I could introduce myself. She told me her name was Monnette Thompson and that her family had moved to Centerville that weekend. We talked all the way to school, hitting it off immediately like old friends. Within days we had become inseparable. The fact that she was a year younger and therefore a class behind me in school didn't prevent us from spending every possible moment together outside the classroom. By the time we finished grammar school there wasn't a nook in Centerville we hadn't investigated.

An adult looking at Centerville in those days would probably have described it as a typical, sleepy, rural Southern town. The population couldn't have been more than 500. (It's only a few thousand now.) The town square still didn't have paved side-walks, but at least the wallowing hogs had been removed and penned up. We had four churches; one school building, which housed grades one through twelve; a train station (important since the train was the only way in and out of town other than by horse-back); a couple of banks and Daddy's lumberyard and sawmill.

The hill where the town stands is completely surrounded by Duck River. Daddy's mill was located on the riverbank, down at the bottom of the hill from our house, west of town. Across the bridge nearest his mill and down a dirt road about three miles is Grinder's Switch, which is really no more than a spur track for loading freight trains. Cars were pulled off the main track there so Daddy could load them with lumber. (After Grinder's Switch became famous as Minnie Pearl's home, many people thought I'd made up the name. But it's very real and looks exactly the same today as it did when I was growing up. I won't say it's small, but when Uncle Nabob saw the first train come through Grinder's Switch, he said, "If that thing ever come through here sideways it'ud wipe us plum off the map!" Several years ago representatives of the L & N Railroad presented the original Grinder's Switch sign to Opryland Park. It now stands at one of the stations on the little railroad that runs through the park.)

Between the hilltop, where our house stood, and the mill below was a ridge that overlooked the river. Daddy had built a dozen or so houses along the ridge for his workers (white and black alike), and the settlement was called Colleytown. Our household help, usually wives and daughters of Daddy's millworkers, lived in Colleytown, and Monnette and I often played there with their children. There were no great antebellum estates in Centerville, but there were no shantytowns either. Instead there were comfortable, well-kept homes of various sizes and shapes scattered about tree-lined dirt streets, where children played and adults called to one another from yard to yard. It was a quiet town, a nice little town, but this wasn't the Centerville that Monnette and I saw.

Though the name doesn't imply it, Duck River is quite beautiful, and Monnette and I loved to cross the bridge by Daddy's mill, then climb the steep, wooded hill on the other side to a special clearing, actually a small meadow, where wildflowers grew in profusion. From that vantage point we could see all of Centerville spread before us across the winding river. We envisioned it as our golden city with golden houses inhabited by the most glamorous and fascinating characters imaginable.

My sister Mary was a strong influence in my life at this time and she encouraged our wild imaginings. Mary was a very dramatic girl, a writer who studied journalism in college and composed deep, romantic poetry. She taught me beautiful poems, which I enjoyed reciting, and one of them had a line that read, "We'll

come at last to the golden town where the golden houses are."
Monnette and I adopted that as Centerville's description, and our
imaginations were so highly developed we could look down
across the river and actually see golden sun rays reflected from
shiny turrets in our magic city.

Everything around us was magic. We'd pick wild violets on the
hillside, then break off the front petal and pretend the flower had
become a king, with his feet resting on a stool. We'd place him on
the ground and imagine he was receiving his court. We spoke all
the parts in dialogue that sounded like conversation from medie-
val times.

Another of our favorite places to play was my cousins' yard, next
door to Monnette's. In the summertime when the yard had just
been mowed we'd rake the grass into long rows (we did the same
thing with leaves in the fall), which made great corridors and
lanes for trenches in war games, or secret passageways in a castle,
or endless settings for the little plays we made up as we went
along.

We also had a wonderful game we played on my front porch.
Because our house overlooked the river, we could stand at a corner where the porch jutted out and easily pretend we were on the
prow of a ship, looking out at the ocean. We'd get all dressed up
in my older sister's clothes—terrific Gatsby-type outfits with
long-waisted dresses, nude stockings and headbands—and we'd
pretend to be elegant ladies walking the deck of a romantic luxury
liner, cruising moonlit waters en route to some exotic port. We'd
pause to speak with our imaginary suitors, all handsome and vying
for our attention and favors. We were so serious, and *so* dramatic!
It's strange but I don't remember the other children ever laughing
at us when we played out these elaborate fantasies. On the contrary, they often stood around watching, hoping we'd allow them
a brief visit to our make-believe world.

We were bad, too! I remember one younger girl who wanted so
much to be a part of our games that she would do anything we
told her to do. So we devised a game for her benefit called Queen.
We'd dress her up in a long gown, put a crown on her head, then
sit her on a throne we'd made from a box and placed under a huge
crepe myrtle bush. We'd let her enjoy her position on the throne
for a minute or two, then we'd shoot her. During the rest of the
game the poor little thing would have to lie there on the ground,
not moving a muscle, pretending to be dead. Of course we had

worked it out so that the game didn't get exciting until after the Queen was shot and naturally the little girl would beg to be allowed to get up and join in. But we'd say, "No, you can't. You're dead. If you don't lie still you can't play!" Looking back it seems so *cruel,* but oddly she doesn't remember it that way. Whenever I see her now she laughs about the fact that she got a lot of rest lying on the ground "dead" while Monnette and I romped around the yard battling dragons.

What I couldn't dream up to do, Monnette could, and no two children ever inspired each other's imaginations more. We're still very close friends. She's Monnette Dewey now, married to a man whose work has taken them to many exciting places, including Cuba during Castro's takeover. But we agree that neither of us has ever had a more dramatic experience in real life than in fantasy back in Centerville.

Possibly one of the most tragic things about the modernization of our society is that children are no longer motivated to develop a strong imagination. They don't have to entertain themselves. Continual, exciting entertainment in living color is just a TV dial away. I don't mean to keep putting down television. It's the greatest thing that ever happened for performers. You can reach a larger audience in one night on TV than you could in a lifetime on the stage, and for a show-off like me, nothing is more appealing than that. But we do pay a price for this incredible invention, and the stifled imaginations of our young is undoubtedly one of the highest.

The only place around Centerville where Monnette and I were forbidden to play was on the riverbank. Duck River could become treacherous after heavy rains. Sometimes the river overflowed its banks and flooded Daddy's sawmill. We didn't mind that a bit because Daddy would let us paddle around the flooded mill in a canoe, and that was great fun.

But we were cautioned not to play near the river even when the water was low, because there was always the fear that a child might fall in and drown. That happened once when I was about seven. A little girl my age fell in the water and disappeared, and the whole town went down to watch them drag the river. It was very frightening, and I got so hysterical Daddy made me go back home. My mother had a terrible fear of the water and never encouraged any of us to learn to swim. Consequently I don't know how even today, and I'm still afraid of the water. Friends laugh at me because I have a swimming pool in my backyard that I paddle around in wearing a life preserver!

However, I did overcome my fear of the river long enough to take a boat ride with a stranger one day. Monnette and I were on our way to our magic mountain across the river, and as we approached the bridge we saw a man rowing by in a small boat. He asked if we wanted to go for a ride and of course we said yes. We were adventurous children, and as our little world was so safe and secure we didn't think a thing about getting into a boat with a man we'd never seen before. We assumed he was from up river somewhere. He rowed us around for about an hour and we had a wonderful time. Looking back, I can't imagine how I had the nerve to get in the boat, considering my fear of water. I think Monnette may have dared me. That was a big ploy with us in those days. You'd do almost anything if someone dared you to. We had a horror of being sissy. Anyway, when I got home and told Mama about it she was horrified. I got a whipping and a stern reminder that I was not to go off anywhere, by land or water, with a stranger. I was too innocent to realize her concern might have something to do with child molestation or any of the other tragedies that can happen to children. At that time I thought she was afraid the stranger might steal me and take me off to be his little girl and they would never see me again.

I didn't fear strangers. I didn't fear anything except the river and rattlesnakes. Hickman County was known as rattlesnake country. And people got bitten, so we were on the lookout for snakes all the time. Daddy had told us about a man who worked for him being bitten in one of the lumber camps. The snake bit right through the man's boot. In those days if you didn't act almost immediately you could die because there weren't any prescription antitoxins. So they rushed this man to the mess tent, where the cook took a knife and cut a gash through the fang marks on his leg. Then the cook killed a chicken and slit it open and laid it on the wound. Daddy said the blood and the meat of the chicken turned black when it came in contact with the wound, which meant the poison was being drawn out. The cook kept killing chickens and laying them on the open cut until they didn't turn black anymore. That meant the poison was all out. I've told that story to several old-timers over the years and a number of them had heard of that same cure for rattlesnake bite, so I guess it was a true story. Anyway, the man lived, so it must have worked that time.

Stories like that stand out in my memory because there was little excitement in Centerville, and Monnette and I considered anything out of the ordinary an event. Going to church was an event, though it was certainly not out of the ordinary. Mama was there every time the doors opened, and we children had free run of the church as if it was a second home, which in a way it was. As strange as it may sound, the church was another place we played. I don't mean we were ever disrespectful in God's house, but we didn't think a thing about going in anytime we wanted and playing the organ or singing in front of an imaginary congregation. I loved that little Methodist church, and I spent a great deal of time there when I was growing up. We went to prayer meeting on Wednesday night and Sunday school and church on Sunday, and when I was small I also went with Mama to her Women's Missionary Society meetings. There was never a question in our family of not going to church. Church was like school. If you stayed home you got a dose of caster oil on the theory that if you were too sick to go to church or school you were sick enough to need the medicine.

When I was real little I sat up by Mama during the service while she played the pump organ. I can remember watching her feet pumping away as she played. She would move up to sit with the choir during the sermon, and I'd get close beside her so I could put my head on her lap and take a nap. I told that story not long ago from the pulpit of my church on Layman's Day. Then I turned to our preacher and said, "I still sleep through the sermons. I just don't have anybody's lap to put my head on now." He laughed right along with the congregation.

Sunday mornings brought a state of cheerful confusion to our house. Mama had a time getting all of us girls dressed and ready for church. We wore button-up shoes, long white stockings and sailor hats with our Sunday-go-to-meetin' dresses. She'd get us fixed up just so, then herd us out to the barouche (or later to the car) and off we'd go. Daddy rarely went with us. He said that was the only time he could get the bathroom.

It's funny that Mama didn't put more pressure on him to go to church, since it was such an important part of her life. But even though Daddy spoiled her in many ways, he was still the undisputed head of the household and she would never have *demanded* that he do anything. His theory about going to church was that he could communicate with God just as well at home. I once heard him say that he knew too many unscrupulous businessmen who were big churchworkers to be much impressed by what going to church did for you. Mama had an answer for him. She said, "You can't judge. Each person's salvation and relationship is with God, and I do not concern myself with the kind of hypocrisy you're talking about. That's between God and the individual. I go to church because I *want* to be there, and it's my business to work out my own salvation."

Daddy said, "Yes, it is. So you work out yours and I'll work out mine."

But even though he wasn't big on going to church, Daddy exerted just as strong a Christian influence on us as Mama did. He was a godly man, a man of faith. He believed in the golden rule and he lived by it. He even risked his life once to confront an angry lynch mob. It happened when I was about 12.

A black man accused of raping a white girl was being held in the courthouse jail, on the town square. The girl had been attacked the previous day on her way home to Grinder's Switch when she took a shortcut through the woods, and the whole town was up in arms. They arrested the black man because he fit a description the girl had given of her assailant. But when she was asked to identify him as the assailant, she said she couldn't.

After the man was put in jail the atmosphere in Centerville became thick with tension. Daddy went into town because talk he'd heard at the mill concerned him deeply—talk of a lynching. Even the word made chills run through me. We were all scared to death, huddled around Mama, waiting for Daddy to come home and tell us what was happening.

By dusk an eerie pall had fallen over the deserted streets. Houses were dark behind locked doors and drawn shutters. As night fell a crowd gathered in the town square—men carrying torches and ropes talked among themselves in low, snarling voices. A lust for violence was spreading through the crowd.

Daddy came home for supper, but didn't eat. After supper he went straight for the high top mantel—above the mirror over the fireplace in the living room—reached up and got down a pistol, checked to see that it was loaded, then put it in his belt. We all knew he kept a pistol up there, higher than any of us could reach, but we had never seen him take it down before. We girls were frightened out of our wits, and Mama was distraught. I had never known her to be in such a state. She knew what Daddy had in mind to do.

"Tom, you are *not* going back to town. You *can't!* Leave it alone. Let them have it out. They'll all settle down and go home soon. It's just wild talk."

"You know I have to go, Tate." Daddy had a tight, drawn expression on his face.

"No, no you *don't* have to go," she pleaded. "You mustn't go; you *can't* go!"

We all knew she was afraid of what would happen to Daddy if he went down there to tangle with a lynch mob, but we also knew it was futile for her to try to stop him.

"Those people are talking about hanging that poor man from the courthouse balcony, Tate." He spoke quietly, but I sensed the effort it cost him not to show the rage he felt inside. "They don't even know if he's guilty, and they want to kill him. I may not be able to stop them single-handedly, but I have to be there to go on record as a man who is against taking the law into your own hands."

Mama turned away, so frightened and upset she couldn't watch him walk out the door.

We heard later what happened in the square. Daddy went around talking to all the men he knew, trying to reason with them, calm them down. He wasn't alone. There were other men in Centerville who felt as he did, and they were also trying to control the mob. The mob leaders wanted to storm the jail, break into the cell and take the man out and hang him. Some of them were beyond listening to reason—until someone came out of the courthouse with the news that the man had been secretly transported to Nashville for safekeeping until his trial. The mob dispersed after that, and the people returned to their homes.

It's a funny thing that I don't remember the trial or whether or not the man was found guilty. What I do remember so vividly was my pride in Daddy that night. They had a saying in the country that there are two kinds of Christians, them that talks it, and them that lives it. Daddy definitely fell into the second category. He didn't pontificate piously on *any* subject, much less religion. But he lived an exemplary life—as a husband, as a father, as a community leader and as a businessman. So the fact that he didn't go to church never made us think he was any less a Christian than Mama.

I felt like Mama did about church, even when I was little. I loved going and I still do. One reason might be that it holds such wonderful memories for me of childhood and that long-lost time of innocence. When I go to church, even in a strange city, I have a sensation of going home. I love to sing the Doxology and repeat the Apostles' Creed. I love to hear the hymns and the words of the Bible. I love the stained-glass windows and the pictures of Christ, the quiet, serene atmosphere that gives me time during a busy week to contemplate my life.

I think Mrs. Floy Thompson's influence had a lot to do with my love of church, and my whole attitude about religion. She was my first Sunday school teacher and an important inspiration during my formative years. She was a wonderful woman who had a special way with little children. We adored her. If Mrs. Floy Thompson said Jesus loved you, then there was not a shadow of a doubt in your mind that Jesus truly *loved* you, loved you in a very *personal* way. Mrs. Thompson taught us about a loving God, never an avenging God. I remember the picture on the wall of the Sunday school room showing Jesus surrounded by little children of all colors and sizes. The inscription read, "Suffer the little children to come unto me." She'd tell us Bible stories and we'd look at that picture and be able to *feel* ourselves sitting around the feet of Jesus, listening to Him talk of God's love.

Sometimes the picture of the children gathered around to listen to Jesus reminded me of us gathered around Daddy at home, begging him to tell us a story. There was nothing we loved more than the tales Daddy could weave, and you could hear our squeals of delight all over the house when he'd say, "Sit down, daughters. I want to tell you about something extraordinary that happened to me today." This was one of his favorite tricks. He'd make up some outrageous story about someone we knew and pretend it had actually happened. He'd say, "On the way home from work I ran into Mr. Harv Grimes, and you won't believe what he told me." Then he'd go into this long, incredible tale and we'd scream and say, "Oh, Daddy, is it true? Is it *true?*" We were never *real* sure if he was telling the truth or not. He'd nod his head and go right on with the story. Then we'd ask Mama if it was true and she'd scold Daddy. "I wish you wouldn't stir the children up like this." Daddy would laugh, knowing how much we *loved* being stirred up.

I always thought Daddy would have made a good preacher because he was such a talented raconteur. There are people in Centerville to this day who remind me of how funny Daddy was and how well he told a story. Unfortunately, those old-time friends who knew Daddy are growing fewer and fewer.

Some of his best stories were about his brother, Uncle Joe, who had gone West as a young man to find his fortune but instead had been killed in a train robbery. None of us had ever met Uncle Joe because he'd left home even before Mama and Daddy were married, but we all had vivid pictures of him in our minds. To us he embodied all the rugged excitement and glamor of the Old West. We could see wagon trains headed across the plains, Indian raids, shoot-outs between the sheriff and the bad guys, gold strikes—all of it as clearly as a movie—when Daddy described Uncle Joe's adventures. Daddy was an avid reader of Western writers and poets, and I'm sure many of his "Uncle Joe" stories came right from the pages of those books. After we were older, Daddy confessed he'd never known exactly what capacity Uncle Joe had been operating in when he was killed in that train robbery. We thought that was hilarious. Poor Uncle Joe!

Daddy was seven years old at the time of the Battle of Franklin, and he could remember it very well. In fact, Daddy talked to us a lot about the War Between the States. He was proud of his ancestors who fought in it, some of them giving their lives. One of those was his uncle, John Shackleford, who was a lieutenant colonel in the Confederate army. He was killed at the Battle of Seven Pines, and his yellowed newspaper obituary, which we still have, extolled his courage and gallantry on the battlefield. Daddy said Uncle John lined his coat with Confederate money to keep the wind out, because "it wasn't worth anything, anyway."

One of Daddy's favorite stories, and ours too, was about an incident that took place during the Civil (or not-so-civil) War. After the Confederate army encamped around the town to prepare for their showdown with the Yankee troops, some of the young soldiers went looking for a home-cooked meal. One such boy from Kentucky ran into Daddy's brothers, and when they discovered his last name was Colley, the same as theirs, they immediately invited him home for supper. After the meal this Colley from Kentucky, whom they had decided was probably a distant relative, gathered them all around the fire to tell them about his war adventures. Daddy said the boy couldn't have been more than 17 and if you knew anything at all about when and where the various battles were fought that he was supposed to have been in, there was no way in the world he could have done all the things he claimed to have done. But he mesmerized those children with incredible tales of his prowess, valor, ingenuity and bravery under fire. To hear him tell it, he was winning the war single-handed. Before the night was over the Colley children considered their long-lost cousin the bravest reb in the Confederacy.

The young soldier spent the night with them. Early the next morning they were all awakened by a little black boy galloping down the streets, slapping an old felt hat on his horse's backside, hollering, "The Yankees is comin'! The Yankees is comin'!" He was no sooner past their house than Daddy and his brothers saw their courageous cousin running lickety-split toward the woods, in the *opposite* direction from the battlefield.

Daddy said that was the first big disillusionment of his life, and whenever someone did something to disappoint him he would say, "Well, that's just like the time our cousin deserted his troops."

Every time Daddy told us that story he would change it or embellish it in some way. We knew it by heart, so we'd correct him, saying, "But Daddy, that's not the way you told us the last time."

"Well, of course it isn't," he'd answer. "Don't you like it better with something new added?" Then with a twinkle in his eye he would say, "Remember, daughters, never let the truth interfere with a good story."

It's advice I've followed all my life.

My mother, Fannie Tate House, my father, Thomas K. Colley, and the house where I was born in Centerville, Tennessee. The curved porch on the left side of the house served as the "prow" of an ocean liner for me and my childhood friend Monnette.

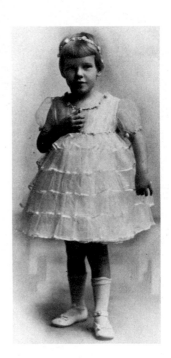

Sarah Ophelia Colley: as a baby with my mother, as a member of my aunt's wedding party and as the most "humorous" in the 1931 Ward-Belmont yearbook— from which a picture of the college's Rec Hall, Acklen Mansion, also is taken. Miss Pauline Sherwood Townsend, head of Ward-Belmont's "Expression Department," fascinated, intimidated and inspired me.

H. OPHELIA COLLEY
HUMOROUS

During my years with the Wayne P. Sewell Company of Roscoe, Georgia: as a demure Southern belle bent on a serious acting career, leading a chorus line of Sewell drama coach trainees and, in a studio shot, as a Sewell director. The publicity photo of Minnie Pearl, her first, was taken in November 1941.

U.S. Army, Signal Corps

On the road: Minnie as a troop entertainer in World War II (two photos) and with traveling companion Pee Wee King (dark suit) after a show with Gene Autry. Pee Wee was featured in the ninth issue of Minnie's Grinder's Switch Gazette.

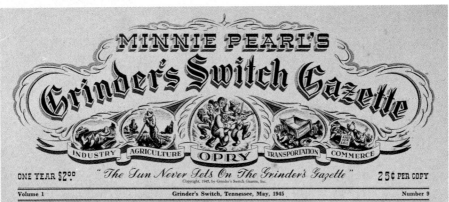

MINNIE PEARL'S
Grinder's Switch Gazette

INDUSTRY · **AGRICULTURE** · **OPRY** · **TRANSPORTATION** · **COMMERCE**

ONE YEAR $2.00 · "The Sun Never Sets On The Grinder's Gazette" · 25¢ PER COPY

Copyright, 1945, by Grinder's Switch Gazette, Inc.

Volume 1 — Grinder's Switch, Tennessee, May, 1945 — Number 9

"DON'T FENCE ME IN!!"

John E. Hood Photo

Story on Page 2

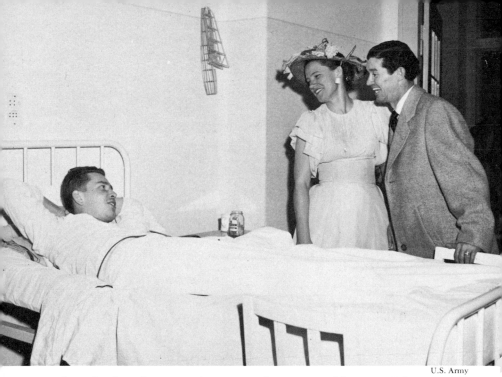

Me and my husband, Henry Cannon, after our wedding on February 23, 1947; with Roy Acuff on an army camp tour of Germany in 1949, and with Red Foley and Rod Brasfield at the Grand Ole Opry in 1950.

Mama with her girls (from left, Frances, Virginia, Mary, Dixie and me) in 1953; me being kissed by Tennessee Ernie Ford and Eddie Arnold on Ralph Edwards' This is Your Life, *my first network television appearance, in 1957; and Henry and me with Sam, our "gentleman" poodle, arriving in our Beechcraft for a show date.*

Gerald Holly, *The Nashville Tennessean*

Me with my men (clockwise from lower left), Hank Williams, at the peak of his career; Elvis Presley, arriving in Honolulu in 1964; Roy Acuff and Red Foley, cuttin' up in 1967; Jim Nabors, on one of our fun-filled trips to Hawaii; and Burt Reynolds, discussing a possible date (well, actually, he was in Nahsville taping a TV special and asked me to drop by—but I knew it was just an excuse to ask for a date).

Joe Rudis, *The Nashville Tennessean*

Charles Warren, *The Nashville Banner*

Three tearful events: my last performance at the old Ryman Auditorium; my 1975 Country Music Association's Hall of Fame award (tearful at the moment my name was called but not later, standing by the plaque and portrait in the Hall); and my 1975 Brotherhood Award from the National Conference of Christians and Jews (celebrated with Henry and Roy Acuff).

Frank Empson, *The Tennessean*

Mike Mauney, *Life Magazine*

Minnie Pearl, in a portrait presented with her Brotherhood Award and acknowledging applause at the Grand Ole Opry.

Chapter Three

BY the time I started school Daddy had added a couple of rooms to the original house. We now had four bedrooms and a big screened-in room we called the summer dining room, in addition to our sitting room, the library and the kitchen. There was a large back porch where we kept the foodsafe, a wooden cabinet used to store foods that would normally be found today in a refrigerator. Things stayed plenty cold in the winter, but I still don't know why the food didn't spoil in the summertime. We didn't have an icebox until later, and I was already grown before Mama got her first electric refrigerator. Our meats were cured outside in the smokehouse, and we had a cellar house built under the ground that doubled as a storm cellar, where we kept home-canned vegetables and stored fresh vegetables, like potatoes and turnips, for the winter.

Dixie and I shared the bedroom next to the only bathroom in the house. Since five girls, plus Mama, all took turns in that one bathroom it's not surprising Daddy had to wait until we were off at church to get in there. The plumbing couldn't be hooked up until sewage and water pipes were laid in Centerville, so for several years after Daddy added the bathroom we still had to use the outhouse and haul water from the kitchen to fill the bathroom tub for bathing.

I loved that old house. It was headquarters for my sisters and their friends. As any mother of daughters knows, one of the greatest untapped sources of dramatic talent in the world can be found among teen-age girls, and with my older sisters so close together in age, our household fairly vibrated with it. Everything was exciting or traumatic, from a first date with a new beau to a misplaced silk stocking. It was a happy house, full of activity, cheerful turbulence and a parade of people. Following the tradition of her youth, Mama held open house on Sunday afternoons so boys could call on Frances, Virginia and Mary. Some of them would come from as far away as Lewisburg or Columbia, which made them seem like glamorous city boys to me. Other young people from Centerville would drop by, and Mama would serve sandwiches and tea. It was an exciting time for me, and I couldn't wait until I was old enough to receive gentlemen callers of my own. I recently discussed this period of my life with my sisters. I found out something I'm afraid I already knew. I was not only a spectator at all these exciting events, I was (much to my sisters' chagrin) an intruder. They say that everytime they turned around a little freckled-face girl appeared, all eyes and ears as tentative courtship moves were made. I know they wanted to wring my neck, but it is significant that they never really slapped me aside. They say they told Mama to keep me out of the way. But Mama was smart; she had a built-in chaperone. I'm embarrassed to say I not only rode in the car with my sisters and their dates, but I sat *between* them!

My favorite room in the house was the library. Not many families living in Centerville at the turn of the century had a special room in their home designated as a library, and we felt very fortunate to have all the wonderful books that Mama and Daddy had accumulated in the big glass-enclosed bookshelves that lined the walls on either side of the fireplace. Among my sisters' friends, there were several who loved reading as much as we did, and our books were loaned freely. It was said that the Colley house was the best library in town. Of course it was also the only "lending" library in town. We didn't get a public library until much later, and our school had very few books that students were allowed to take home.

Our library had a window seat, which I considered my own special place. The window overlooked the river, winding down below, and the steep hill Monnette and I loved rising on the other side. I used to curl up in that window seat and, with a new book, lose myself in dreamworlds for hours. But that wasn't all. It didn't take much imagination to make the window seat a stage. All you had to do was remove the cushions and it became a perfect platform from which to perform. It was made to order for me. My audience, usually composed of my sisters and their friends, would sit on the oriental rug while I stood on my little stage to do my latest reading or dance. No wonder I was precocious. They encouraged me in every way, applauding and carrying on as though every silly thing I did was marvelous.

When the weather was bad we played on the oriental rug, using its unusual pattern as a giant gameboard, whiling away hours in front of a cozy fire.

Looking back, I wonder how Daddy stood being surrounded by such unceasing activity, dominated by so much girlish silliness. But it never bothered him. He would often doze in his favorite chair with all of us talking and giggling at his feet. There was a pennant on the wall in one of the rooms that read "B.P.O.E.," which stood for something to do with the Elks Lodge. But Daddy said it meant Best People on Earth, and we knew that's how he felt about his household. He was always the calm eye in the center of our storms of activity.

Summertimes were best. After Frances and Virginia went away to college they'd bring home girlfriends during vacation, to stay for weeks at a time and our home was like a dormitory. I remember it as a constant round of parties and dances, with the girls looking so pretty in their pastel summer frocks, being courted by handsome young men in ice-cream suits and dapper straw hats.

Once in a while Mama and Daddy would get dressed up to go to a party themselves and we all thought they were the handsomest couple in Centerville. We especially approved of the parties at the Nunnelly place, because we were invited to go along. We'd leave in the barouche about dusk, all dressed up in our best finery. The Nunnelly plantation was several miles from town, a grand antebellum estate with a huge colonial mansion. When the Nunnellys entertained, they did it on a lavish scale, which made a lasting impression on us children. I remember the elegant drawing rooms with lighted tapers and the smell of the beeswax they used to polish their fine, imported furniture.

Daddy used to tell us a story about Mr. Nunnelly that we loved. He was a typical Southern landowner, lord of the manor, but a kind and courteous gentleman who placed great value on good manners. A tenant farmer who worked his land came to call about business one day, just as the Nunnelly family was sitting down to their midday meal. Mr. Nunnelly invited the man to stay for dinner, and this nice sharecropper, who wasn't accustomed to eating off fine linen, china and crystal, felt embarrassed and out of his element. Sensing the man's discomfort, Mr. Nunnelly did everything possible to make his guest feel at home. The meal was served family style, with a servant bringing the various dishes to the table which were then to be passed around. But when a compote dish of homemade jelly was placed in front of the man, he mistakenly thought it his serving portion, so he began eating it from the dish. Daddy said Mr. Nunnelly went right on talking, never missing a beat, meanwhile motioning to the servant to bring *everyone* a small dish of jelly. The children were horrified and didn't want to eat it, but Mr. Nunnelly stared them down, so they followed the man's example and began spooning up jelly from their bowls. Later they were all sick and told their mother they never wanted to eat that kind of jelly again. I have thought often that Mr. Nunnelly's quick thinking that day epitomized Southern hospitality. His guest never knew he'd done anything wrong.

While my older sisters passed long summer twilights in flirtations in the parlor, or on the front porch swing, Monnette and I received imaginary callers of our own in the playhouse Daddy had built in the backyard. Or we'd sit on the "golden stairway" (which was actually a sequence of wooden steps set in the steep hillside leading from the road up to our side yard) and count fireflies as we watched carefree couples stroll past en route to Coble & Peeler's Drugstore for chocolate sodas and cherry Cokes.

It was a romantic time, and, since I was a very romantic little girl, all of this made an indelible imprint on my mind. Imagine, then, how thrilled I was to learn that my oldest sister, Frances, was getting married and that the ceremony was going to be held in my favorite place, our library!

I was about seven, and the flurry of planning and preparation going on at home was almost too exciting to bear. I wanted to be in on every discussion and decision, and consequently stayed underfoot more than ever for fear I'd miss out. Aunt Dixie, Uncle John's wife, was in charge of floral arrangements, and on the morning of the wedding when I walked into the library and saw the finished results of her weeks of preparation, I gasped in delight. The room had been transformed into a fairyland of flowers and greenery, with the fireplace, where the couple were to stand and exchange their vows, completely hidden behind a bank of pastel blossoms and lacy fern.

My excitement mounted as, first the wedding party and then the guests began to arrive. Frances' bridegroom, Gordon McDaniel, a handsome young man from Franklin, was being kept in another room so there would be no chance of his seeing the bride before the ceremony. He appeared dutifully nervous, which I found very cute. Mama had kept me out of Frances' room while Frances was dressing—she had enough to think about without me adding to the confusion—so I hadn't seen her in her gown. Then my cousin began playing "Here Comes the Bride" on the piano and Frances walked into the library on Daddy's arm. She looked so beautiful in her wedding gown it almost took my breath away. I didn't take my eyes off her until I heard Daddy's response to the preacher's question "Who gives this woman in marriage?" His voice sounded strained and funny as he said, "I do." I looked at him sharply and saw him step back and turn his head slightly to the side. Then I realized he had tears in his eyes! The sight momentarily burst my bubble of romantic illusion. I felt a lump in my throat. Daddy got out his handkerchief and tried to wipe away his tears without being seen. Watching him like to have killed me. I had never seen my daddy cry, never even thought about the possibility, and I couldn't bear it.

Before the wedding Frances had kidded me about crying at the ceremony. She said, "Aren't you going to cry buckets of tears when I get married? I'll be disappointed if you don't, because it will mean you don't love me." I was so crazy about her—she had practically raised me—and she knew I'd hate to see her go, but I had been too caught up in the excitement of the preparations to feel the full impact of her leaving. Then, when I saw Daddy cry, it struck me suddenly that our close family, this secure haven of mine, was about to change. For the first time we were being split apart, losing one of our own. I began crying too, out of sympathy for Daddy, and also because I was suddenly shaken, hit by the realization that my family wouldn't be together forever, as they had been all my life.

Later that afternoon we all went down to the railroad station to see Frances and Gordon off on their honeymoon. Gordon was associated with the Nashville, Chattanooga, and St. Louis Railroad, and they had sent a private car all the way from Nashville and attached it to the regular 4 p.m. train that passed through Centerville each day. That was the first time a private coach had ever come to town, and we were enthralled by it. I'll never forget seeing my sister, looking so radiantly happy, with her bridegroom sitting beside her on a plush sofa in that luxurious car. The hand-polished panelwood walls reflected soft light from the Tiffany fixtures, which seemed to bathe the room in a golden yellow glow.

That was my first exposure to real first-class luxury travel. This was the crème de la crème—J. P. Morgan and Nelson Rockefeller didn't ride any more luxuriously than my sister traveled that day, and I distinctly remember a little voice somewhere deep inside saying, "This is for me!"

My desire to go first class in the outside world was reconfirmed a few years later when my second sister, Virginia, got married.

Unlike Frances' small, sweet wedding at home, Virginia was having a grand affair at the church, a morning wedding to be followed by a reception breakfast at our house. Again, I was excitedly caught up in plans and preparations. My sister Dixie played the organ so Mama could sit in the front row of the church as mother of the bride.

Virginia wore a beautiful, pale pink chiffon wedding gown with a matching horsehair picture hat trimmed in flowers. Mary was maid of honor, and her gown was a soft lime green. Mama got mad with her because she came down the aisle crying. She said, "I didn't spend all that money on a dress to have you ruin the looks of it by screwing your face up." I think Virginia wanted us all to cry at her wedding as we had at Frances', but the big church ceremony just wasn't as touching as the more intimate one at home, even though we hated for her to go just as much.

That wedding took place more than 50 years ago, but I can still remember the dress I wore as though it were yesterday. I thought it was prettier than either Virginia's or Mary's. It was powder blue georgette with a Peter Pan collar and short puffed sleeves trimmed in ecru lace. It fell straight down from the collar, in the fashion of the twenties' flapper dresses, with a skirt that flared out from an insertion of lace around my hips. Oh, did I think I was something!

Bill Burns, Virginia's bridegroom, was one of the most attractive men I'd ever seen. He and his groomsmen—all big-city boys from

Columbia, Tennessee—wore morning suits with gray gloves and ascots, and they all looked like prince charmings to me.

My aunt from Nashville had arranged for a caterer to do the food for the reception. I had never heard of a caterer in my life. There was no such thing in Centerville. When we returned home after the wedding and I saw the buffet table laden with these incredible dainty little ice-cream figures shaped like ladies' slippers, lilies of the valley and tulips, I was just as impressed as I had been with Frances' private Pullman car. There were little finger sandwiches cut into various interesting shapes and miniature individual cakes adorned with roses and cupids. It looked like a feast in fairyland. To this day I can't imagine how they brought all those ice-cream figures down from Nashville, 50 miles away, without their being ruined. We had no refrigeration, so they had to have brought them in that morning by car. In my young, impressionable mind that fancy food represented another world, a world I very much wanted to see more of. Suddenly I had a prescience of jets, limos, hotel suites, room service, menus with no prices and all the other accoutrements of the big time. And I made up my mind that I *liked* it and *wanted* it. (Now I realize how transitory that all is. I've seen more unhappy people in that luxury world than I care to remember.)

Chapter Four

THERE was another family wedding that I recall vividly, but for an entirely different reason.

When I was about four, my mother's youngest sister asked to have me in her wedding. A cousin my same age was coming down with her family from Baltimore, and they thought it would be cute to have both little girls in the ceremony. The wedding was to take place at the home of another of Mama's sisters in Nashville, where an impressive winding staircase afforded the perfect backdrop for the bride to make a dramatic entrance. She was to come down the stairs to the music of the wedding march while my little cousin and I followed behind holding the long train of her formal white gown. The night before, we had rehearsed the descent down the stairs over and over, until the adults felt fairly secure that we children knew exactly what to do.

The next afternoon at dusk, as the wedding was about to begin, everyone lined up upstairs, ready for the grand entrance. Mama struck the first chords of the wedding march on the piano and we started slowly down. I was wearing a little pink tulle dress with dainty pink and white satin rosebuds trimming the neckline and skirt. Mama said she and Daddy, who was one of the groomsmen, were so proud of me. We got about halfway down the stairs, with the guests below looking up enthralled at the bride, when suddenly I stopped dead in my tracks and began hollering at the top of my lungs. My outburst brought a quick halt to the wedding processional. At first everyone thought something was wrong with me, but it was soon apparent that I was simply having a tantrum. My mother was mortified. She told Daddy to take me outside immediately and spank me. The wedding resumed without me, but I had broken the romantic spell and I'm sure my aunt never forgave me for it. (Looking back on that episode I am forced to admit I just might have pitched that fit to upstage the bride. I hated to have the spotlight on someone else, even at that tender age.)

When Daddy got me outside, he sat me down on the back steps and said, "Phel, *why* did you do that?" I'm told I answered, "I already married. I don't wanna marry again." I thought I had done my part the night before with all that rehearsing, and going through it again that afternoon was keeping me from playing. Typical of Daddy, he wasn't mad. He understood a four-year-old's impatience. He said, "Well, tell you what. Let's walk down the street and see if we can find an ice-cream cone." And we did. It's no surprise I was as spoiled as I could be.

That was one performance the family wanted to forget, but they were usually delighted with my precocity. My first appearance before an audience (other than my family) took place when I was 18 months old. Miss Daisy Nixon, Centerville's leading (and only) piano teacher, was holding a recital at her studio above her husband's grocery store. Since all four of my older sisters took lessons from her, I doubt that she had much choice when they suggested I go out to do a little song and dance they'd taught me at home. Everyone thought it quite remarkable that I had memorized the words to a song at such a young age. I don't remember this, of course, but in years to come my sisters told me I didn't hesitate a moment when they said, "Go on out there and sing." I marched on stage and did my number as unselfconsciously as I did it at home on the library window seat. My family should have seen the handwriting on the wall right then, but they never dreamed my showing off for friends and relatives would lead to a lifetime of doing the same thing in front of strangers.

I can remember singing and playing piano at World War I bond rallies when I was no more than six or seven. Mama was big on civic responsibilities, so you can imagine how active she became in working to help the war effort. She would take me to the town square where a platform had been erected and draped in red, white and blue bunting. A piano had been put up there so Mama could play popular war songs to get the people's patriotic spirit going before they started the sales pitch for bonds. She'd offer to let me sing and play for the price of a bond, and I'd do songs like "Over There" and "If He Can Fight Like He Can Love, It's Good-bye Germany." Dixie taught me that one because she thought it was so cute to hear a little girl singing a song about a sweetheart. I loved the applause and didn't care whether they bought bonds or not, as long as they cheered for me.

I tried to get my own job performing at age 10, but Mama soon put a stop to that. I didn't receive enough allowance to go to the movies as often as I wanted (which would have been daily if it had been left up to me), so I made a deal with old Mr. Rulander who ran the theater. I told him if he'd let me in free I'd play background music during the films. He quickly agreed because he didn't have a regular pianist (undoubtedly owing to lack of funds). I'd play real sad songs during the sad scenes, romantic music during the love scenes and fast, exciting music during the action. Remember, they were silent movies, so any sound at all was an improvement. I did this for several weeks before Mama found out about it, when she suggested, very firmly, that I was much too young to be hanging out at the movie house playing piano.

A couple of years before this a woman had come to town to visit relatives for the summer, and word soon got around that she was an "expression" teacher. She would be called an acting coach today, but in those days the word *actor* still had naughty connotations. She agreed to give expression lessons to some of the children in Centerville while she was on vacation, and of course I was among the first to sign up. She was young and attractive, a delightful lady, and I was fascinated by her. She taught us cute little poems and monologues, which enlarged my repertoire considerably and made me more insufferably eager to show off than ever.

Much later, when I took expression in high school, I learned poems that I knew Daddy especially liked so I could recite them for him. One of his favorites was "That Old Sweetheart of Mine," by James Whitcomb Riley. Mama would play "Love's Old Sweet Song" softly in the background while I gave the reading. It began,

As one who cons at evening
O'er an album all alone,
And muses on the faces
of the friends that he has known,
So I turn the leaves of fancy,
'til in shadowy design,
I greet the smiling features
of that old sweetheart of mine.

The cadence of the poem fit perfectly with the melody of "Love's Old Sweet Song," and Daddy would sit back in his chair and listen with the most peaceful, loving expression on his face.

All the way through the poem you think the writer has lost his love, and then in the very last stanza it says,

But wait! I hear a footstep.

And he feels the soft touch of a hand on his shoulder as he turns to see the charming face of the woman he married so many years before—"that old sweetheart of mine."

I was always delighted that it turned out that way because I wanted everything to have a happy ending. Like Daddy, I was a romantic. I had read so many fairytales about romantic princesses that I could see myself in their glass shoes. I knew I wasn't pretty then—I had freckles, a knobby little body and straight, reddish blond hair (it seemed I was always blowing bangs out of my eyes) —but I never doubted that some day I would turn into a beautiful princess. I had heard my sisters say I was adorable for as long as I could remember, so it came as a shock to me—when I was about seven or eight—to discover others thought of me quite differently.

In those days ladies dressed up in the afternoon and went calling on one another. If a friend wasn't home, a servant answered the door and took the ladies' calling cards, placing them on a silver tray on the front hall table. One particular day Mama told me to answer the door if anyone called and say she was dressing and would be down in a minute. Two ladies came to the door and I invited them in, showed them to the library and excused myself. They thought I was out of earshot, but I had paused by the hall table to examine a calling card left the day before. I heard one of the ladies say, "My, she's a plain little thing, isn't she?" The other lady agreed.

The words *plain little thing* stung, but I knew instinctively she was telling the truth. I went on outside and sat on the steps, looking across at the river, thinking about what she'd said. I didn't cry or anything, but it surprised and disappointed me to realize I was plain. I had honestly never thought of myself in that way. In fact I probably thought I was really cute, even though I knew I wasn't as pretty as some of my girlfriends. What that woman said made a deep impression on me, and it was actually a help many years later when I finally had to face the fact that my future lay in comedy, not drama. Remembering her words made it all come together, because I knew I could never be the beautiful lady leaning over the balcony tossing her scarf to the handsome knight passing below on his magnificent white steed.

I should have known my forte was comedy much earlier than I did. Something happened in high school that ought to have told me I had a natural talent for making people laugh, but it didn't. At the time it hurt too much for me to see anything valuable in the experience.

A beauty contest was being held to raise money for the school, and as president of the PTA, Mama was in charge of the event. It was just a local contest, but people turned out to see things like that then because there wasn't anything better to do. I would never have considered entering the contest, knowing as I did by then that I was no beauty, but as it turned out I had no choice. Mama came to me about 6:30 the evening of the contest and said she'd just gotten word one of the contestants was too ill to appear, so I would have to take her place. I said, "Mama, I *can't* be in a beauty contest. Get someone else to do it." She said, "I can't. Anyone I could ask at this late date would get her feelings hurt because she hadn't been asked at first." When Mama's mind was set on something, there was no point in arguing, so I rushed around trying to decide what dress to wear. I didn't know what to do with my hair, but I thought I might get by if I put on theatrical makeup like I'd used in a couple of high school plays. I had a good figure by then, and I knew how to walk across a stage with confidence.

I went down to the auditorium with Mama. When I walked backstage some of the others said, "What are you doing here?" in a tone that implied I surely must be there for some purpose other than competing. I explained what had happened and there were a few giggles, but I shrugged them off. After all, these were my friends and I knew they didn't mean to be cruel. I got in line where the absent girl was supposed to have stood. Mama marked her name off the emcee's list and scribbled mine in above it. Then she gave him the list and went to the piano. The contestants paraded out one by one as she played "A Pretty Girl Is Like a Melody." (To this day, I can't hear that song without a twinge of embarrassment.) When my turn came, the emcee said, "And now ladies and gentlemen, representing the Centerville Ice Company, we have . . . Ophelia Colley????" The way he put those question marks in his voice after my name was all the encouragement the audience needed to start laughing. They *roared,* or at least it seemed to my sensitive ears that their laughter was as loud as a roar. I wanted the floor to open up and swallow me. Now I *love* it when people start laughing the minute I walk on stage, but not then. I was playing it straight, and they were falling out of their seats laughing over it. I decided, "Well, I'll give them a show." So I did a few turns, holding my head high and my back straight, and they laughed all the more. I thought, "Oh, Lord, just let it be over and I'll *never* let myself get into something like this again."

Afterward everyone said. "You were so *funny* in that beauty contest," and I managed to smile, but all the time I was dying inside. I asked Mama, "How could you make me get into that contest? Didn't you know those people would make fun of me?" She brushed it off as though it didn't mean a thing. "Oh, daughter, they weren't making fun of you. They thought you were funny. There's a difference." Of course I didn't see the difference, and I felt humiliated for days afterward.

But that experience didn't diminish in the slightest my urge to be on stage. I did my utmost to become a part of every production put on in Centerville and most of the time I managed to get right in the midst of things, because what I may have lacked in talent I more than made up for in enthusiasm and willingness to perform even the most menial tasks. I'd do anything, as long as it was connected with a Show. But, ironically, I never got to be a part of my favorite annual production.

Each year our church put on a Christmas pageant that we looked forward to as the highlight of the season. It was the same play every year—the story of the birth of Christ—with different people playing the roles of Mary, Joseph, the shepherds, the wise men and the angels. I was always too young to play Mary, and I obviously didn't qualify for any of the male roles, but it didn't occur to me until much later to wonder why I had never been chosen to play an angel. I suspect it had something to do with my personality. But by the time I became aware that I had been shamefully overlooked all those years, I was too old to play an angel anyhow.

However, not being in the pageant never dampened my enthusiasm for attending. Even though we knew the story by heart and could quote the dialogue right along with the actors, it was still the most wonderful event of the year. I can remember the costumes. The shepherds always had on flannel bathrobes with towels wrapped around their heads, held in place by braided cord. The angels were dressed in sheets with wings of fluted, white crepe paper, trimmed in gold, attached in back.

One year the pageant was more exciting than ever because a real baby played Jesus, instead of a doll. The woman playing Mary had given birth to a son a few weeks earlier and she used her own little baby. When she sang "Away in a Manger" in her beautiful contralto voice it was so moving we all wept. The scene is still clear in my mind, even though it took place fifty years ago. I know, because today that baby is a man in his early fifties who still lives in Centerville.

The pageant was held on Christmas Eve, which was the happiest time of the year for all of us. Mama served a big meal early in the evening, and my sisters invited their beaus and other friends. The house was alive with Christmas spirit, and the girls giggled and pretended to be annoyed when the boys caught them under the mistletoe. After supper we'd walk slowly to the church, singing carols all the way, enjoying the cold, crisp air and, sometimes, the beauty of moonlight reflecting on the snow-covered streets and lawns.

There was always a huge Christmas tree at church, lit by hundreds of small tapers. It's amazing a tree never caught fire, because every year the tree was ablaze with burning candles. Most church members brought their family gifts to exchange under the tree, and some competed for the status of receiving the most presents. So Mama would only let us bring one gift each to the church, saving our big presents for Christmas morning at home.

Then we'd get up at dawn and run in to wake up Mama and Daddy. Daddy would moan, "Oh, *please*. Just give me my socks and ties and let me go back to sleep." But he always got up and went to the library to light a fire and take the chill off the room, while we, dressed in our robes and slippers, all huddled together giggling and squealing, waited in Mama's room until the library was warm. Then we'd rush in to open our presents, which Mama had set out in stacks on the window seat with our names on them. Each of us always got at least one new game and one new book, in addition to all sorts of other surprises and things we'd asked Santa to bring. Our stockings, hanging from the mantel, were jammed full of nuts, sweets and fresh fruits. I'll always associate Christmas morning with the smell of oranges because that's the only time during winter we ever saw them in Centerville.

And throughout the festivities we were aware of the most divine smells coming from the kitchen, where our cook already would have started Christmas breakfast, a very special meal every year. In addition to the usual—country ham and hot biscuits—on Christmas we had such treats as scalloped oysters and waffles covered with creamed chicken. The table was set with Mama's finest china, crystal and linen, and we had a wonderful time together enjoying that meal.

After breakfast we bundled up in our overcoats and headed down to Colleytown with our cousins (Uncle John and Aunt Dixie's three children), who joined us in exchanging Christmas presents with Daddy's and Uncle John's workers. There were a dozen houses in Colleytown, and we knew all the families down to the smallest child. Nearly all the women worked at our house at one time or another and some of the men as well, doing repair jobs, or acting as the houseman. We played with the children, black and white, and there was never any question of difference. In fact, throughout the year one of our greatest treats was getting to go home with Nanny, or whoever happened to be working at the house, for midday dinner. We had as much fun in Colleytown as we did anywhere in Centerville. Daddy and Uncle John were so well liked that the people there felt as much affection for us as we did for them. Daddy treated all his workers as gentlemen unless someone proved to be otherwise, which was rare. My father was a man who respected human beings no matter what their race, religion or economic status. (One of the things that made me fall in love with my husband is that he is like Daddy in that way. Henry Cannon respects the dignity of every man, and so did my father.) Anyway, on Christmas we went from house to house, exchanging store-bought presents for gifts of jams and jellies and other homemade things, and it was always a wonderful occasion.

After we returned from Colleytown, we either got ready to go to Aunt Dixie's house for our big holiday dinner or waited for them to come to our place, as we took turns each year. Mama baked cakes for weeks again—fresh coconut, Lady Baltimore, fruitcake, chocolate layer and a jam cake made with a gingerbread batter that contained nuts and a filling of homemade blackberry jam, all covered in caramel icing. It was luscious! She also made plum pudding, which Daddy laced with brandy, much to her disapproval. Daddy kept his whiskey in a demijohn (a wicker-covered decanter) on the top shelf of his wardrobe. It was supposedly there for medicinal purposes only; at least that's what he always told Mama. But we knew better. Daddy wasn't a drinking man, but I wouldn't be surprised if he didn't take a nip before bedtime now and then. I know he used to spike Mama's boiled custard, because he got such a big kick out of the preacher's reaction to it. As we lived next door to the parsonage, the preacher was a frequent visitor, and Daddy always offered him boiled custard—which he invariably drank with gusto, saying, "Mister Colley, didn't I detect a little something other than eggs and milk in there?" With Mama's and Aunt Dixie's elaborate Christmas feasts, we'd finish the holiday eating ourselves sick in the afternoon and picking at leftovers again in the evening.

When I was growing up, the emphasis at Christmas was on celebrating Jesus' birthday in the spirit of love and giving, not on giving material things, as we do today. Most of the things we gave and received in the family were hand-crafted and homemade, which gave them more meaning than if they'd been bought.

I do remember one very special "store-bought" gift that caused such a trauma I didn't get over it for quite some time.

I was about six or seven and what I wanted most in the world that Christmas was a doll buggy. That might seem like an ordinary gift today, but back then you rarely saw a little girl in Centerville pushing her doll along in a *buggy*. Some children had wagons, which they *pretended* were buggies, but it wasn't the same thing. I wrote "doll buggy" at the top of my Christmas list to Santa, and hoped and prayed he would remember it when he came down the chimney Christmas Eve.

Sure enough, when I ran into the library Christmas morning the first thing that caught my eye was the most beautiful little white wicker doll buggy I had ever seen. I was ecstatic! And I couldn't wait until after breakfast so I could get my playmate from next door to come over and see it. She came as soon as we finished eating, eager to see my exciting gift. I was showing off my present proudly when suddenly *she sat down in it!* She was a heavyset child and her weight was too much for my dainty little buggy. It went crashing to the floor, wheels flying in all directions, with my surprised friend still stuck inside. When we finally extracted *her* from *it,* the doll buggy had definitely come out on the losing end. It was broken to pieces. Daddy tried to fix it, but it never was right. I was inconsolable. I learned something from that incident, but I'm not sure what—whether it was not to put so much stock in material goods, or not to invite chubby little neighbors over to play with your Christmas toys!

Chapter Five

MY sisters were all very different, and each influenced my life in a special way.

Frances, who was 14 when I was born, was like a second mother to me. She was loving and affectionate, more like Daddy in personality than were the other girls. She was more practical and less frivolous than Dixie, for example, not so outspoken as Virginia and less a dreamer than Mary. By the time I was old enough to remember, she was already out of high school and working as a stenographer for a lawyer in Centerville. She had gone to Athens College for a year, but she wasn't too interested in school.

It was Frances who gave me my first close look at romance. She had been dating since I was a toddler and was the first of my sisters to fall in love and get married. I'll never forget how excited we all were the night she got her diamond engagement ring. The next day was Sunday and I sat by her in church, taking notice of the fact that she wiggled her fingers and stared at her ring throughout the entire sermon. When she wasn't admiring it herself, she draped her arm gracefully over the back of the pew so the people in the row behind her could get a good look at the sparkling diamond, which seemed enormous to me. She was so cute, so typical of a young girl in love, that it never occurred to any of us she was being ostentatious, showing off that way. (Of course it *would* have occurred to Mama, but she was up front playing the organ and didn't see a thing.)

After she married, Frances moved to Franklin, but she came home to have her first baby. This was customary in those days, as almost no one went to a hospital for delivery. I had seen pregnant women before, with their bodies enlarged and their stomachs stuck out, but it seemed strange to see my own sister looking out of shape. I suppose I realized the baby was inside her stomach, but I didn't believe for one second that it had gotten there the way a little girl at school told me babies got inside their mothers. I not only didn't believe it, I thought it sounded ugly; so I pushed it out of my mind completely. I was thoroughly innocent, and not just about sex, which was never discussed in our home, even among my older sisters. My life was so cloistered that even a word like *divorce* was completely foreign to me. The first time I heard it, Mama and Daddy were talking about a distant relative who lived somewhere else. Daddy was visibly saddened. Divorce sounded as frightening to me as death. There had never been a divorce in Centerville.

On the day Frances gave birth to her baby I could feel the tension and excitement mounting in the house from early morning. I knew right away something was different when Frances didn't get out of bed for breakfast. There were whispered conversations all around me and a sense of urgency. About noon Mama called Monnette's mother and said, "I'm sending Ophelia over." Normally, she would never have had to *send* me to Monnette's. But I knew something big was going to happen that day, even though I wasn't sure what, and I didn't want to miss it. Monnette and I played away the afternoon with one eye on my house. By dusk I was really getting restless and anxious to get home. Finally Mama called and told Mrs. Thompson to send me on.

As soon as I got there I was taken into Frances' bedroom. She was lying in bed with this precious, tiny baby in her arms. Mama pulled back the receiving blanket and showed me her little feet, and I couldn't believe those tiny toes! She was so perfect, the most beautiful baby in the world, I thought. (And I tell my niece Virginia Bowman that, to this day.)

Frances hired a nurse, Mattie Otey, to stay with us for a couple of weeks and help with the baby. I would hear a tiny cry early in the morning, and I'd run to Frances' room to find Mattie sitting close to the fireplace, holding little Virginia so her tiny feet were exposed to the warmth of the fire. Mattie would let me touch the baby's feet and play with her little fingers, and I thought that was wonderful. It never occurred to me to question where the baby came from or how it got there. It was like a miracle, and I had no trouble accepting miracles because I learned all about them in Miss Floy Thompson's Sunday school class. When it was time for Frances to go, I hated to see her leave with the baby. But at least I still had three sisters at home.

Virginia was already teaching then. She had earned a degree from Goucher College in Baltimore, then gone on to get her Master's in Library Science at Peabody College in Nashville, but nevertheless was teaching Spanish and French at the local high school. Virginia was, and is to this day, one of those people who can be funny without knowing it, because she's so candid and outspoken. She has a caustic wit, but she can express gentle humor, too, as she did often, years later, when she wrote some of Minnie Pearl's best material for me.

As a girl, Virginia had a reputation for being headstrong and independent. I don't mean she ever caused discipline problems at home, but among her peers she was considered strong-willed and uncompromising. I'll never forget the time she stood up to a *preacher,* refusing his call to "save her soul."

Centerville was having one of those old-timey, protracted revival meetings that ran for days. Evangelists came through town to conduct revivals a couple of times a year, and this particular man was a real hell-fire-damnation preacher, who shouted and carried on about sinners burning in hell for eternity. I was about seven or eight, and he scared me to death because I was not accustomed to hearing that kind of preaching from our regular minister.

Mama was playing for the revival, and Virginia had gone to hear the sermon with a group of her girlfriends. The evangelist got carried away on sin. He condemned every kind of sin known to man, shouting louder by the minute, until eventually he got down to card playing.

He said, "There are women in this church who play cards, the game of the devil, every week, and every one of them are sinners in the eyes of the Lord." Now, Virginia was sitting in the back row with her Wednesday-evening bridge club. These girls all looked at one another guiltily as the preacher raved on about the evils of card playing, except Virginia. She sat staring straight ahead. Then he said, "Now I'm going to give the invitation while Mrs. Colley plays, and I want all you card-playing sinners—the Lord knows who you are—to come down here and ask forgiveness and promise you will *never* play cards again." Virginia's friends all got up and started down the aisle. He had worked everybody up so much they were afraid not to. But Virginia knew as well as anything that those girls would be right back playing bridge the next Wednesday, so she didn't budge.

I turned around and saw my sister sitting there alone and I was horrified. I just knew she was going straight to the devil. When the preacher saw one lone sinner stubbornly holding back he worked even harder to get her to come forward, calling out to the entire congregation to pray for her soul. Virginia said later that she wasn't about to give up bridge so she didn't see any point in being a hypocrite about it. Mama agreed with Virginia, and she didn't like the idea of the preacher (who had no idea his "sinner" was Mrs. Colley's daughter) pointing the finger at one of her own in front of the whole congregation. When finally the preacher realized he couldn't intimidate Virginia into coming forward he concentrated on praying for the ones he'd successfully summoned. And when they got back to their seats they were suitably chastised. "You should have gone down," they whispered. "No, I shouldn't have, either," Virginia said. "And neither should you, unless you're giving up bridge club. Now I won't have to break a promise next Wednesday, but you will."

After the service Virginia went forward to speak to the preacher. Undoubtedly he expected some sort of apology, or at least a request that he pray for her soul. Instead, she told him she didn't appreciate being singled out as a sinner in front of her family and friends, and that she had no intention of giving up bridge until she had more evidence than his say-so that the Lord considered it a sin. Virginia was as outspoken and opinionated as Mama, and just as skilled in cutting through to the core of a matter.

Mary was different. She was the dreamer, the romantic. She lived in a fantasy world and encouraged me to do the same. Mary was always writing stories and poetry. Someday she was going to write the Great American Novel.

Her two best friends, Grace Thompson and Katie Derryberry, were also budding young writers, so the threesome made up a literary-sounding nom de plume—Sarah Baxter Wood—which they used as their collective by-line. They sent volumes of stories

and poems off to every imaginable publication, signed and sub-
mitted by Miss Wood. Then they haunted the post office for
weeks, sure that our postmaster, who knew everyone in town,
thought they were using the U.S. postal service fraudulently.
Sarah Baxter Wood never did get anything in print, but Mary,
using her own by-line, had a short story published in an obscure
magazine when she was in high school. She received $1.65 in
payment for it, and we were all so proud.

Mary's poetry was surprisingly deep and melancholy for a
young girl. The following, which was written when she was about
16, is a good example:

ALONE I WATCHED OLD SUNSETS
by Mary Wood Colley

Alone
I watched old sunsets slowly die and trail
Their flaming colors
'Cross a curving sky,
And saw the moon, all new and trembling shy
Be born and then grow old
As you and I.
I was afraid
Because I was alone
To face a new and flaunting spring.
Summer would come
And bring
New days of languor—and of dreams
And autumn then
Would set the world on fire.
Why did I fear
New seasons and new years
And shrink when winter came again
With frozen tears?
I was alone with beauty night and day—
Who knows what Beauty whispers
If alone we walk her way?

As this poem might indicate, everything Mary did was dramatic.
I'll never forget the morning she and Grace Thompson were sit-
ting at our kitchen table reading poetry while they ate breakfast.
They were putting heart and soul into every line. Our old cook,

Essie, was puttering around the kitchen, not paying any attention to them, when Mary came to the line "I'm sick, sick with an old longing." She put so much anguish into "sick, *sick*" that Essie didn't wait to hear more. She went running out of the kitchen calling, "Miss Colley, Miss Colley, come quick! Miss Mary's done took sick!" Mama came running to the kitchen to find the two girls sitting calmly at the table reading poetry. We laughed about that for weeks.

Mary later received her degree in English from Agnes Scott College in Atlanta. Then she went on to New York, where she worked on her Master's at Columbia before marrying James Kershaw. She never lived in Centerville again, but she visited every year and she always had some new story or poem to share with me.

Three of my sisters were widowed—Virginia's husband was killed in an accident when her twin daughters were just three years old, Frances' husband died when her two children were in their early teens and Mary's husband passed away in 1964. Only Dixie lived out her life with her husband by her side. Her marriage to Wash Shouse had been a long and happy one when she died of cancer in 1967. It's ironical that she was the most adventurous among my sisters when she was young, yet she's the only one who never strayed from home. She married her high school sweetheart and they raised their two children on a farm near Centerville in Shipps Bend. Dixie was so beloved in her community that they named a new bridge in her honor after she died. Every time I go home and cross the Dixie C. Shouse Memorial Bridge I think how surprised she would have been at receiving an honor so important. I can just hear her say, "What are you talking about?" I doubt that there is another bridge in the United States named for a woman who was not a philanthropist, who was never prominent in politics or civic affairs, who was simply a housewife and mother—but was so well loved by her neighbors they gave her a lasting memorial.

Dixie was my idol. I adored her. I loved all my sisters, but I was closest to Dixie because we were closer in age, and we were the only two left at home after Frances, Virginia and Mary married and moved away.

Dixie was seven years older than I and she started dating when I was about eight, a very impressionable age. We slept in the same room in the same bed, and she always woke me up when she came in from a date. We'd lie there and whisper and giggle with the dying firelight flickering against the bedroom walls, and I thought she was the neatest thing that ever was. I wanted to be just like her. I copied her in every way I could. When she started wearing makeup and bobbed her hair and got her first bra I couldn't wait to do the same. I watched every move she made. Those were the days of short dresses and flapper clothes, Dixieland jazz and the Charleston—the height of the Roaring Twenties —and Dixie was Thoroughly Modern Millie. She was a swinger, but she was good. She didn't do anything wrong—none of us did —but she loved to date and dance and dart around in open-top cars with boys in raccoon coats. I remember when she was dating the high school football star and he gave her his letter sweater with three stripes on the arm. Oh, how I wanted to grow up *quick,* so I could get a letter sweater too!

Once I caught Dixie smoking. Daddy had just left for work and you could still smell his pipe smoke in the living room. Dixie thought that would be a good time to sneak a cigarette. I watched her light one up, take a big puff, then blow the smoke up the fireplace chimney. Mama walked in just at that moment. Dixie got so shook up she put the burning cigarette in her sweater pocket. Mama sniffed and said, "Do I smell wool burning in here?" Dixie said, "No, ma'am, it's just Daddy's pipe. I've gotta run now or I'll be late for school." And she dashed out the door with a hole burning right through her sweater. Normally, I thought smoking was cheap and unladylike—we all did—but anything Dixie wanted to do was alright with me. She was laughter and excitement; she was youth on a spree.

Dixie played beautiful piano. She had studied all her life, but she also had a natural ear and could play anything from the classics to the hottest jazz in town. In high school she played with a local combo called Hard Tater and His Syncopaters, named after the leader, "Tater" McWilliams. I'm sure it isn't true, because Mama wouldn't have allowed it, but my memory tells me there was a dance somewhere every night. Parents would open their homes, and the young people would dance to records they played on old wind-up Victrolas. Or sometimes they'd have live music featuring the Syncopaters. I know we had a dance at our house nearly every weekend. Mama would roll up the rugs and we never knew how many teenagers were going to show up or how many girls would end up spending the night. Sometimes Mama would find girls at the breakfast table she didn't even know were in the house. And I was right in the middle of it all, eating it up.

Dixie caused me to get more than one whipping, but even that was alright. The first time it happened I was only about seven. Mealtime was usually a pretty loose affair at our house. It was a fun time, with the whole family sitting around the table laughing and talking. We discussed everything and Mama and Daddy *listened* to us, which means so much. We even played games at the table. We'd stick a fork in a biscuit and dance it along the table-cloth, having imaginary conversations with these fork people that we thought were hilarious. So silly.

But on this occasion we were having a very dignified couple over for dinner and we'd been warned to mind our manners. Mama was very proud that I could say grace as well as the older girls, so when we were all seated she said, "Ophelia will say the blessing." Dixie sat right across from me. We bowed our heads. But instead of repeating the same prayer we always said at meal-time, "O Lord, make us thankful for these and all our many blessings," I said, "Now I lay me down to sleep; I pray the Lord . . ." and then I realized I was saying the wrong prayer. I looked up quickly, terribly embarrassed by my mistake. Dixie said, "Well, I don't believe it," and just fell out laughing. Of course that's all it took for me. I got the giggles. I could have killed Dixie, but I couldn't stop laughing, and neither could she. Mama spoke up sternly, "Ophelia, you and Dixie are excused!" We left the table still giggling. As soon as dinner was finished Daddy took the company into the library and Mama took me and Dixie to the woodshed. I was screaming, "It was Dixie's fault; it was Dixie's fault." Mama said, "I'm not whipping you for saying the wrong prayer. That was an honest mistake. I'm spanking you both for making a joke over a religious ceremony. You were being sacrilegious, and it was *not* funny." Mama thought some things were above humor.

I'll never forget the last whipping Dixie ever got. It was a prime example of the solidarity Mama and Daddy always presented to their children. Dixie was about 17 and really living it up. She had been going out night after night on a continual round of flapper parties, and Mama had had about enough. Dixie was never much of a scholar, and Mama thought she ought to spend more time at home with her studies. One morning, after having been out the night before, Dixie began talking about the dance she was going to that evening. Mama interrupted, saying, "No, you're not going anywhere tonight. I believe it's time you stayed home for a change." Well, Dixie raised the roof. "They're *expecting* me!" she wailed. "I have to be there to play the piano or there won't be any music." Unmoved, Mama said, "Let them play the Victrola." Dixie pleaded and begged, and I was backing her up all the way. Then Dixie said something smart to Mama, who cut her down with a look. "No child of mine ever gets too old to be whipped," she said, marching right out the back door to get a switch. When she started whipping Dixie I threw a fit and tried to grab the switch out of her hand, kicking at her feet, pushing her, which was a mistake. The minute Mama finished switching Dixie, she switched me. Then she sent us both to our room.

We cried until we were worn out. Then Dixie said, "Just wait until Daddy comes home. Mama had no business whipping me. I'm too old to be whipped and Daddy won't like that." Later, as soon as we heard the iron gate clang shut when Daddy came home to lunch, we started bawling and squalling all over again. We vied to see who could cry the loudest. We thought Daddy would come running in to the room thinking one of us had been killed. But he knew better because Mama always called him immediately if someone got hurt. (With five daughters there were numerous accidents, and there's no telling how many times that poor man jumped on his horse and galloped up the hill in the middle of the day to look at a cut finger or a scraped knee.)

Daddy took his time coming to our room. When he opened the door we were both lying on the bed, crying hysterically. He didn't rush over to us. He just stood there in the doorway, a big, calm, quiet man, and said, "What seems to be the matter here?" He was way ahead of us. Dixie began pouring out this long sad tale between racking sobs, while I tearfully agreed to everything she said. Daddy listened until she'd finished. Then he said, "Well, first I want you both to stop crying and wash your faces and come in and sit down at the table and eat your dinner." Dixie said, "Aren't you going to say anything to Mama about whipping us?" Daddy said, "You just do what I told you to do." While we were washing our faces we said, "Maybe he's in the kitchen right now telling Mama she was wrong." But we knew better. We came to the table and ate our lunch and not one word was ever mentioned again about the whipping. And Dixie didn't get to go out that night, either.

If Mama and Daddy ever had a disagreement of any kind over the raising of their daughters we were not aware of it. They always presented a solid front to us, and it was a good way to grow up because it gave us a sense of security and safety you don't find in a home where the parents argue over their children. In fact, Mama and Daddy never argued about anything in front of us, except politics.

Daddy was what they called a Yellow-Dog Democrat. That was an old Southern expression which meant he was such a staunch Democrat he'd vote for a yellow dog if it was running on the party ticket. Mama voted for the man. When Al Smith ran for President on the Democratic ticket, there was a lot of controversy over his nomination because he was Catholic and we'd never had a Catholic President. Daddy was going to vote for him no matter, because he was a Democrat. But Mama wasn't so sure. Daddy said, "Tell you what. Let's don't either one of us vote. It'll work out the same way because if we do vote we'll just cancel one another out." Mama agreed. She stayed home that day. But Daddy went ahead and voted! Oh, I'd never seen Mama so mad. She fumed and fussed. But Daddy just laughed. He told her, "A woman should never believe *everything* a man says."

We girls just loved that. He teased Mama about it for years afterward. As I've said, she was on the go a lot because she was involved in practically every church, civic and school activity in town, so any time something would come up about the election Daddy would say, "Oh, yes. I believe that's the day your Mama stayed home."

Chapter Six

I was like Daddy in many ways—I think I got my sense of humor from him—but when it came to wanting to *go*, I took after Mama.

By the time I reached high school the throttle was wide open and I was going full-speed ahead. Because my family was one of the most prominent in Centerville, I was invited to as many social functions as I could handle, which also had a lot to do with the size of my hometown (like Minnie Pearl, who, when asked if it's true she's been kissed by every boy in Grinder's Switch, says, "Well, Grinder's Switch ain't such a big town").

I was never the student that Virginia and Mary had been, but I somehow managed to be named valedictorian in the eighth grade, an honor I accepted proudly. My sister Mary had written me an impressive valedictorian address, which began dramatically: "Someone has said that to travel hopefully is better than to arrive, but after traveling hopefully for eight years, I cannot believe anything could be better than to have arrived at this graduation day!"

The only thing that marred that occasion was the fact that Mama and I had a huge argument over whether I would wear white knee socks or silk stockings to the graduation exercises. (I should say *I* had the argument. Mama never argued, she decreed!) In Centerville, Tennessee, in 1927, girls did *not* put on silk stockings until a certain age. I was the youngest girl in the class, and Mama said

I wasn't old enough to wear silk stockings. She said I would wear my white knee socks, as always. I knew I'd be the only one there in "babyish" socks, and the fact that I had to stand up in front of everyone on stage to give my valedictorian address made it even worse. I begged, I pleaded. But Mama was adamant. I said, "But *Mama, all* the other girls are wearing silk stockings. I'll be the *only* one different." She said, "But you are *not* every other girl, and you *are* different. You never will be just one of the other girls. You are an individual, and you do not have to follow the crowd." (Later on I was to hear her say that about a lot of customs and practices of my teenage associates. Just because others smoked or took a drink didn't mean I had to be like them. I was *not* to try to copy others; I was to be myself!)

Even in white knee socks, my eighth grade honor made me feel special and enabled me to enter Hickman County High School (which was in the same building that housed Hickman County Grammar School) with some small measure of credibility among my teachers. I wasn't pretty, but I was well liked and popular with my peers. I had enormous energy, pep and vitality, which helped me to get elected cheerleader, a privilege I accepted with total dedication.

Hickman County High had a pretty good football team—some of those big farm boys were tough and fast—and if hollering from the sidelines had anything to do with their victories, I can personally take credit for quite a few touchdowns. I pranced up and down in front of the stands in my red plaid accordion-pleated skirt, white shirt and red galluses, my bobby sox and white oxfords, and I screamed, I jumped, I whistled, I yelled. Half the time I'd go home from a game so hoarse I could barely speak. I had no way of knowing it then, but I was doing irreparable damage to the one instrument I needed most to realize my dream of becoming a great dramatic actress: I was ruining my voice.

Of course school spirit was not the only motive that inspired me to be the most enthusiastic cheerleader on the team. Leading cheers before a bleacher section of football fans put me right out there on display in front of everybody, which was exactly where I wanted to be. I could show off to the nth degree with everyone's approval. It was heaven.

Of all my activities at this time, none was more important to me than my expression lessons with Miss Inez Shipp. Miss Shipp taught in her home near the high school, and twice a week I'd go there in the afternoon to learn readings and scenes from plays, stage presence, voice inflection, timing—all the things that make up the study of acting. My dream for my future by then was full-blown, and as real to me as anything that was happening in my everyday life. *I was going to be one of the greatest dramatic actresses of my time.* I was going to out-Bernhardt Bernhardt. There was no doubt in my mind that I could accomplish this goal. After all, hadn't I been performing since I was 18 months old? And didn't everyone in my hometown say I had dramatic talent? In my own mind I was already an actress. It was just a matter of honing my talent to a fine, sharp edge. I don't think it would have fazed me if my friends and relatives had told me to my face that I was dreaming a fool's dream. I wanted so desperately to become a dramatic actress that it was an actual physical longing deep inside me, and I had convinced myself that it was meant to be. It was my *destiny*.

Mama and Daddy knew that I was interested in dramatics and that I loved my lessons with Miss Inez, but I did not confide to them my audacious dream. I knew instinctively that they would not approve of their baby daughter heading out into the big, wild world to pursue a career in *show business*. Monnette was the only one who knew my secret. And she shared my belief that my dream would come true.

Miss Inez also encouraged me. She didn't flatter me, but she let me know she thought I had a certain amount of talent. She was impressed by how easily I could slip out of my own personality and take on traits of whatever character I was playing. I was never self-conscious about giving it my all. My overdeveloped imagination made it possible for me to lose myself completely in any role she gave me, and if the part called for the tears to stream down my face, I could let them flow with no trouble at all.

During this same period I also became acquainted with the Wayne P. Sewell Production Company from Atlanta, Georgia. Actually, I had first come in contact with this organization when I was 10 or 11 years old, through some of their directors who came to Centerville from time to time to put on a musical production for the PTA.

The practice of bringing productions to rural towns and using local talent as the performers was prevalent during the twenties and thirties, and it was a popular form of entertainment. Mr. Sewell's company was the biggest and best known in the South.

Here's how it worked: A promoter would arrive in a town and contact the president of some local civic or religious organization. He would sell that group, say the Lions Club, on the idea of staging a "professional musical production" as a fund-raising event. The Sewell Company agreed to provide the director, the costumes, the play and the music. The organization would then provide the cast, made up of local talent. It was also up to the group to find the director a free place to stay while she was in town. The event would be set for several months ahead. The promoter would leave and go on to sell some group in the next town. At the appointed time, the director would arrive and put the show together. The Sewell Company and the local club would then share the profits from the show.

A cute, bright Sewell director—they were all young ladies in their twenties—came to Centerville almost every year, and I was always fascinated. I not only took any role I could get in the productions, no matter how insignificant, but I also followed the director around everywhere. I ran errands, I did favors, I sold ads for the programs, I even helped sell tickets at the door. Mama usually played for the shows, so it was a busy time for all of us when a Sewell director was in town.

I would ask the girls a million questions about their work and their lives, and they were all very patient and sweet. They told me about all the towns they visited and the adventures they had, and I hung on their every word. It sounded to me like the most glamorous existence imaginable. (Little did I know there was another side to this life, but later I was to spend six years finding it out.) I dreamed of studying at the American Academy of Dramatic Arts, but in the back of my mind I also thought it would be terrifically exciting to work as a Sewell director someday.

Between my local performing experiences, my lessons with Miss Inez and the brain-picking job I'd done on all these Sewell girls, I thought I knew a good deal about dramatics by the time I was 17. You might even say I was a bit conceited about my ability in that area. I was certainly convinced that I was the best actor in Centerville, so I wasn't surprised when the Socratic Society chose me to represent them in the Annual Oratorical and Declamatory Contest.

The Socratic Society and the Argonaut Society were the high school literary groups, and every year two boys and two girls from each club competed in a declamation contest, doing a scene from a play or a reading of some kind. It was a great honor just to be chosen to participate because it was a popular annual event, and half the town turned out to see the contestants perform. The prize was an engraved medal, and I could already envision it hanging around my neck. Monnette was chosen to represent the Argonauts, which meant we would be competing against one another for the first time in our long, close friendship. (This didn't bother me because I knew I was going to win.) We decided not to tell each other what reading or scene we'd selected to do because we thought it would be more fun to find out on the night of the contest.

If I had had any sense at all, I would have taken advantage of my natural flair for comedy, for "cuttin' the fool," and chosen a humorous monologue. But no, I was into *drama*, so I went all the way . . . I chose a reading from the last scene in *Madame Butterfly*, in which the heroine commits suicide.

I went to Miss Inez's house every afternoon that spring to work on my reading, and by the time the contest rolled around I had it down pat. Every voice inflection, every movement of my hands and motion of my body was calculated to milk the last ounce of sympathy from the audience for this tragic girl who had lost her lover and could not face life without him.

Mama had hired a local seamstress to make me an evening dress of pink and blue organdy, with rows of ruffles down the skirt, fashionably cut knee-length in front and floor-length in back. Mama said it looked "Frenchy." I never did know exactly what that meant, but I took her word that I was dressed appropriately for my big night.

I can't recall being nervous on the night of the contest. I knew my reading so well I could say it in my sleep, and I was looking forward to showing off my dramatic talent before a full house. So I sat on stage calmly as I awaited my turn. Another girl went first, then a boy, then it was my turn.

I walked slowly, purposefully to the center of the stage on steady legs beneath my pink and blue ruffles. I paused dramatically, just long enough to set a serious mood, before beginning my reading. I began softly, building steadily for 10 minutes with studied timing to the poignant climax where Madame Butterfly takes up the sword to kill herself. By this time I was completely lost in her desperate plight. She draws her fingers along the blade of the sword, bravely reciting the words she sees inscribed there: "To

Die with Honor When One Can No Longer Live with Honor."
She lifts the sword above her breast, about to utter her last im-
mortal words. She opens her mouth to speak . . . but no sound
came out. Silence. You could hear a pin drop. Seconds, minutes
dragged by. Still no sound from Madame Butterfly. *My mind had
gone completely blank!* My knees turned to jelly. I counted the
footlights. I broke out in a sweat. I imagined that the judges,
seated in full view in the front row, had turned to whisper to one
another. I wanted to *die*. I knew exactly how Madame Butterfly
felt. Death by the dagger was infinitely preferable. Finally, after
what seemed like an eternity of silence, I stammered out the last
lines of the reading and stumbled back to my seat. I was a shambles. I couldn't even look up at the audience to acknowledge the
polite applause they accorded me.

A boy went on next, but I was so mortified, so thoroughly disgraced, I didn't hear a word of his reading. Then it was Monnette's turn. She had picked a funny monologue about a little
stable boy and a horse race. She did a terrific job with it, and
before she'd finished she had the audience in the palm of her
hand. They *loved* it, and it was obvious by the applause that she
had won, even before the judges announced their decision.

I don't remember feeling jealous over Monnette's victory,
though I probably did. I only remember how hurt I was and how
shocked and ashamed that I could do something so *stupid* as to
forget my lines and blow the whole thing. Mama and Daddy were
sympathetic and understanding. Daddy said I was obviously very
talented and the only reason I lost was because two of the judges
were from Columbia, Tennessee, which was such big horse country they had erected an equestrian statue right in the middle of
town. He said they'd been partial to Monnette's reading because
it had been about a horse race. It was so sweet and so typical of
his supportive attitude toward all his girls.

I've emphasized the story of my demoralizing defeat at the declamatory contest because it came to me vaguely that night that
you had a better chance to be a winner if you didn't try to play it
so straight and heavy. Monnette's reading had made them laugh;
they had had *fun* listening to her. She brought them *enjoyment*,
and she would probably have won even if I hadn't blown the best
part of my reading. Years later, thinking back on that traumatic
incident made it easier for me to accept comedy as a career. Possibly the Lord was already trying to show me then that I didn't

have the talent to become a great dramatic actress. But if He was, I wasn't listening.

The only thing that saved that night from complete disaster was that Mama allowed me to go to a public dance for the first time, where a handsome young man gave me such a rush I momentarily forgot my earlier humiliation.

I must explain that even though I was popular in my own crowd and dated fairly regularly, I was not a smashing success with the opposite sex. I tried too hard. I had grown up with these boys, played cops and robbers and cowboys and Indians with them, and we were buddies, but I didn't know how to *flirt*. I would always get tickled at the flirting stage because the insincerity of it just destroyed me. I was not a social flop, but I was a flirting flop. And boys love flirts because a plainspoken girl takes them off-guard, whereas a flirt builds them up. (Monnette and I weren't made aware of the power of flirtation until a new preacher with a glamorous daughter our age moved to town. She knew the ropes. She was the one who caused our boys to stop acting silly and start looking dumb. She was a classic beauty in the Merle Oberon tradition, and all she had to do was lower her eyes demurely to make the boys come completely unglued. I couldn't have been demure if I'd known how. I had already grown to full size, and if you're five foot eight and wear a size 9½ shoe you're going to have a very hard time looking demure!)

Monnette and I were uncomplicated, silly and carefree. But the preacher's daughter was sophisticated and coy. (When we saw how she affected those boys we'd known so long, we realized there was something more to life than sharing a cold glass of lemonade with them after a hot tennis match.)

Ordinarily Mama wouldn't have let me go to a public dance, but this one was chaperoned and it was being held at the Knights of Pythias Hall, a local men's organization, and she knew there wouldn't be any alcohol or rowdy behavior allowed. I was dancing away with some boy from my class when suddenly a *stranger* cut in on me. That in itself was a new experience, since the only dances I'd ever been to were held at my house or in the homes of friends. He was exceptionally handsome, with blonde hair and Paul Newman-blue eyes, and I was quite literally swept off my feet. He was a terrific dancer and proceeded to waltz me around the room as though our feet weren't touching the floor. I did have a good figure, even though I was no beauty, and I was a good dancer, so it didn't occur to me to doubt this young man's sincerity when he started shooting me a line a mile long.

He told me I was the most attractive girl he'd ever seen, and the most beautiful dancer, and that I had the greatest figure and the cutest personality! I absolutely swallowed it hook, line and sinker! I thought I had reached a new plateau, that I was obviously much more attractive than I had imagined, and I wondered what was wrong with all those Centerville boys that they hadn't noticed it. I went home in a cloud.

The next day I told Monnette everything this boy had said to me. Monnette wasn't right sure about all this. She looked at me out of the corner of her eye, very dubious about my conquest. She didn't doubt he'd said all those things, she doubted the truth of them. She knew me and she knew I wasn't all that cute, so she concluded he must be out of his mind. Neither of us was aware that boys sometimes tell out-and-out lies to get their way with a girl. Our local boys had never done that.

My new conquest had made a date with me for the next week, and he brought a friend for Monnette. When he arrived in a black Buick roadster with red leather upholstery, I almost fainted. I was terribly impressed. But it didn't last. We had fun for one or two dates, but he soon got bored when he discovered his line wasn't getting him anywhere, and I never heard from him again. I hadn't even kissed a boy at that time (my first kiss came after I'd gone away to college), and this young dude in his fancy car had more on his mind than kissing. I wasn't sure what the results of a kiss would be. Mama had never made that clear, but something always stopped me.

Even so, there was nothing more important to Monnette and me than boys, with a capital B. We had some cute boys in Centerville and some funny boys, but no real Romeos. We'd known them too long for them to pull that stuff on us. Therefore you can imagine our excitement when a whole new batch of young men arrived in town to supervise construction on Highway 100, which was going to cut through Centerville, connecting the town for the first time to a main route between Nashville and Memphis.

Under normal circumstances Monnette and I would never have been allowed to date any of these young men, because, to quote Mama, "Nobody knew anything about them." But there were not enough rooms at our one hotel to accommodate these temporary residents, so several families with large homes took them in as boarders. One of these young men, a graduate engineer who was in charge of a portion of the highway construction, took a room at my aunt Dixie's house, and I found plenty of reasons to go over there. When he'd been in town long enough for the family to get to know him and reassure themselves that he wasn't "fast," I was allowed to date him.

I thought I was really something, going out with an "older"man. He was probably only in his early thirties, but I was just 18, so he seemed much older and very sophisticated, a man of the world from Nashville, the big city! He had a green Buick convertible, and he often let Monnette and me borrow it while he was working. We drove it around town with the top down, calling out and waving to friends. It was terrific.

It was through him that I had my first exposure to big-city dating, as opposed to the country variety I was accustomed to. He and one of his buddies on the job invited Monnette and me to drive to Nashville to have lunch. They said they'd take us to the Hermitage Hotel, where there was an *orchestra* that played at noon. At first we just knew our parents wouldn't let us go. Nashville was a two-hour drive away, and we'd never been allowed to go out of Centerville on a date. But they finally agreed because we were to be back before dark. (Apparently Mama thought you couldn't do anything wrong in the daytime. And she always made me come home from dates by 10 p.m., as though I couldn't do whatever I wanted to by then. When I teased her about it later, she would say, "The defenses are more apt to be down after midnight.")

On the Saturday when we set out for our big luncheon date in Nashville, Monnette and I were delirious with excitement. We acted so silly on the drive it's a wonder those men didn't turn around. When we arrived at the Hermitage, our dates ushered us into the elegant old dining room, where the maître d' seated us next to the orchestra. The music was soft and romantic and the atmosphere was very Continental, but the sophisticated diners—ladies in fancy hats and gentlemen in tailored suits—seemed oblivious to their chic surroundings. Monnette and I longed to be equally blasé, but we were so enchanted we kept kicking one another under the table to call attention to anything the other might have missed.

We were just beginning to relax when the waiter brought us the menus. We took one glance at them and froze. I looked at Mon-

nette and she looked at me. It was exactly like a scene from La-
verne and Shirley. We had never seen anything like these fine,
big, parchmentlike menus, written in *French*, the courses divided
into sections—appetizers, salads, entrees, vegetables, desserts.
We didn't even know what half the names meant, much less how
to go about ordering. Fortunately my date asked if we'd like him
to order for us. "Oh, *yes*," we chorused, relieved beyond words
that we weren't going to have to muddle through it alone and
make fools of ourselves.

He went down the menu section by section, asking if we'd
prefer soup or fruit cocktail as a first course, salad next, and so on.
Then he passed our choices on to the waiter. We watched him
closely to see how it was done. When he'd finished he gave us an
invaluable piece of advice, one I have since passed on to inexperienced young people often. He said, "When you go into a restaurant where the menu offers so many dishes it's confusing, ask the
waiter's advice. Any good waiter is prepared to help, and he will
enjoy being asked." It's surprising how many people don't know
how to do that, even though dining out is so commonplace today.

Monnette and I talked about our luncheon date for weeks, gloat-
ing over how superior we were to our friends, who still thought it
was a big deal to share a banana split at the Liberty Pharmacy.

Because I was dating an "older" man, I naturally didn't want
him to think of me as a baby—a high school kid (which is exactly
what I was)—so when he invited me to go to a dance at a roadhouse in Dickson, I wasn't about to admit there was no way Mama
would ever give her consent. Instead I devised an elaborate plot
to get out of the house, even though it entailed my lying to my
father, something I had never done before in my life.

The date was on a Tuesday night in the summertime. I waited
until after Mama had gone to her Eastern Star meeting before
getting ready, which left me only about 30 minutes before I was
to be picked up. I rushed around getting into my one-and-only
evening dress (the pink-and-blue "Frenchy" number I'd worn at
the declamatory contest), fixed my face and hair to look as sophisticated as possible, then put on my wrap and walked calmly into
the sitting room, where Daddy was reading the *Saturday Evening
Post*.

"You look mighty pretty, honey," he said. "Where are you
going?"

"I'm going to Dickson to a dance." I couldn't look at him. I pretended to be glancing at another magazine, trying to sound nonchalant.

"Oh, really?" he said. "Who's giving the dance?" He assumed it was at someone's home because we didn't usually go to public dances.

"Well, they're holding it at the Wayside Pavilion," I said. He looked surprised. "Does your mother know about this?" I answered, "Yessir," still not looking him in the eye.

"Well, I can't imagine her giving her permission, but if she did I'm sure it's alright, so you go ahead and have a good time."

Oh, I cannot describe the feeling of shame I felt for telling that lie! Looking back I can recall that Daddy had a sad expression on his face, and I think he knew at that moment I was lying to him. But he didn't stop me from going. I believe he wanted me to have the experience, hoping I would learn a lesson from it.

I knew I was going to get into serious trouble when I got home; I knew I'd be punished for what I was doing. Yet I was determined to go to that dance. I was willing to pay the price in order to have the adventure, which reveals something about my nature. I am a very stubborn person. I am not proud of it, but I can be as hard-headed as the oldest mule. I was certain that I was going to have a wonderful time, that it would be worth the consequences. What I hadn't counted on was that my conscience would start ticking the minute I walked out the front door.

We were going with another couple from Centerville, a brother and sister I'd known all my life, but even their familiar company didn't ease my guilt. On the drive to Dickson I pretended to be as carefree and happy-go-lucky as ever, for I would never have admitted to a soul that I'd lied to my father. But inside I was suffering pangs of remorse.

I told myself I'd relax when I got on the dance floor and heard the music of a professional pop band from Nashville. But the Pavilion turned out to be a shock for my country innocence. For the first time in my life I was thrown into a honky-tonk—a dark, overcrowded room, with blaring music, loud voices and the smell of stale beer and whiskey. *Girls* were drinking white corn liquor out of fruit jars, and chasing it with Coke. I had never seen *anyone* take a drink in my life, much less a woman. I couldn't wait to get out of that place and back to my nice, safe world.

We didn't get home until after midnight, which would have gotten me in trouble even if I'd been out with Mama's approval, and every light in the house was on. I knew Mama was waiting, but I didn't let on, and she let my date get back to his car before she started in on me. Mama was a voluble, articulate woman, and she could pierce your heart with words when she wanted to. I just wanted to go to bed and hide my head under the covers, but she gave it to me with both barrels. She kept it up, letting me know in no uncertain terms how disgraceful my conduct had been and how hurt, how disgusted she was to learn I was capable of telling such a bald-faced life. The last thing she said to me stung me the most. "Your father is terribly disappointed. He will speak to you in the morning."

The thought of facing Daddy was more than I could bear! I lay awake half the night crying in shame, dreading it, wondering what on earth I could say to make it up to him.

The next morning I stayed in bed, hoping he would be gone to work when I got up. But he waited for me in the parlor. Eventually I had to get up. I felt queasy and shaky all over. But I took a deep breath and entered the parlor, starting to apologize before he could say anything.

"I'm sorry about last night, Daddy," I said. I was already in tears, although he hadn't said a word.

"Phel, I'm *really* disappointed in you," he replied. I remember so distinctly that he didn't even raise his voice.

I was crushed! Daddy had never said anything like that to me in my life. But there was more to come.

"You not only went to a place you had no business going, you *lied* to me. And if there is anything in the world I dislike, it's a liar."

Oh, Lord, I wanted to die. Now my daddy hated me. I was so stricken I could hardly speak.

"Is there anything I can do to make you like me again?" I sobbed.

"I didn't say I didn't like you." He looked as stricken as I. "There is something you must remember. Your mother and I want you to be happy and to have fun, but we also want you to take care of yourself." And he turned and walked out of the room.

I cried that whole day. Mama didn't mention it again, which indicated she knew how ashamed I was because she usually harped on things. Daddy never brought it up again either, but that was like him. Once he'd had his say, he was finished on a subject. But I never forgot the expression of pain and disappointment on his face when he left for work that morning, and I never lied to him again as long as he lived.

Chapter Seven

I entered my senior year of high school in September 1929 with no doubt about my future or the wonderful times that lay ahead. My plan was to earn my college degree, then go on to study at the American Academy of Dramatic Arts or the Pasadena Playhouse, where I would polish my talent until it shown brightly enough to attract the attention of Broadway directors. I had sense enough to know that landing the first job wouldn't be easy, but after that, the sky was the limit!

One month later the stock market crashed, and when January 1, 1930, dawned, Americans had said good-bye to more than an old decade. It was as if the country had been forced to grow up suddenly, propelled overnight out of its irresponsible teens into frightened middle age.

The impact of the crash didn't hit me personally until after the first of the year. Money was now being discussed in our home for the first time. Daddy's business had been hard-hit and was sinking fast. No one was building because no one had the money to build. Lumber orders were being canceled left and right, with no new ones coming in. Workers had to be laid off. I knew Daddy felt as bad about that as he did about the hardship the Depression might bring to his own family.

Until this time, I had never really thought much about money, one way or another. It was just taken for granted that if we needed something, or wanted something within reason, Daddy would get it for us. We were not rich, and we did not live extravagantly, but we were comfortable and none of us had ever wanted for anything. Now we had just enough to get by, which made a noticeable difference in our lifestyle. We had less help at home. I had to be careful not to run my silk stockings, which had always been plentiful before, or scuff my shoes, which now had to last more than one season. We had to shop for bargains, and we bought much less of everything. And there was certainly no money for anything as costly as the education I desired.

Daddy had prided himself on being able to send his daughters to the colleges of their choice, and all my sisters had gone to expensive schools, with Virginia and Mary earning degrees. Now he had a daughter who not only wanted a degree, but after that, dramatic training as well. And there was no way he could afford it. I imagine Daddy's most difficult time as a father was when he had to tell me we didn't have the money for the education I wanted. When he and Mama said I would have to make a choice between two years at Ward-Belmont, the most fashionable finishing school in the state, or four years at the University of Tennessee, I knew their disappointment was as great as my own. I felt as bad for them as I did for myself. Besides, I was still overflowing with youthful optimism. Secretly, I was sure *something* would turn up to enable me to finish my education and go on to study dramatics.

Even though the Depression was uppermost in the minds of the adults, I don't remember its preventing us teenagers from having fun during our senior year. We still went to dances and parties and acted just as silly and crazy as ever. And we were very excited about being the first class to graduate from Hickman County High wearing caps and gowns. Mama played "Pomp and Circumstance" on the auditorium piano as we marched misty-eyed down the aisle to receive our diplomas. We all cried and had a wonderful time.

I had chosen two years at Ward-Belmont, even though it cost as much as four years at the university, because Miss Inez told me they had an exceptionally good drama department under the direction of Miss Pauline Sherwood Townsend. Miss Townsend was well known throughout the South for her work in the performing arts, and she was highly respected both as a director and an educator. She was a graduate of the Currie School of Expression in Boston, which in her day was even more prestigious than being an alumna of the American Academy of Dramatic Arts. I wanted the opportunity to study with this woman I'd heard so much about, and I knew she was interested in having me as a student because Miss Inez had written her about me and she had responded graciously.

Dixie had gone to Ward-Belmont for one year, and I knew a little about it from her. She hadn't been happy there, but that had had nothing to do with the school. She didn't want to be separated from her high school sweetheart (whom she later married), so she wouldn't have had fun anywhere away from Centerville. But I felt I would fit right in at a college where dramatics was considered important enough to attract and hold someone of Miss Townsend's reputation. Even though Ward-Belmont was much better known as a fine finishing school for young ladies than for its drama department (even today in the South, a Ward-Belmont background is of social importance in some circles), the idea of going to a cloistered girls' school didn't bother me. I was accustomed to restrictions because I'd grown up with them at home, so I did not foresee any problem in adjusting to campus life.

My first inkling that I might be out of place at this fashionable school arrived in a letter the summer before I was to enroll. The letter included a list of things I was to bring with me, including the minimum wardrobe requirements. I couldn't get over it! The list seemed to go on and on. I remember it included a good black dress and "at least one" evening gown. I had only one evening gown, and it wasn't new, and we all knew that the $1,200 tuition for the first year, which was as much as the annual income of many families in 1930, was all that Daddy could afford. There was no money left over for me to buy a lot of clothes. So Mama and I put together my best things from high school and then purchased necessities, like new underwear and shoes, along with a couple of dresses. The only splurge was the new coat Daddy bought for me—black wool with a red fox collar! I thought it was a knockout!

I hadn't been at Ward-Belmont 24 hours when I *knew* I was out of my element. The school had been in existence since before the turn of the century, and even the campus itself was intimidating. The atmosphere was solid, substantial, *old* money.

The main building had originally been the Acklen Mansion, a noble, three-story structure built in 1850 and designed by an Italian architect who had followed the design of a Venetian palace.

The building is more Renaissance than antebellum, though it does have a broad Corinthian colonnade, front and back, like those often seen on old Southern mansions. It its day, it had been the scene of some of the most celebrated parties in the state, with guests making two- and three-day journeys to attend a ball there. At that time it was surrounded by 150 acres of woods, rolling green hills, gardens and a wildlife preserve that included a bird sanctuary and a zoo. Most of the land had been sold off by 1930, but Ward-Belmont still occupied some 35 acres of the original, with the grounds and gardens kept as well manicured as a private park.

Entering the campus from what is now Nashville's famed Music Row (Sixteenth Avenue South) you drove along a private tree-lined road, slowly rising for about two miles, into a clearing, where you caught your first glimpse of the majestic white mansion on the crest of a hill. It was an awesome sight.

The office of Miss Emma I. Sisson, Ward-Belmont's formidable dean of residents, was located in the mansion, and as new students had to check in there, it was the first building I entered on campus. What struck me immediately was the subtle, indefinable scent of wealth. It had the same aroma of beeswax I associated with the Nunnelly home, but there was something else, which much later I realized was the smell of dried eucalyptus. (Today many dried floral arrangements contain eucalyptus leaves, but back then they were used mainly by sophisticated decorators who catered to the very rich.) By contrast, my own home smelled of logs burning in the fireplace and good food cooking.

The next thing I noticed about the Acklen Mansion was the *quiet.* Many students were walking back and forth in the hall, yet it was as quiet as a library, even as a monastery. Everyone spoke in dulcet tones, just above a whisper, and moved at a very precise, carefully measured, ladylike pace. As I soon discovered, there were very strict rules about dress and comportment in the mansion. But, comparing my first impression with the noisy, active household I'd come from, I felt like I'd been dropped into a funeral home.

I walked through the rooms that first day wide-eyed and open-mouthed. The furnishings and appointments were sumptuously beautiful: baroque gold-leaf moldings bordering the 14-foot ceilings, doors inlaid with leaded Venetian glass, enormous crystal chandeliers, splendid European antique furniture, classical mar-

ble statuary, magnificent oriental rugs. Everything looked freshly
scrubbed or painted, as indeed it was, and every surface that was
supposed to shine gleamed. To me, it looked more like a European palace than headquarters of an American girls' school, and it
was every bit as intimidating as it was meant to be. While America
was in the throes of a major financial depression, Ward-Belmont
remained aloof, untouched, an oasis of Bourbon opulence.

It was an absolutely perfect setting for Miss Sisson, who carried
herself as regally as any queen. She was a coldly beautiful woman,
who always held her head high and her back ramrod-straight. Her
manner, her bearing, even the way she folded her hands in her
lap, exuded complete self-assurance, which, of course, made a
new student feel more insecure than ever.

Although the mansion served as living quarters for the president of the college and his family, as well as housing Miss Sisson's
office and a few dormitory rooms for upperclassmen, it was pri-
marily used for receiving gentlemen callers and for the social
activities, all chaperoned by austere faculty members wearing
long black dresses. Typically unawed, the students called it Rec
Hall, short for recreation hall.

Even before I found my way to my room I was terrified. I had
never seen so many well-dressed girls in one place in my life.
Everything about them—clothes, haircuts, vocabulary, even the
way they walked—reeked of money. It was hard to believe that
just a few miles away, in downtown Nashville, people were actually standing in breadlines. The Depression apparently had not
hit families of Ward-Belmont students. But then, of course, only
the very wealthy could afford to send their daughters to Ward-
Belmont. Very *few* girls were there because their parents had
scraped to send them, as mine had.

Two large dormitory wings, called Fidelity and Founders, had
been added to the mansion, and my room was in the former. It
overlooked the academic building and other dormitories across a
wooded parklike area containing lifesize statues of animals, several gazebos and a large, circular, tiered fountain from which
water flowed day and night onto a pool of lily pads. No wonder
the school was so expensive!

My roommate turned out to be a girl from Texas. Her family
had the kind of money you read about in novels. She came from
oil, and the crash hadn't stopped those gushers. After I unpacked
(it didn't take me long) I sat down to watch her unload a steamer

trunk and a pile of luggage. I had never seen so many clothes in my life outside a department store. All four of my sisters put together hadn't taken that many clothes away to college. She pulled out outfit after outfit, all coordinated with different shoes, bags and gloves, several black dresses and a half-dozen formals. Her closet was soon stuffed to overflowing, so I offered to share mine, where there was room to spare. The pièce de résistance was when she brought out not one, but *two* full-length fur coats. One was a snazzy-looking fashion fur to wear around school and the other was the most gorgeous full-length mink I'd ever seen. My black cloth coat with the fox collar paled in comparison!

My roommate wasn't flaunting her wealth or her wardrobe. She was simply accustomed to having beautiful, expensive clothes in abundance and thought no more about it than I had thought about money before the Depression. (Later, after Christmas, I learned that one of my classmates had gotten a mirrored marble bathroom as a present from her family. She said it was something she had always wanted because she loved to look at her white body against that black marble! I was aghast. It sounded indecent! At home we felt privileged because the plumbing had finally been hooked up and Daddy could tear down the outhouse!)

That first night in the dining room, where round tables had been set with lovely linens, beautiful china, sparkling crystal and gleaming silverware, I sat with girls who talked of debutante balls, vacations in Europe, winter homes in Palm Beach (or Palm Springs), English nannies and upstairs maids and charge accounts that had been opened for them in Nashville's smart boutiques. As one of them pointed out, it wouldn't be as chic as shopping in New York, Paris, London or Rome, but it beat being stuck with no charge account at all.

I sat like a lump, listening and feeling lower by the minute. I had nothing to contribute to conversations of this kind. These girls had come from cities, where there were very definite strata of society, and they'd been skimmed off the top. By comparison, I was a country bumpkin. I couldn't have felt more out of place if I'd been on Mars.

Later, I realized that many of those very wealthy students were terribly unhappy. Often they had been raised by governesses and shuttled off to boarding school while they were still very young. They needed the protection of their wealth because they didn't have a sense of security or identity without it. I was far richer than they, just from the wonderful relationship I had enjoyed with my parents and my sisters, but I couldn't see that then. Then I was *miserable,* and my misery grew with every passing day. Nobody has to tell me at this point how stupid I was. Looking back on it, I know this was a direct result of being spoiled all my life. Now when I go to college campuses and see unhappy, maladjusted students I relate to them instantly. I know many of them are quite the opposite from the overindulged child I was, but the unhappiness gets to me. I long to reassure them that time will take care of it, as it did with me, but they probably wouldn't listen to me any more than I would have listened then.

Ward-Belmont didn't have national sororities, but they had student clubs which varied in popularity and leadership, and every new girl wanted to be asked to join one of the ones she considered the best. The clubs had Greek names, and each had its own stucco cottage on the back campus. "Rushing," the period when the clubs invited new students to parties and teas to look them over, began the second week of school. To put it mildly, I was not rushed to death. While everyone around me appeared to be caught up in a frenzy of rush parties, I moped around feeling sorry for myself. I wanted to go home so badly I could taste it. But Ward-Belmont had a rule (a very wise one) that freshmen (or Senior-Mids, as we were called) could not go home during the first two months of the fall term. I talked to Mama and Daddy on the phone, but after being so determined to go to Ward-Belmont, I didn't want them to know I hated it, so I pretended things were great.

Mama and Daddy would never have guessed how lonely and insecure I felt because they thought their "general manager" could handle any situation. In fact, no one from Centerville would have recognized the morose girl I'd become. It's no wonder I wasn't invited to a lot of rush parties. Who wants to be around a sniffling, long-faced, sad-eyed girl too busy wallowing in self-pity to see beyond her own gloom!

I'd go to chapel and hear the familiar hymns I had sung at home and it would make me so homesick I'd hurry back to my room and fall on the bed in a flood of tears. I'll bet I cried more those first weeks at college than I'd cried in all the rest of my life. I'm sure my roommate thought I was crazy. She *loved* the whole scene. If only I had paid more attention to my personality and worried less about my wardrobe and "country girl" background, letting those strangers see the side of me that was full of fun and pep, I would have done alright. But I wasn't capable of thinking objectively. It was like the bit Rod Brasfield (my beloved Grand Ole Opry friend who worked double comedy with me) used to do with Minnie Pearl. He'd tell Minnie about his new girlfriend, and he'd say, "By Ned, buddy, Miss Suzie bought a new pair of slacks the other day." Minnie would say, "Oh, really. How'd they look?" "Well, let's put it thissa way," he'd answer. "If Suzie had more hindsight than she did foresight, she never would'a bought them slacks!"

I didn't have the hindsight, or the foresight, to see what kind of impression I was making. All I knew was I'd never felt so alone in all my life, even though I was only two hours from home. I might as well have been on the other side of the earth, and I missed my friends and family with a longing that was a constant, aching emptiness in the pit of my stomach.

Nor did my first few sessions with Miss Townsend improve my spirits. She was so overwhelming I would have been scared to death if we'd been introduced in Miss Inez's parlor back in Centerville. She didn't exactly sweep into a room—because she was physically handicapped and moved with difficulty—but her personality was so powerful, her spirit so indomitable, her manner so dramatic, that she swept her audience, whoever it might be, into the distant background. She terrified me.

She had deformed ankles, the result of a birth defect, which would have forced an ordinary person to move in an awkward manner. But Miss Townsend had a theatrical flair that enabled her to disguise her handicap so well you forgot it in no time. Her dresses were always floor-length, black or navy blue, trimmed in spotless white, with full gathered skirts that swooshed when she moved so you couldn't be certain if she was shuffling her feet along or lifting them up and down. But her appearance above the waist was so striking your eyes were galvanized. She had a handsome patrician face and gloriously thick, snow white hair, which she wore piled high in a bun on the top of her head. She had an enormous bosom, and a back as straight as a board. She carried herself with an authority that demanded absolute respect. So she also fascinated me.

The first time we met she said that Miss Inez had written about me and told her I had considerable talent. "I'm looking forward to working with you," she said crisply. Then she asked me to do a reading for her so she could assess my ability. I chose something

(I don't remember what, but it wasn't *Madame Butterfly*) that I thought might impress her, and she gave me her full attention until I was finished. Then, in an ominous tone, she wanted to know what I had done to strain my voice. I wasn't even aware my voice had been strained. I said I didn't know unless it was yelling so loud as a cheerleader. (Her own voice was a perfectly tuned instrument, which she played with virtuoso skill, so that even a slight inflection could create a mood or convey an idea.)

"Cheerleader!" When she repeated the word she made it sound both contemptible and as hopeless as an incurable disease. "Well, I can certainly tell it. You've ruined the timbre of your voice, which is an essential tool for any dramatic actress." She then informed me, as tactfully as she could, that we had a *great* deal of work ahead of us.

I walked back to my room on the verge of tears. As though I weren't miserable enough already, Miss Townsend, the only reason I had come to Ward-Belmont to begin with, had as much as told me I didn't have the equipment to realize my dream of becoming a great dramatic actress. I had never been so depressed.

My other teachers only reinforced my feelings that I did not belong, that I would never fit in. My gym teacher, Miss Morrison, was just as intimidating as Miss Townsend. She had the personality and bearing of a drill sergeant. Although I had played tennis at home and was a good dancer, I had never been really athletic, and I was certain Miss Morrison saw me as a clumsy oaf. In her presence I always felt as though I had two left feet and had been put together with mending tape. And I wasn't the only one. When she was 82 (she's in her nineties now), 900 Ward-Belmont alumnae gathered in Nashville for a reunion with Miss Morrison as their guest of honor. Some of the girls put on a skit with her, and she got on stage wearing her original gym-class outfit—black bloomers, black stockings, high-top tennis shoes. She was just as stern and forbidding in the skit as she was in real life, and we weren't at all sure whether she knew we were teasing her. She still had the same effect on us that night, even after all those years. It was hilarious to see grown women—many of them grandmothers—pouring drinks in flowerpots and furtively crushing out cigarettes as Miss Morrison walked through the assemblage. Not one in 900 had the nerve to face her with a drink or a cigarette in hand!

Dr. Rhea, my English professor, chopped me down to size my

first day in her class. I had gone into her course with more confidence than in any other because I had always gotten A's in English at home. (Agnes Barnwell, my high school English teacher, had been my sister Mary's good friend, and we often had played tennis after school. She thought I had a flair for writing and especially liked the humorous pieces I turned in, often reading them aloud to the class.) The first day in Dr. Rhea's class we were asked to write an autobiographical sketch so she could get to know more about us and at the same time judge our knowledge of spelling, punctuation, sentence structure, etc. I thought, "At last! Something I can do and do well!" I wrote what I thought was an hilarious account of my life in Centerville, and turned it in, confident that I would impress at least one teacher on campus. But when the paper came back, it had so many red marks, it looked like a roadmap. In addition there was a note: "Miss Colley, someone has apparently misinformed you. From this paper I perceive you've been given the idea that you are funny. *You are not.* But even if you were, no amount of humor could cover up the fact that your carelessness and/or lack of knowledge in grammar, spelling and sentence structure are inexcusable for anyone claiming a high school education!" She implied that my beloved Hickman County High School should never have been accredited!

My first encounters with all these women intensified my homesickness almost beyond endurance. In Centerville I had always had a warm, affectionate relationship with my teachers, and for that matter, with all figures of authority. But most of the teachers at Ward-Belmont, including the dean of women, had a stern bearing and superior attitude that immediately discouraged any attempt toward friendship. (And yet, I grew to love them all. In later life I often met fine dramatic actresses who had this same cool, aloof manner, and I learned that it was often a facade they had developed to cover up shyness, uncertainty and timidity.)

Chapter Eight

MY depression lingered day after day. I walked around
under a cloud of gloom, simply going through the
motions of attending classes, keeping to myself in the dorm, making no effort whatever to get into the swing on campus.

Then one day, toward the end of the first month, I wandered
down to one of the student clubs, which were always open during
the rush season. I knew a piano was there and I just wanted to sit
down and play out some of my misery. I love music so much that
it can always give me a lift, and I desperately needed one. I was
glad to find the cottage empty. I didn't feel like making small talk,
and I certainly wasn't up to performing, even for an audience of
one or two. I sat down at the piano and let 'er rip. I knew the
music and words to all the popular songs of the day, and I was
banging out the liveliest ones, singing at the top of my lungs,
when I suddenly got the feeling I was being watched. I turned
around to see three girls sitting across the room on the sofa. They
hadn't been there before, and I had been too caught up in the
music to hear them come in. I stopped playing instantly, embarrassed that I'd been observed and wondering how long they'd
been there and whether I'd been making a fool of myself. (This
may sound strange, coming from someone who has played comedy more than 40 years, but I have learned that most comics dread
being laughed *at*. The ones I've talked to about it agree that this

is a paradox. Despite the brass and egotism it takes to enable us to go out in front of an audience and "make fools of ourselves," there is also an ingrained sensitivity about being laughed at! Don't ask me why. But even then I was a latent comic, so I had this characteristic.)

"Hey, don't stop!" One of them got up and came toward the piano. "That was great! Why haven't we seen you playing at any of the rush parties?"

"No one ever asked me to play," I answered meekly.

"Well, how on earth could they ask if they didn't know you played?" hooted another girl from the sofa. They were so relaxed, so "in"! It killed me!

Soon they were all gathered around the piano urging me to play this song or that one. They wanted to know my name, then introduced themselves as Hot, Dot and Annie. *Hot, Dot* and *Annie!* Even their names were cute, and they were the liveliest threesome I'd seen since leaving Centerville. I knew they were seniors even before they told me. Even the most sophisticated newcomers didn't have their kind of casual confidence. They said they thought I'd be great fun to have at a party. Would I come along with them to a rush party that evening? *Would I?* If they only knew! If I'd had any money I would have *paid* them to take me.

I wasn't able to tell them at the time, but Hot, Dot and Annie saved my life at Ward-Belmont. If they hadn't taken me under their wing, I honestly don't know if I would have made it through the first year. They were terrific girls (as I told two of them publicly at a recent reunion), and so sweet to take a sad-faced little underclassman as their protégée. I soon learned they were among the most popular girls on campus, and also three of the funniest, but *nice* girls, and responsible, too. They introduced me around, took me to parties, saw that I always had a part in the Saturday-night campus entertainment programs and sponsored and supported me in every possible way. They asked me to join their student club, the Agora, which was the one I had secretly longed to be in, and by Thanksgiving, when we were allowed to go home for the first time, I had my old enthusiasm back and was well on my way to becoming a popular girl on campus. (By the end of the first term I had been elected to the student council as dormitory proctor, which was both an honor and a responsibility, since you were elected by the students but held accountable by the dean of women's office.) I soon forgot all about my sparse wardrobe. In fact, my one coral, cowl-necked evening dress became a dormitory joke. We'd be dressing for a formal and someone would ask, "Well, what are you wearing, Colley?" And I'd say, "Oh, I think I'll be different this time and wear my coral number." It was amazing, really, how soon clothes became unimportant to me, for which I give my mother and father credit. They had given me a good sense of values. I'd only "betrayed" them those first weeks because I was out of my element.

Before we were allowed to go home for the Christmas holidays, we had to gather in the auditorium to hear Miss Sisson's famous speech "The Conduct of Young Ladies While Traveling on Public Conveyances." Most of the girls had come to school by Pullman, and would be returning to their hometowns the same way. But they were now "Ward-Belmont girls," which meant anything they did or said was a reflection on the school. Miss Sisson's talk left nothing to chance. She gave us specific instructions to follow en route to and from campus.

"When a young lady travels by public conveyance there are certain rules that are *not to be broken*," she began. "A young lady *always* carries a book to read so that her eyes are cast downward at *all* times. A lady *never* meets the eyes of a strange man, and under *no* circumstances does she change expression!" (Even if the train is derailed, we wondered?) She cautioned us *never* to smile at a strange man. Speaking to one was so far out of the question she didn't even bring that up.

Her tone and manner in delivering these rules implied they were designed not only to reflect Ward-Belmont's high standard of conduct but also to protect us from Heaven-knows-what dreadful thing that might happen to a young girl who dared to look a strange man in the eye. (I am reminded of the story Mama used to tell about the mother who left her children at home alone while she went to the store. "Don't stuff beans up your noses," she warned, along with her other admonitions. When she came home the children had naturally stuffed beans up their noses. They told her they never would have thought of it if she hadn't suggested it. We Ward-Belmont girls were a lot like those children. When Miss Sisson warned us of the perils of traveling in a Pullman car, we could hardly wait to see what would happen!)

After Miss Sisson's talk the senior girls had a wonderful story to tell. The tale apparently had been circulating around Ward-Belmont for so many years it had become a tradition, one that was always told to new students after Miss Sisson's proper-conduct speech, if not before. It seems that two Ward-Belmont girls were sharing a Pullman sleeping berth en route home for the holidays. One of them got up in the middle of the night to get a drink of water. Returning still half asleep, she climbed into the wrong berth. She was cold, so she snuggled up against her companion's back and whispered, "I'm freezing. Let's sleep spoon fashion," whereupon the man beside her turned over and clapped a hand over her mouth. "Ssssssh!" he whispered. "You are in the wrong berth. I don't want you to embarrass yourself, so slip out quietly and find your friend. Then you can sleep spoon fashion!"

The next morning in the dining car the two Ward-Belmont girls were still talking about the frightful mistake of the night before when a man walked up to their breakfast table, stopped, smiled, picked up a spoon from the table and placed it carefully inside another spoon. Then he walked off without saying a word. Supposedly the girls went so completely to pieces that neither of them could remember afterward what he looked like.

Oh, we thought that was the most *romantic* story! And naturally the next year, when we were seniors, we repeated it to the freshmen just as it had been told to us.

Once I got into the swing at Ward-Belmont, no one had more enthusiasm for campus life than I did. A deep camaraderie develops among the denizens of institutions where strict rules are enforced by stern authority. Prison inmates, army recruits, sanitarium patients and boarding school students all have one thing in common—a cohesion that comes from living in close quarters and under the same rules and authority. Ward-Belmont was no exception. We shared unforgettable experiences that bound us together for the rest of our lives. Even now I can't meet a Ward-Belmont alumna without immediately knowing certain things about her and feeling a kind of conspiratorial intimacy. None of us, for example, will ever forget the humiliating ritual of our Sunday-morning inspections. Before being "released" to attend church (wearing our obligatory black dresses, hats, gloves and stockings) we were lined up to face forbidding, stiff-backed matrons who scrutinized us closely. First they dabbed at our lips and cheeks with immaculate white linen handkerchiefs to make certain our faces bore no trace of make-up. Then they flicked up the hems of our dresses with a blackboard pointer to see if we were "connected" underneath. This was long before the days of panty hose, or even garter belts, so our stockings were precariously held up by garters, which had to be rolled high enough on our thighs to meet our bloomers. It was absolutely unacceptable for *flesh* to show between stockings and underpants. To this day Ward-Belmont graduates tease one another about being "connected." And will any of us ever forget the Saturday-night dances, held once or twice a month, for which we dressed *formally* in order to dance only with one another! My dancing has never recovered, as, being tall, I invariably had to lead.

Dating at Ward-Belmont, not surprisingly, took ingenuity. No one wanted to meet a beau in Rec Hall, where couples were obliged to sit in "uncompromising positions" on straight-backed love seats (inappropriately named) under the ever-watchful eyes of a platoon of chaperones. Thus the only way to have fun on dates was not to date on campus. So we devised elaborate schemes to escape our restrictions. The first requirement was to make friends with a day student at whose home one might visit on Saturdays until 10:30 p.m. As there were only about three hundred day students to a thousand or more boarders, the girls who lived in Nashville were in great demand.

I was lucky. I had been assigned a seat in French class next to a day student named Ruth Carlin. She was an adorable girl and very popular with the Vanderbilt boys. (Vanderbilt, one of the oldest and most prestigious universities in the South, was only a few blocks from Ward-Belmont, and was looked upon by us as the most exciting place in Nashville.) Ruth and I soon became good friends. We kept up with all the popular songs and had a wonderful time playing double piano and singing all the latest hits. She often invited me to her home on weekends, and set me up with a number of cute boys.

The first time she arranged a blind date for me I was still upstairs when the boys came, and I heard Ruthie say, "You're gonna have a great time with Ophie. She's not real pretty, but she's the funniest girl at school." Then she looked up the stairs, saw me coming down and called out, "Say something funny, Ophie." Her meaning was clear to me. I knew how I looked. I'd just left a mirror!

One of the young men I met at Ruthie's house gave me my first real kiss. One night we drove to Percy Warner Park, where we parked. My date leaned over and put his arm around me, pulled me toward him and gave me a real, knockout movie-star kiss . . . none of that spin-the-bottle, post-office kid stuff, like in Centerville. This was the curl-your-toes take-your-breath-away kind. I thought it was the greatest thing that ever was, and I fell wildly in love on the strength of that one kiss. We dated off and on all that semester, but by the end of the first term I had a mad crush on someone else. I was too fickle to stay in love for long, and having too much fun to be serious about any one boy.

Meanwhile I was becoming well known on campus (thanks to Hot, Dot and Annie), mainly because of my participation in the little programs put on every Saturday night. Because my craving for the spotlight had not diminished since leaving home, I thrived on the attention these extracurricular activities brought me, but Miss Townsend took a dim view of them. She felt such things were frivolous and unnecessary. I thought they were essential, because they gave me an enthusiasm for campus life I never would have had otherwise.

Miss Townsend's reputation as a teacher was justified. She was fantastic. She was a Christian woman who earnestly believed it was a sin not to use our God-given talents to their fullest. Only by stretching ourselves to the limit could we repay God for His gifts. Anything less was shameful, a flagrant display of ingratitude. I worried about her classes more than any others. Impressing her was foremost in my mind. But she was a perfectionist, and no matter how well you thought you'd done a reading or a scene, she always wanted and expected more. She could reduce me to tears with the slightest criticism. And she believed in criticism. She would pick to pieces something I'd done, and then, when she saw the hurt and disappointment on my face, she'd say, "Colley, if I didn't think you had talent . . . if I didn't think you could do this better . . . I wouldn't fuss about it. I wouldn't care. I only criticize people about whom I care, people who have potential." But her words did little to appease the frustration I felt at never being able to satisfy her, to measure up to her exacting standards. Now I realize that great teachers like Miss Townsend instill in their pupils this eternal reaching for the stars. Never satisfied with the lowlands, they must stretch endlessly for the heights. She *never* let us rest on our laurels. I learned only recently that her own secret dream in life was one that she could never have realized, yet it didn't daunt her spirit. Someone who had known her well told me she used to say, "In my next incarnation I am going to be a dancer." Trapped inside that lame body was a potential Margot Fonteyn longing to get out.

It may sound ludicrous to Minnie Pearl fans, but my most intense dramatic training at Ward-Belmont was in Shakespeare. If you were majoring in dramatics, you had to minor in Shakespeare,

under the aegis of the English department. So I studied Shakespeare not only with Miss Townsend, but with my teacher of
Shakespeare, Miss Scruggs, as well. She also was a marvelous
instructor. The drama department and the Shakespeare department coproduced Shakespearean plays twice a year, and I took
part in all these productions, playing the lead in *The Taming of
the Shrew* in my senior year—Petruchio, that is.

The highlight of any Ward-Belmont drama student's final semester was the one-woman recital each graduate had to give before the student body, faculty, family and friends. This was a Big
Night on Campus. Everyone wore formal attire—tuxedos and
long dresses—and Miss Townsend's little studio on campus was
always filled to capacity. I performed all the parts in a three-act
play (which I had cut to one hour) called *The Charm School*. I
don't recall feeling stage fright that night, but I do remember the
excitement—adrenaline pumping through my veins in a jet
stream! The audience gathered outside the studio before the recital, then Miss Townsend invited them to take their seats. Mama
and Daddy looked so elegant, and I was so proud of them. When
everyone turned to go inside, Daddy lingered a minute and bent
over to kiss my cheek for good luck. He said, "Stay in there with
'em, Phel. And don't forget your great-uncle John sold newspapers on a street corner of St. Louis." It was his way of telling
me to keep my head. How many times since in my life, when I've
been tempted to be impressed by people or my surroundings, has
the sweet voice of my father echoed in my mind to that refrain! It
was the only indication Daddy ever gave that he was afraid my
head might be turned by the pomp and affluence of Ward-Belmont.

Recital night was a small triumph for me. I felt confident, prepared, effective. But most of all I had a strange presentiment of
other nights to come, when I might make an audience forget for a
while and go with me to a never-never land of entertainment and
happiness.

When graduation day came in the spring of thirty-two it would
have been hard to imagine me as the same girl who had entered
that college two years earlier. Nobody cried louder or harder than
I did as we stood on the steps of Academic Hall at sunset and sang
our Alma Mater, "The Bells of Ward-Belmont." At the traditional
ivy-planting ceremony we watered the young plants with our
tears. So I cried coming in, and I cried going out!

Chapter Nine

WHEN I graduated from Ward-Belmont in the spring of 1932, I had to face the fact that no long-lost rich uncle was going to provide the money I needed to continue my education in dramatics. I knew that I had only one option—I had to get a job. Moreover, I had very little choice as to what kind of work I could do because I wasn't qualified to do anything but teach dramatics, piano and dancing. Reluctantly (oh, *how* reluctantly) I opened a little studio in Centerville in connection with the high school.

I had reached an impasse in my life and teaching was simply a way of holding on until I could get out on my own and pursue my career as a performer. My dream of becoming an actress had not diminished in the slightest, but the route to my goal was obviously not going to be the direct flight I had once envisaged. I knew there was no way I would be allowed to leave home before I was 21. In the early thirties, a girl didn't strike out on her own before she was of age. It simply wasn't done. I wouldn't even have suggested it to Mama and Daddy because I knew it was out of the question. But I was living for the day when I would be old enough to leave. Meanwhile, I was restless, bored, discontented and terribly impatient to have this dull interval of my life over.

The hometown that had once offered me both adventure and security now seemed like a prison, holding me back from the challenges and attainments I felt sure awaited me in the world. My friends either were still away at college or had married and were raising families. I felt stranded, cut off from all that was new, fun and exciting. Centerville hadn't changed, but I had. And I knew for certain that something I had always suspected about myself was an indisputable fact: I would never be content to remain in my hometown to work or to marry a local boy and settle there to make a home. This was no reflection on Centerville. I still loved it as much as ever. But I realized that fulfillment lay elsewhere. I didn't want to hurt Mama and Daddy—I knew they were already hurt enough over the fact that they hadn't been able to give me the full education I wanted—so I tried to keep my restlessness and impatience to myself.

As my studio year ran concurrently with the school year, I was already locked into a new term when my twenty-first birthday finally arrived in October of 1933. All that fall and winter I worried about what I could do to earn a living (other than teaching), where I would find work and what to do with my life. I had the Sewell Production Company in the back of my mind, even though the idea of working as a director for them was quite a comedown from my dreams of starring on Broadway. It was like aspiring to the lead in a network television show and settling for a five-minute spot on a small local radio station. What I really wanted was more training, but since that was out of the question, I thought I would at least be doing something theatrical if I worked for Mr. Sewell.

I wrote to him in the spring of 1934. I mentioned Mama's name because, although he had never met her, his directors, I knew, had always praised her. I also persuaded both Miss Inez and Miss Townsend to write letters to him on my behalf. He responded quickly, saying that he had already filled all his openings for coaches for the first summer session, but that I could join the company in August and train on the road with one of his directors. The letter instructed me to report to Coach Sally Pippin in Hendersonville, North Carolina, on the afternoon of August 24.

Mama and Daddy knew I had written Mr. Sewell, but they may have thought I wouldn't be accepted, because it wasn't until I received the letter that it hit them I was actually leaving home. They brought up every kind of argument imaginable. Daddy was even more adamant about it than Mama. She had spent time around the various Sewell girls when they came to Centerville, and knew most of them to be nice and well mannered. Daddy came up with a thousand reasons why I shouldn't leave—I was too young, I was too inexperienced, I had never been anywhere, I didn't know how to handle money, etc. He was older by then, 77 or 78, and in retrospect I'm sure the main reason he didn't want me to leave was because I was his last child, his "baby," and he was reluctant to let go, knowing he had only a few years left. I loved him so much I probably would have given in had I not felt so *suffocated* in Centerville.

Finally they resigned themselves to my leaving, but all that summer Daddy would bring up things at the dinner table which indicated his concern. He'd say, "Now don't trust people too much. You're too trusting, and you have to be careful. You have to be careful of men." (It is significant that Daddy never really discussed the "pitfalls of sex" with me. I realize now that this omission was a sign of confidence in me. Knowing him, I can see it would have been beneath his dignity to catalogue these so-called pitfalls. It would, in his estimation, have implied that I was unworthy of his trust in me. I sometimes wish, however, that he had advised me more. Mama's dire predictions left me cold, but his careful suggestions would have impressed me. And, goodness knows, I needed them.) He also made it clear that if I couldn't live on my earnings he would *not* send me money, even though he could tell by reading my contract that my income was going to be meager. I listened to all his objections, consciously playing down my enthusiasm about leaving because it would have hurt him to know how anxious I was to go.

All summer I was caught up in a whirlwind of activity as I got clothes together and planned my departure. I had left home only once before, for Ward-Belmont, but that was nothing compared to this breakaway. Still, I seriously believed that something would happen during my time with Sewell that would catapult me into the glamorous world of Broadway. I would be discovered! (How many times would that hope spring up in my lifetime. And it is only from the vantage point of age and experience that I can look back and see what a God-given blessing it is to have that attitude. How many times those hopes were dashed, only to rise again!)

My sister Mary's wedding—to a charming and brilliant Floridian named Jimmy Kershaw—was the high point of that summer. It was a gala affair, romantic and happy. She had been working away from home since she graduated from college, so I didn't feel the terrible wrench that I felt when my other sisters married. And, besides, my own days at home were numbered.

Finally in August my big day arrived. I said good-bye to Daddy at home, and Mama drove me to Nashville, where I caught the train for Hendersonville. I barely suppressed my excitement until we parted.

I had never ridden in a Pullman car before, and this new adventure, coupled with my excitement about getting out on my own, was enough to keep me floating for the first half of the trip. But as Hendersonville drew nearer I began to have feelings of trepidation about facing the future alone. I had only $100 in my pocket, an enormous sum in those days, but I had to make it last until I finished training and had been paid for my first road engagement. I knew I couldn't write home for more if it ran out; Daddy had made that perfectly clear. However, it wasn't the lack of funds that really worried me. (This was undoubtedly due to the triumph of youth and ambition over common sense.) Nor was I concerned about my ability to direct the Sewell plays; I knew I could handle that. What did worry me was my lack of experience in the outside world—meeting strangers, handling people, traveling alone, conducting *business.* I had never done any of these things and I wondered about my ability to carry them off smoothly, with as much easy-going confidence as I had observed in the Sewell girls who came to Centerville.

An element of "fear of the unknown" also nagged at the back of my mind. I was embarking on a journey through unfamiliar, uncharted territory. I wasn't just taking a new job. I was taking on a new lifestyle, one as far removed from anything I knew as Peking is from Pittsburgh. I tossed and turned all night in my Pullman berth, having grave second thoughts about what I was doing. I was glad Daddy didn't know. He was already worried enough, even though I had put up a brave, and jaunty front.

I arrived in Hendersonville in a downpour. By the time I got off the train, located my luggage and found a cab, I was no longer the adventurer who had left Nashville the day before. I was a cowering Milquetoast. I had been told to report to Mr. Bob Cawthon at the Skyland Hotel. There was no bellboy at the door when the taxi left me off there, so I struggled inside with my bags and looked around anxiously. The lobby was as gloomy as the overcast sky outside. No lights had been turned on and no people were there to liven up the atmosphere. The place was completely empty, except for one man behind the desk. Even from a distance I could see that he was attractive—dark, mid-thirties, good-looking. I approached him cautiously, but with what I thought were firm, purposeful steps.

"My name is Ophelia Colley," I said. "I am here to see Mr. Bob Cawthon. Can you tell me where to find him?"

The young man leaned seductively across the desk. "Baby, you're looking at 'im."

I jumped back. His response completely threw me. I had not expected to find a representative of Mr. Sewell behind the desk at the Skyland Hotel, and I had never heard his kind of cocky, familiar, show-bizzy talk from a man before. I was fresh out of Ward-Belmont, where I'd been told not even to look a strange man in the eye!

When he saw that my nervousness was genuine, he tried to put me at ease by explaining he was filling in while the desk clerk took a break. Then he called for the bellboy (more senior citizen than boy) to take my bags upstairs and told me the other girls who had come to be trained as coaches were already waiting in my room. I still wasn't real sure about him. He had made me feel like the chicken cornered by the fox, and when I glanced back over my shoulder he still wore that rakish grin. Heavens, I was accustomed to being formally introduced, then slowly (very slowly) working toward a comfortable rapport with the opposite sex. This was my first brush with the instant familiarity so prevalent in show business.

During all my years with Mr. Sewell, as long as I knew Bob Cawthon, he never let me forget that first meeting. In fact he worked up a regular routine about it, which he delighted in "performing" before other Sewell girls. Mr. Sewell himself loved to see him do it and often requested it! Bob would begin by describing a dark, rainy afternoon, with him alone in the lobby. "Suddenly I looked up from the desk and saw this timorous, frightened creature *creeping* toward me," he would say, as he imitated someone creeping. "She was wide-eyed with fear, shaking all over!" Then he would raise his voice to a high squeak: "Ah—ah—ah—I'm—er—O—O Ophelia Colley. And I'm h—h—here to s—s—see Mr. Bob C—C—Cawthon." He would go through his little act, stuttering, squeaking, shaking, until he had his audience on the floor, at my expense. After I was well established with Sewell, the new girls ate it up when Bob told this story because they were all scared to death and couldn't imagine that I had ever been. To them I appeared a model of gregarious self-assurance.

Bob and I became good friends, even though he teased me unmercifully during the 10 days I stayed in Hendersonville. He would pull the other girls aside in my presence and say (in a tone that implied unspeakable lechery), "You know *I* have a room here at the hotel, too. *Ophelia* knows! She visited me there last night." He loved to shock me, to see me cringe, blush, protest, and the more upset I got the more he carried on. I thought, "If my daddy could hear this man, he would *kill* him!" A sophisticated girl would have seen through Bob in a minute. He wasn't a lecher at all; he was a tease. But he was the first man I had ever met who dropped sex casually into conversation in a joking way—that macho approach to parrying I was to run into on the road time and again.

In the hotel room where Bob told me to go I found four or five other girls in the same shape I was in—scared! They were all from little towns around the South, all wondering what they had gotten themselves into. (The advertisements Mr. Sewell ran in small community newspapers were so enticing, it was easy to lure these girls away from home.) We sat around on the small beds that had been crowded into the sample room (a large room usually engaged by traveling salesmen to set up their wares, like a meeting room would be today), all talking at once, trying to take comfort in the fact that we shared the same anxiety about our future. But we didn't have long to fret. That night we were given scripts of *Dixie Blackbirds* to memorize for our first production.

The production was typical of the minstrel shows of the day. Nine men in blackface sat in chairs on the stage, four on each side of an interlocutor. They told jokes back and forth between the scenes and skits (blackouts, or olios, as they were called) that made up the show. Our coach, Sally Moore Pippin, was wonderful. We loved her immediately! She was a pert little girl, overflowing with pep and personality, and she had a wonderful figure. We Sewell girls stayed awake late talking about how great she was and wondering if we'd ever attain her self-assurance. She seemed to know *everything,* and we knew nothing. But she was so patient we felt inspired rather than intimidated.

The morning after we arrived we donned shorts and tap shoes and reported to a large conference room in the hotel basement, where Sally began teaching us the dance routines to *Blackbirds.*

She put us through our paces while at the same time rehearsing her local cast for their upcoming production of the show, and for the next 10 days she worked us like dogs! By some miracle, at the end of that time she had taught us the entire show—dialogue, songs and dances. Sally had her hands full trying to get her Hendersonville cast into shape while simultaneously training a group of new coaches. (It may have been too much for her. After the show she stayed on in Hendersonville and married the leading man! I still see her when I visit my sister who lives there.)

Sally kept us on our toes all day and Mr. Sewell put us to work at night, over books, ledgers and paperwork. He had come up from his headquarters in Atlanta to make sure we were as well schooled in the business end of our job as we were in coaching. We were all fascinated by him. He was a dashing man, very dramatic-looking, given to wearing Barrymore-ish suits, capes and smart hats. He wore pince-nez glasses à la Teddy Roosevelt, and had the same type of speaking voice as FDR. He was the archetype of the old-time theatrical agent.

My image of the Sewell Company's operation was based solely on what I had seen in Centerville. The girls who worked there had all been vivacious and talented, and they appeared to be thoroughly happy in their work. To my naive mind it seemed like a job that would make anyone happy—singing and dancing their way across the South, Pied Pipers of entertainment, leading the local citizens through lighthearted routines in delightful little productions that everyone raved and laughed about for weeks afterward. I was totally ignorant of the enormous amount of work that went on behind the scenes to make this unique production company successful, or of the hardships these girls faced on the road. (But even if I had been told the worst, it wouldn't have discouraged me. I would have thought, "Well, it won't be that way for me." For me it was going to be different, *better*.)

Mr. Sewell and his wife, the former Hettie Jane Dunaway, had started their company in the twenties, and it was the only one of its kind in the South. They had met when both worked for the Chautauqua Circuit, a classy road show where Mr. Sewell had been a booker and Mrs. Sewell had performed in a one-woman show. She had been a star on the circuit, one of the most popular "platform readers" of her day and a talented performer. When they married they formed a production company that would send shows throughout the South into rural towns and communities where very little, if any, entertainment was available. Mrs. Sewell wrote all their original productions and in the beginning was also in charge of their training school for coaches in Roscoe, Georgia. Hers was the creative contribution to the partnership, while Mr. Sewell was the brains behind the business operation.

In many ways Mr. Sewell was ahead of his time as a business-man. He was shrewd. He used psychology at every turn, long before it was a household word or even became widely accepted as a subject in college. He trained us all, coaches and promoters alike, in Dale Carnegie's method of dealing with people: "Sell yourself first." Carnegie's book *How to Win Friends and Influence People* had already made an impact on the country, and Mr. Sewell considered it the bible of selling. (Years later, after I had made a name on the Grand Ole Opry, I was playing the Astor Roof at the Hotel Astor in New York when I was given a note saying Dale Carnegie and his wife were in the audience and would like to meet me. I was flattered to death to learn they were fans of Minnie Pearl's, and delighted to have the opportunity to tell him how much his philosophy had influenced my life.)

Mr. Sewell's operation was set up so that about 10 bookers (also called promoters or advance men) were going from town to town at all times persuading different organizations to sponsor shows. Concurrently, he would have as many as 150 coaches in the field in other towns putting on the shows previously booked by these men.

When a promoter hit a town he would contact a representative of a school or civic or church organization and sell them on the idea of sponsoring a show to make money for their club treasury. The organization would sign a contract that stipulated that it would be responsible for furnishing a place to put on the show, a cast, an accompanist, food and lodging for the director and some-one to take said director around town and help her sell advertising for the program. In return, the Sewell Company would send the sponsoring organization a "winsome" director, who would bring costumes, scripts and music and would coach and rehearse the cast, direct the show, sell ads for the program and pay the club its share of the box office returns before leaving town.

Sewell and the local organization split the cost of printing the programs, but the ticket money was divided 60/40—60 percent for Sewell, 40 percent for the club. We directors were paid out of Mr. Sewell's percentage, which meant our weekly salary varied. But we didn't take our cut when we counted out and divided the ticket money. We sent the entire 60 percent to Sewell, who then mailed us a check covering our share to a town further down the line on our schedule. This was not only a means of keeping his girls honest with the box office receipts (not that Mr. Sewell distrusted his coaches), but it was also as close as he could get to a guarantee that each girl would stay on the road until the next town. He had a big turnover among his coaches, but no matter how disenchanted a girl might be, she was more likely to go on to her next assignment if she knew a check was waiting.

My salary on the road averaged about $10 per week. No Sewell coach could hope to earn much more than that. We were fed and sheltered by strangers in towns where we worked, so we usually ate well and had a place to sleep, but we had no money. I remember feeling rich if I had a few dollars in my purse. But the whole nation was suffering a depression, so we were no worse off than most.

Mr. Sewell's promoters did a great job of selling each show. They made it sound like the local organization could make quick, easy money without the usual hassle of planning and preparing a fund-raising event. They told the customers that basically all they had to do was round up a certain number of prominent citizens to play the leading roles (this was important because the town would turn out in full force to see the mayor, chief of police or a judge "cuttin' the fool"), then furnish the coach with room and board, and she would do the rest. Unfortunately, by the time Mr. Sewell's "winsome" directors hit these towns, weeks, or even months, later, the organization had often cooled on the idea. Sometimes new officers had been elected who didn't even know that their predecessors had signed a contract with Sewell.

A few days before a coach was scheduled to arrive in a town, a wire was sent to the person who had signed the contract, requesting that someone meet the director's train or bus. There was no return address on the telegram, so the group couldn't cancel if they wanted to (another example of Sewell psychology). I can't count the times I got off trains and stood on cold, windy, deserted platforms, one eye on the huge costume trunk that accompanied me everywhere, looking in vain for a face wearing that questioning Are you the one? expression. On some occasions no one showed up at all and I was left to my own devices to locate my contact in town. At other times I knew the minute I saw the look on the face of the person meeting me that I wasn't wanted, that the play wasn't wanted, that all they did want was for me to get on the next train and get out of town. In both cases I knew immediately, without being told, that nothing had been done to prepare for my arrival. That meant I had to resell them on the idea of the show (selling myself first!), then help them round up a cast, losing a precious day or two before I could start rehearsals. I had to work harder than ever then to get the production together on time because my schedule was firm and inflexible. I was allowed ten days in each town, and if five of those were wasted getting the people organized, that was my problem. I still had to be in the next town on the date agreed.

The first few hours in a new town were the most critical. The president of the organization, his committee, the people I was staying with, all had to be won over and resold or there was the chance they might cancel the play. No play, no pay—at least not for that week. The pressure on me at that point in each town was incredible. My energy level had to remain at fever pitch, and I smiled until my jaws ached. Even worse (at least for me) was the possibility of becoming a failure in Mr. Sewell's eyes.

I had to cancel only two productions in the six years I was with Sewell, and circumstances made that unavoidable. One was during my first year on the road, in 1934. I arrived in Clover, South Carolina, to find the town up in arms over a textile strike. There were cotton mills all over that part of the country, and this was when unions were just beginning to move in and organize factory workers in the South. There was a bitter fight going on. The protesting mill hands paraded up and down at night with torches, and you could almost smell the fear in the air. People were told to stay off the streets, but that only made them more anxious to see what was going on. One night violence erupted all along the picket lines and nine men were killed. Everyone was too scared to rehearse the play, so I had to cancel. I was scared, too. But I also thought it was the most exciting thing in the world to have a job that put me right in the center of the action.

Even when I was met by a smiling committee who had done all the groundwork and when everything went smoothly from beginning to end, I still ran myself ragged. Teaching a group of amateurs (chosen more for local prominence than talent) to sing, dance and act in 10 days wasn't a coach's only headache. The costumes, for example, were a constant source of irritation. Each cast member had to get his own costume cleaned before the show, but I was responsible for keeping them in one piece, which meant finding a reliable alteration woman who would not tear them up while letting out and taking up seams. But of all the countless little jobs connected with putting on these plays, the one I hated most was selling program ads. The program listed the cast of characters along with local advertisements. It was very hard to convince merchants that this was worthwhile advertising. The programs were used only that one night, and very few people read anything other than the names of friends and relatives appearing in the play. Most businessmen considered buying an ad in the program purely a contribution to the organization that was sponsoring the show, and the fly in the ointment was that *I* was taking part of this contribution out of town with me.

I also hated the fact that I had to smile all the time. Even if you were sick or ready to drop from fatigue you had to *smile*. You were representing the Sewell Company every moment, even if you were in church. Mr. Sewell insisted that his coaches attend church on the road, and sing in the choir if possible, because it generated interest in the play. Seeing a stranger in their midst, members of the congregation would inquire about her, and someone would say, "Oh, that's the director from the Sewell Company who's here to put on that play next Friday night." I learned to make eye contact and smile in every encounter (the very opposite of Miss Sisson's lectures!), and sometimes I felt I would *die* if I didn't quit smiling and let my mouth rest. For six years I suffered from a chronic case of dry teeth!

I had been scared to death when I left Hendersonville on the train to take over my first coaching job in Valdosta, Georgia. I worried all the way there, certain I'd never be able to remember all that had been crammed into my head (and feet) in 10 short days and desperately afraid something terrible would go wrong and I wouldn't know how to handle it. I was more concerned about being efficient at business than anything else. Nothing in my training at Ward-Belmont or my teaching job at home had equipped me to handle business matters, especially in a position of responsibility for success or failure, profit or loss.

I was frantic to prove myself in every way because Mr. Sewell had singled me out in Hendersonville and made me a conditional offer I was determined to see come to fruit. I had noticed him watching me when he sat in on dance rehearsals, but I knew I was a good dancer, so I assumed that was what interested him. Then after four or five days' training he approached me one evening after our business class and asked if I would join him for dinner the following night. It was such a surprising gesture, such an unexpected invitation, it's a wonder I didn't suspect him of ulterior motives, but I didn't. I was so innocent then. Instead I was thrilled that my new boss was giving me special attention and delighted that I was going to be treated to a meal in the Skyland dining room, which seemed elegant and expensive. (We had been eating all our meals at a boarding house down the street where the food was starchy and the prices cheap.) Once we were seated, Mr. Sewell didn't waste any time getting to the purpose of his invitation. "Miss Colley, I've been watching you closely these past few days, and I think I have more in mind for you than just being a coach." (This would have certainly triggered suspicion had I not been so naive.) "I think you have an exceptional talent for this type of work, and there's going to be an opening this summer in my organization that might interest you."

He explained that his niece, Marjorie Dunaway, who ran the main coaching school in Roscoe, was getting married, and that he would be needing someone to take over her job. "Would you be willing to work as hard as necessary to learn all eight of our productions so you could train the new coaches during the summer months, then go back on the road during the winter season?" he asked. I could hardly believe he was making this offer to *me*, a rank beginner, who didn't even know *one* production yet. I knew there must have been coaches out in the field who had been with him long enough to prove their ability, so I was doubly flattered. I was so excited by his offer I would have agreed to try if he'd asked me to jump over the moon. This was the biggest event of my life! (What Mr. Sewell had seen in me was an inherent conscientiousness—a legacy from Mama and Daddy—and the energy, enthusiasm and vitality to inspire other girls.)

"Now, you realize we will be watching you this season on the road," he cautioned. "And whether you get the job will depend on how well you do out there. But I just wanted to make sure you'd be willing to take on this challenge should it be offered to you."

A few days later, with his words still ringing in my ears, I arrived in Valdosta for my first assignment. I was met at the train by a Mr. Theo Coleman of the Lions Club. His group was sponsoring

the play. He was very nice and invited me to dine with him that
night so we could discuss preparations for the production. He had
already lined up the cast and the chorus (I was to learn that this
caliber of efficiency was the exception rather than the rule), and
everything was ready for me to start rehearsals the next day. Mr.
Sewell had warned all the new coaches who trained in Hendersonville not to say we had just started with the company. "Tell
them you've been putting on these plays for *years*," he instructed.
I wasn't prepared to go that far, but when Mr. Coleman asked me
how long I'd been at it, I managed to mutter, "Quite some time."
Little did he know that I was a nervous wreck thinking about
what lay ahead for the next 10 days.

As I had anticipated, I found the coaching part of my job easy
compared to the business side. But somehow I muddled through.
And 10 days later I put on my first play. It was a huge success, and
I remember that everyone was very sweet to me when it was over.
I tried to be charming. (Well, I *had* to be!) I left Valdosta thinking
that the nicest people in the world lived there.

Mr. Sewell always asked the sponsoring club to write him a
letter evaluating the coach who had been sent to their town. The
next day the Valdosta Lions Club sent a telegram (very unusual)
with glowing compliments about Miss Ophelia Colley. Bless
them! I was so proud. I wish I had gotten that wire and framed it!

The next few months became a blur of one small town after
another. I loved the attention I received in those places. As I
gained confidence in my ability to pull an amateur cast together
into an entertaining production in a ridiculously short time, I
grew to enjoy thoroughly the coaching part of my work. As a director, I relied more on showing performers how I wanted a show
done than on telling them, and it pleased me and fed my ego that
they were absolutely awed by my ability to play all the parts, do
all the dance routines, sing all the songs, play all the music on the
piano and prompt them without a script.

Persuading stiff, self-conscious businessmen to loosen up and
throw themselves into their parts or training clumsy, uncoordi-
nated children and students in dance routines was not easy. But it
was a challenge I liked, because it was great fun to see them
finally start to enjoy themselves when they realized they could
actually perform. There were always parts for children in the productions because Mr. Sewell knew it would bring parents, grand-
parents and aunts and uncles to see the show. "One on the stage,

three in the audience," was his motto. The experience I'd had teaching at home helped me get performances out of children that I might not have gotten otherwise, and often they turned out to be the hits of the shows.

Going into these small towns as a director made me feel important. I liked the fact that I was a little different from the local people in that I seemed to be bringing a breath of fresh air from the outside world, like the Music Man coming to River City. I was bright and peppy and happy. And it was no act. I *was* happy, and wrote glowing letters home about my exciting life. At the same time it was the hardest work imaginable. The sheer physical exertion alone was enough to put you to bed. Only a very young, very energetic person could have gotten through it—keeping up a whirlwind pace for 10 days in a town, then packing up the old costume trunk and back on a train or bus for the next town, no rest between stops, no days off except at Christmas, smiling, selling, rehearsing the same routines over and over, town after town.

Every 10 days I would think I had faced every conceivable crisis. Then a new one would arise. I learned to deal with jealous wives, panting husbands, stuffy teachers, hypocritical preachers, pompous businessmen, scared children, bossy mothers, shy young farm boys, young and old, rich and poor. Mothers were almost always jealous about the positions of their children in the show. Each one insisted her little Suzie or dear Freddy be in the *front* row of the chorus. Then they would want me to stay after the others were finished to give their child individual instruction. If the children were sweet, the mothers took the credit; if they acted like brats, it was my fault for not having better control over them.

Most men I met on the road immediately categorized me as a "show girl"—i.e., different from their wives, mothers, sisters or girlfriends. Bob Cawthon's initiation proved helpful. I realized these men saw me as a sophisticated woman (Ha!) and therefore felt less inhibited around me than they did around their hometown girls. I had to learn to fend off passes without bruising egos, an essential trick for any female who wants to be successful at a job that requires her to travel alone from place to place. Having a sense of humor about it helped. It would have been disastrous had I adopted a hostile, prudish attitude. And yet I had to remain ladylike and deserving of their respect. I knew they didn't mean anything by their come-ons. And they seldom got ugly about it. Very few of them ever tried to force themselves on me.

In fact, I had only one really ugly experience involving a man during the six years I traveled for Mr. Sewell, and it was so sad, so *tragic,* that it upsets me to think about it even today. I was staying in the home of the woman who was president of the organization sponsoring our show in that town. She was a kind, soft-spoken lady who lived in a neat little two-bedroom house with her husband and her teenage daughter. There was no guest room, so I had to share her daughter's bed. She was a nervous adolescent but sweet, and I liked her. The first night, I was sound asleep beside her in the double bed when I was suddenly awakened by the horrifying sensation of hands groping at my body. I was terrified! I thought it was the girl. But as I started to scream I felt her hand clamp over my mouth and realized she was on the other side of the bed from where the hands were reaching under the covers.

"Ssssssh, Sssssssh, *please* don't scream," she begged. "You'll wake Mama."

In the dark I could see no more than a shadow bending over my side of the bed, but I knew it was a man. When he heard her whispered plea he jumped back quickly and hurried out of the room. After he'd gone I jumped out of that bed as fast as I could and turned on the light. The girl was crying. "It was my daddy." Her voice was barely audible. She was so pitiful, so ashamed. "He's been coming in here at night since I was 13, but I can't tell Mama. It would kill her. So I'm just biding my time until I'm 18. Then I'm going to leave home and get away from him. He gets drunk and doesn't know what he's doing. But I hate him just the same," she sobbed.

I sat up the rest of the night. The next morning I left the house before breakfast and made arrangements to cancel the show and leave town. I went straight to Atlanta and told Mr. Sewell in no uncertain terms that he could have his job if I was expected to stay and put on a show under those circumstances. He was very kind. He calmed me down, then sent me on to another town. I never found out if the woman understood. I'd made up some excuse for leaving, I don't remember what. The woman didn't protest or ask questions. I always wondered if maybe she knew the truth but just didn't want to face it, or was afraid to. I hope she didn't know. And I'm glad Mama and Daddy never knew of this. I shudder to think what Daddy would have done!

Looking back I can honestly say that the hardest work I've ever done in my life was during the six years I spent with Sewell. I consistently faced more difficult and disheartening situations than at any other time; I had more eye-opening experiences; I was alone, constantly broke, sometimes mistreated, often scared, never relaxed. But it was also the most important, invaluable training period of my life. No other job could have taught me as much that would be useful to me throughout my career. I also had more fun than I could have imagined. Last, and most important of all, it was during this time that I found Minnie Pearl. So with all this in mind, I can only describe my Sewell years by borrowing a line from Dickens: "It was the best of times; it was the worst of times."

Chapter Ten

BY the end of my first winter on the road, Mr. Sewell had sent word that his offer for me to take over the training school in Roscoe, Georgia, was still open if I was interested.

Interested! I can't put into words how excited I was about the prospect of becoming the director of the Wayne P. Sewell Training School! I thought I had really come up in the world. And I guess I had, when you consider I'd been teaching at home just one short year before.

I reported to the school in May of 1935, and was pleasantly surprised to find the Sewells had an impressive setup. The Sewell plantation was located outside of Roscoe, a small town about 40 miles south of Atlanta. Mr. Sewell's older sister lived in the lovely, large old farmhouse that had been in their family for generations, along with hundreds of acres of rich bottomland where they grew cotton. There was an atmosphere of rural gentility about the place. Unlike Centerville, which was a new settlement by comparison, this was the Old South, where plantation life hadn't changed much since before the Civil War.

Mr. Sewell had built a 10-room dormitory about 100 yards from the family home, where the coaches lived while they were training. There was also a warehouse on the property for storing costumes and stage equipment, and a small, rustic theater for rehearsals. Closer to town, on a separate parcel of land, Mrs. Sewell owned a park known as the Hettie Jane Dunaway Gardens. These gardens, which were beautifully landscaped and impressive enough to attract visitors from all over the state, represented her own personal domain, where her maiden name and her Chautauqua Circuit fame lived on. The park boasted a fine tearoom and the Patchwork Barn, a theater so named because the decor featured patchwork quilts hung on the walls like paintings. There were also cottages on the property where guests could stay overnight. Mrs. Sewell charged 50-cents admission to the park, which included a guided tour she sometimes conducted herself. There were living quarters behind the tearoom, where she and Mr. Sewell stayed when they were down from their elegant apartment in Atlanta. (They rented a whole floor in the Ponce de Leon apartment building on Peachtree Street across from the Georgian Terrace Hotel, where they lived and he had his offices.) During the summer months Mr. Sewell had to be in Roscoe several nights a week to conduct business classes for his new coaches.

When I arrived in Roscoe, Mrs. Sewell's niece Marjorie Dunaway was already there, ready to teach me the seven other shows that filled out the Sewell repertoire. I liked Marjorie immediately. She was a beautiful young woman—dark brown hair and large dark eyes, a clear, translucent complexion and a willowy figure. She also had the most exquisite speaking voice I had ever heard. She was very much in love and already making plans for her wedding to a local man that summer.

When I found out Marjorie had just come from doing a show on *Broadway* (where she had actually had a *speaking* role!) I was absolutely in awe. I *idolized* her and pumped her to death day and night, asking a million questions about theater in New York. To me she represented the sophisticated, glamorous world of big-time show biz. Everything about her impressed me, even the fact that she wore a leotard to our dance classes. It was so *New York!* She rekindled the flame of my burning desire to be on the stage, to see my name in lights on the Great White Way, and she was such an inspiration I absolutely surpassed myself to win her approval. Imagine having to learn seven hour-and-a-half-long musical productions—every word of dialogue, every dance step, every song—in just six weeks. Had I not been inspired by my teacher, I never could have done it. She was a marvelous boost for my ego. She complimented me and encouraged me continually, and she was a wonderful audience for my clowning. I could make her fall out laughing with a silly dance or some dumb routine, and I gloried in her response.

Those six weeks with Marjorie were the hardest concentrated work I've ever done in my life, but thanks to her high spirits and down-to-earth congeniality, it was also great fun. I've had some difficult times during my 40 years in show business, committing things to memory on short notice, but nothing like that. We worked 10 hours a day, and at night I would fall into bed exhausted, my head spinning with songs and routines. Half the time I didn't know which song went with which production.

My graduation test was a two-hour recital, or one-woman show, which I performed in front of Mr. and Mrs. Sewell. I stood on stage while Mrs. Sewell threw cues to me from the audience: "Give me the stuttering scene from *Black-Eyed Susan;* let me see the opening dance routine from *Rosetime;* sing the love ballad from *Miss Blue Bonnet."* Miraculously I got through it without a mistake, greatly relieved and proud that I had lived up to Marjorie's expectations.

When my first batch of girls arrived the following week to be trained as coaches I was ready and eager to prove myself as director of the Sewell Training School. Actually, my job included more than training these girls. I was also in charge of the dormitory where we all lived and therefore responsible for them day and night. I was only 22, a little young to be a housemother to so many girls from different towns and backgrounds and with so many different motives for being there. Some simply wanted to get away from the dull routine of small-town living; others were running from broken engagements or unhappy love affairs; a few were pregnant; some were chasing vague dreams of a career in show business. But I felt equipped to handle the duties required of me because Mama and Daddy had taught me that when you accepted responsibility you were honor-bound to live up to it. In that area, at least, I was mature for my age, and I'm sure Mr. Sewell had sensed this before he offered me the job. During the next five years more than 1,000 girls passed through that training school, and I learned enough about females to last me the rest of my life. I met girls who lied, feigned illness, tattled, schemed, gossiped and griped constantly. Some were frightened and lost and pitifully insecure. But the majority were nice. They were sweet and funny, supportive of one another, and eager to please their director.

There were 12 training sessions every summer, with about 20 girls in each session. This meant they had only 10 days under my tutelage to learn the plays they would be taking on the road. (The girls had no voice in selecting which play they were to learn, nor did I. Mr. Sewell made up the schedule according to what production needed new coaches at that time.) I had to work the girls hard in order for them to assimilate so much new information in such a short time. In fact, the work was so hard some of them dropped out before the week was up because they simply couldn't take it. Remembering how much fun Marjorie had made my training period, I tried to keep my classes relaxed, interjecting humor, and even silliness, whenever I could.

If we had any time off on Sunday afternoons, I'd take the girls out riding in the Model-T Ford Mr. Sewell had put at my disposal. We'd have a good time driving around the countryside, half of them hanging out of the car like the Beverly Hillbillies. Sometimes we moved the training sessions over to Mrs. Sewell's gardens. While there, we slept in the guest cottages, took our meals in the tearoom, and rehearsed in the Patchwork Barn. If construction work was going on in the gardens (Mrs. Sewell was constantly making improvements and additions) or the cottages were rented out, we trained at the old Sewell place, living in the dorm, eating at the Sewell home and rehearsing in the little rustic theater nearby. Having two locations made it nice for me because I didn't have time to get bored with one place before moving my classes to the other. Having two distinctly different jobs during the year also was good. I'd no sooner start getting tired of the hectic pace of the road than I'd return to the school for another summer season. Then, by the end of the summer, when I'd had it with the boarding school atmosphere, I'd be ready to hit the road again.

I soon felt right at home at the coaching school, even though there were times when my relationship with Mrs. Sewell was not as easy as I would have liked it to be. It could have been that she resented my taking over a part of what had always been a family operation, her special "baby." All those plays were her creations, her "children," and it wasn't easy for her to sit by and watch a stranger take them over. Certainly I couldn't have replaced her niece Marjorie in her affection. No one could, as they had been very close.

Mrs. Sewell might also have envied my youth. She had been a *star*, and a striking beauty in her younger days. She was still a handsome woman, but she was matronly, and makeup could not hide the telltale signs of age. She wanted very much to be young again. It was sad. Now that I am past the age she was then, I can fully understand how she felt. But for her it was even worse because her beauty had faded along with her youth. Having never been a beauty, I didn't have that loss to contend with as I grew older, but I've known many, many women who did, and their suffering is very real. There *are* compensations for not being beautiful, but it's hard to convince a young girl of that!

Mrs. Sewell never confronted me with her jealousy. She was too proud for that. Her hostility came out in more subtle ways. Often, as she escorted visitors through her gardens, she would stop by the Patchwork Barn while I was holding a dance rehearsal with my students. She would invite the people inside to watch. After a few minutes she would say, in a disgusted tone, "Colley that's *not* the way I intended this dance to be done." That gave her an excuse to get up on stage in front of these strangers and show them that she could dance, too. She always made a valiant effort to move gracefully through the routine, but there is no way an overweight 55-year-old woman is going to look lithe, young and supple in motion, no matter how well she once danced. We would stand up there in our perky little shorts—a group of energetic, firm-thighed, slim-waisted girls—watching her push and strain to make it look easy, and we felt embarrassed for her.

It was a shame Mrs. Sewell let her anxiety show, because she was such a charming, talented woman she didn't need to feel threatened by anyone. She had many qualities that I admired and envied, including a lovely, light and facile speaking voice. She was also a fine actress, and she could drop into characterization in a second. She was a clever writer, composer and lyricist, and all the original musicals she had penned for the Sewell Production Company were bright and entertaining. I was awed by the variety of her talents and wanted very much for her to like me. But I couldn't get past the barrier she had put in my way. Fortunately I was protected from her criticisms by the armor of youth, and it is a very strong armor. She couldn't shake my confidence as a coach because I knew I was good at what I was doing. I loved it so much that I absolutely bloomed. It wasn't until much later, toward the last of my six years with Sewell, that the work began to get routine and the fun went out of it.

In later years, after I became Minnie Pearl, Marjorie brought

Mrs. Sewell to see me work, and she was very complimentary. I realized then that any conflict between us had been resolved by the passing years, and I appreciated that.

In contrast, Mr. Sewell and I had a fine rapport (Mrs. Sewell may also have misinterpreted that, but she had no reason to), and his attitude toward me made the difficulties easier. He was a very attractive man, and he did have somewhat of a reputation with the ladies, but our relationship was always strictly business. He had a great sense of humor, and we laughed over many situations at the school that could have been depressing if he had taken them too seriously. We always had inside jokes about the different types of girls who came to the school. I used to compare the coaches going into the field to the Foreign Legion because so many of them had joined to get away from problems at home. Two or three times a month, after Mr. Sewell's first business meeting with each new class, we'd get together and go down the list of girls one by one. Then he would categorize them. Even on such quick observation, we got so we could put them into three classes; those who would never make it through training, those who would quit the job after one or two assignments on the road and those who would be good for the long haul. The third category was always the smallest! It was the kind of job that required great stamina, unwavering dedication, relentless optimism, a dogged sense of humor and almost limitless adaptability, and you just didn't find too many young girls ready to give all that in return for the salary of a nine-to-five secretary!

Despite my lack of rapport with Mrs. Sewell, one of the most rewarding experiences I had during this time involved working very closely with her on a special project, which began in the following way.

There was a small community of black families who lived in cabins on the Sewell plantation and worked in the cotton fields. These people were very important to Mr. and Mrs. Sewell. Some were descendants of slaves who had been on the plantation before the Civil War, and a closeness that was warm and comfortable had developed over the generations between these workers and the Sewell family. I got to know them by visiting their church with Mr. and Mrs. Sewell. We spent many inspiring Sunday evenings at that little church way out in the country in the middle of a cool pine grove. They always welcomed us warmly and made us feel like special guests. I loved their church services.

I'll never forget Deacon Rowe, a much respected old gentleman who appeared to have a straight line to Heaven. At some point during each service, Deacon Rowe would stand up from the congregation and talk to the Lord. He always closed his prayer with the same line: "Oh Lord, prop us up on our leaning side." I love that expression and have often thought of it in my own prayers. We all have a leaning side, and there have been many times when I needed to be propped up on mine to keep from falling over!

But for me the high point of these services was the music. They sang the most moving old spirituals, with the beat and rhythm of that deep-rooted Southern black gospel sound that spawned so much American music, from blues to rock n' roll. Church wasn't the only place you could hear their marvelous voices raised to the heavens. Every afternoon at dusk, as they were leaving the fields, the workers sang their way home, and whenever we were within earshot of the sound we stopped whatever we were doing to listen. It was like stepping back in time—at first the distant sound of one or two voices, then others joining in to swell the chorus as they reached the line where they waited to have their cotton weighed. Then, as they left the fields, the tempo of the music picked up in a joyful, "going home" beat, which made you want to move your feet and clap your hands. I'm sure it was the music of these people that inspired Mrs. Sewell to write her all-black operetta *Glory Train*. It was my favorite of all her productions, and I looked forward to working on it more than any other.

Glory Train was presented by the field hands every summer at the Patchwork Barn in the Hettie Jane Dunaway Gardens. The show always played to a packed house because it was so enjoyable it attracted the same audiences over and over again, as well as new visitors to the area. The old audiences knew what to expect so they really got with it.

The show opened with part of the cast dressed in their Sunday best, filing down the aisles singing a spiritual they often sang coming in from the fields in the afternoon:

> *When de sun go down, brother*
> *When de sun go down,*
> *We gonna rest so sweet and easy*
> *When de sun go down.*

When they reached the front of the theater they sat in the first three rows, which had been cordoned off for them, while Deacon Rowe prayed. This established the fact that they were in church. Then the lights would go up on stage to reveal other men and women dressed in white choir robes, singing in high voices like angels. The stage represented Heaven. Hell was down in the orchestra pit where Leon (Mr. Sewell's chauffeur) played a marvelous devil in white-tie and tails, leaping out to sing jazzy songs of temptation as he tried to lure the church members away from Heaven. As the church members tried to get past the devil, they'd sing:

> *One mornin' soon I hear the angels singin',*
> *One mornin' soon I hear the Lord a 'callin'.*

And the angels in Heaven would sing back:

> *You can't hide, sinner,*
> *Fly to the mountain, you can't hide;*
> *Fly to the mountain, you can't hide,*
> *Can't hide, sinner, can't hide. . . .*

One woman with an incredible soprano voice would take the "can't hide, sinner, can't hide" higher and higher above the other voices, with the music swelling until it flooded your senses. By the time the chorus of little angels filed down the aisles the audience was completely enraptured. (One of my jobs was to get these children lined up in the foyer before they made their entrance.) These six- and seven-year-olds were dressed in little white choir robes and they were adorable. They came down the aisles in twos, doing a little step we'd taught them and singing:

> *D'ere is one, d'ere is two,*
> *d'ere is three little angels;*
> *D'ere is four, d'ere is five,*
> *d'ere is six little angels. . . .*

And every time they'd sing "little angels," they'd throw their arms up in the air and shake their hands above their heads. They put everything they had into that entrance, never missing a step or a beat, and the audience would go wild. After they got on stage, the church members would finally make their way past the devil, who would then slink away in defeat. Leon was a wiry, lithe man who made a perfect devil, playing the role in that snappy, cocky way that Sammy Davis, Jr., used playing Sportin' Life in the film version of *Porgy and Bess.*

The finale consisted of the cast moving in a shuffling fashion back and forth across the stage, almost like a congo line, but making the sound of a train, with their hands on one another's shoulders, singing:

> *Get on board, little chillun,*
> *Get on board, little chillun,*
> *We're bound for Canaan Land.*

Their full, clear voices took on a joyous sound, getting louder and livelier until the whole theater seemed to vibrate with music. It was one of those shows that left you wanting to sing and dance and "make joyful noises unto the Lord." I've never seen happier audiences anywhere than the ones who filed out of the Patchwork Barn after a *Glory Train* production.

Chapter Eleven

MR. Sewell never gave his "winsome" directors an advance road schedule. We didn't get our next assignment until we had already started the current job. Then a route sheet would be sent from headquarters in Atlanta telling us where to report the following week.

In January of 1936 I received notice that my next assignment was in a little village near Sand Mountain in northern Alabama. At that time, this was rugged, remote country, not unlike the Appalachians in Tennessee and Kentucky. I was to put on my play at a large consolidated school which was 15 miles from the nearest transportation facilities in Cullman, Alabama. I wrote to the principal of the school, whose name was on the Sewell contract, and asked that he meet me at the Cullman railroad station at a certain time and date.

My train pulled into the little depot in the middle of a blizzard. I was the only person who got off. It was about three o'clock in the afternoon, and already almost dark, with snow falling so heavily I could hardly see. I automatically looked down toward the baggage car first. (Sewell girls learned very quickly that the costumes were even more important than their own luggage.) There stood the huge trunk down at the far end of the deserted platform, surrounded by swirling snow. As the train pulled out of the station I looked around anxiously to see if anyone had come to meet me.

There wasn't a soul in sight. I had never felt more alone in my life, or less independent, especially since I had only $7 in my purse. I hurried, half-frozen, into the depot. The stationmaster was just about to close up for the day, as no other train was due in until morning. He seemed surprised to see me, as though he hadn't expected anyone to be stupid enough to travel during the heaviest snowfall of the year. I inquired if anyone had been there asking about arriving passengers.

"Ain't seen no one all afternoon," he answered.

I told him I had to get to the school at the village up in the mountains. "Are there any taxis in town?" I asked.

He looked at me as though I were crazy. In those days it would have been unusual to hire a cab for a 15-mile trip even in good weather, much less during a snowstorm. (He would really have wondered about my sanity if he'd known I had only $7 to my name!)

"There's usually a man on the other side of the station with a car to hire out," he said finally. "Let me see if I can find him." Then he wanted to know if the trunk sitting outside on the platform belonged to me. When I told him it did, he said, "Guess I'll have to bring it in here for the night." I knew I couldn't tip him, but I couldn't lift that huge trunk either, so I had to let him carry it inside. I felt ashamed that I didn't have any money to offer him, and too embarrassed to tell him so.

In a few minutes he came back with a little old man who looked a lot like the movie comedian Percy McBride. I told the old man where I wanted to go and asked how much he would charge to take me.

"The road's awful bad up thar," he said. "Don't know if'n I kin make it."

"But I've *got* to get up there," I pleaded. "How much will you charge to try it?"

"Reckon I'd have to have $10 fer that," he answered.

It was not an unreasonable price, considering I was asking him to drive a ramshackle old car up a mountain road during a snowstorm. But I didn't *have* $10.

"Will you take $5?" I asked hopefully.

"Oh, no," he shook his head. "I'd have to have more'n that."

We haggled back and forth. I knew I couldn't give him all I had and leave myself penniless, so I held out for $5. I was still too proud to come right out and admit I was broke. Finally, he accepted grudgingly. I blithely told the stationmaster I would send for my trunk the next day, and we took off.

The trip turned out to be one of the most harrowing journeys of my life. We had to drive a narrow, winding mountain road that would have been scary even in clear weather. All the way there the old man told me stories about the wrecks they'd had on that mountain, pointing out each precise spot as we slid around curve after curve. Every time we'd start up another incline he'd say, "Don't know if we kin make it up this'un." I sat gripping my seat, white-knuckled, all the way. It took us more than an hour to drive 15 miles. At last he pulled up in front of the schoolhouse. I paid him the $5, but I again felt embarrassed that I couldn't afford to tip someone who deserved it. (If I'd known then what I know now about my experience in that little settlement, I'd have given him every last cent I had.)

By this time it was well after four o'clock and almost completely dark. I stood and watched him drive off down the mountain, not knowing where I'd be staying that night, wishing desperately that I didn't have to go inside and throw myself on the mercy of strangers. (It was times like this when I wondered why I'd ever left the safety and security of Centerville!) When I went inside the school building, and looked up and down a long, empty hallway, it was clear the students had already gone. None of the classroom doors were open. The place appeared empty. Then I heard voices coming from one of the rooms. I looked through a glass partition and saw a group having some kind of meeting. I knocked and the man standing before the group saw me and came to the door. I told him I was looking for the principal.

"That's me," he said.

"I'm Ophelia Colley from the Wayne P. Sewell Company in Atlanta," I said. "I sent you a letter that I was arriving today to put on the play *Flapper Grandmother* for your school."

His expression told me exactly how he felt about that news. It was one of those times when I knew instantly that I wasn't wanted. I couldn't have been more unwelcome.

"Well, I'm sorry, but I'm here." I told him.

"I did get your letter," he admitted, "but with the weather like this I didn't think you'd come."

"I *had* to come." There was no point in trying to explain. They simply didn't realize that once a contract had been signed, no disaster or diversion mattered. *Somebody* was going to show up to put on that play!

"Come on inside," he said, thoroughly annoyed with the intrusion. "I have to finish this teachers' meeting. Then we'll talk." I followed him inside and sat down. The teachers all turned around to stare at me. He didn't explain who I was or why I was there. (Later he told me, "When I talked to that booker last summer, January seemed very far away. I had all but forgotten about the contract until I received your letter.") Finally, after he finished his meeting, he introduced me to the teachers, who were very nice. He said, "Miss Colley here is going to put on a play for us."

"I would also like somewhere to stay," I interjected frantically. "Is there some place available nearby?"

The response to my plea was silence. There *was* no place for me to stay. Back in the thirties when the WPA built consolidated schools in remote areas they also attached dormitories, called teacherages, where the teachers lived. The teacherage at this school was full, and the principal explained apologetically that he had no place for me at his home. There I was with $2 left in my pocket and Cullman 15 miles away by an icy road that would certainly be impassable at night. By this time it was already dark. Eventually, someone suggested a family that lived in a mountain cabin about a mile from the school. "I'll bet they'd take you in," the principal said.

After that he loaded me and my beat-up suitcase into his car and drove down a winding, snow-covered mountain road to a typical rural log cabin. It had two rooms on one side—a kitchen and a bedroom—and another bedroom on the other side. The two sides were separated by an open breezeway, or dogtrot, that ran the depth of the house.

The principal led me around to the back of the house and knocked on the kitchen door. A tall, thin lady in her seventies came to the door. She wore a clean, faded print dress and an apron, and you could tell she had worked hard all her life by the lines in her face and her worn hands. Her gray hair was pulled up in a knot on the back of her head, like Granny in the Beverly Hillbillies. She greeted the principal very hospitably.

"This is Miss Ophelia Colley, and she has come here to put on a play for the school," he said. That didn't seem to register with her. "Yes?" she said.

"She'll be here for a week putting on the play, and we want her to stay with you," he explained.

"You mean, live here?" she asked.

"Well, just for 10 days," he answered. "Don't you have an extra room?"

She thought for a second, then replied, "Well, we have Brother's room. I reckon he could sleep in the lean-to out by the kitchen."

I thought, "The accommodations aren't going to be too great on this job, but at least she's kind enough to take me in." It was still snowing, and I was tired, hungry and desperate.

"If you'll let her have that spare room we'll pay you for it," the principal said. That made her feel better. But I could tell she had already decided to take me in whether he paid her or not. Her kindness had been apparent from the moment she opened the door. I liked her, but I had no way of knowing she would change my life. I didn't suspect for a moment that I was looking at a woman who would provide me with the framework of a country character named Minnie Pearl. And I certainly had no premonition this woman would bring me all the pleasure, recognition and security I still longed for through a dramatics career, or that she would become my alter ego.

(I must emphasize how unusual it was for someone in an area like this to be asked to take in a boarder. Those fine mountain folks knew what it was to help a stranger in distress, but that's not the same thing as letting someone come live in your home. After I got to know this sweet lady I realized she must have thought the principal was out of his mind when he showed up at her door in a snowstorm asking that she rent out her son's bedroom for 10 days. I've often wondered what they paid her—probably not more than $1 a day. But she was game!)

The principal brought my suitcase inside, then told me he would pick me up the next morning at eight, on his way to school. When he'd gone, this nice old lady led me to a room across the dogtrot, where there was a bed piled with quilts and a washstand with a bowl and pitcher on it. It was very cold in the room and she began making a fire in a tin stove that looked like a big lard can lying sideways. I noticed that her son's clothes were hanging on nails around the wall. Among the overalls and shirts was a World War I uniform.

"Is your son in the national guard?" I asked, making conversation.

"No," she replied. "He just lives here with us."

"I thought because of the uniform. . . ." I pointed toward it.

"Oh, he swapped for that," she explained.

I didn't pursue it. Instead, I asked how many children she had.

"I've had 16 young'uns and never failed to make a crop," she answered proudly.

(Years later, when planned parenthood became a big thing, I thought about that statement. This woman didn't know anything about modern birth control, yet she'd worked it out so her babies came between planting and harvest so she was always able to help her husband out on their truck farm back of the house.)

Her husband and son shortly came in for supper. The old man, who looked about 75 years old, was tall and spare. His shoulders were stooped, but he still looked strong, a hardy mountain man. Brother (I never heard him called anything else, which is where I got the idea for the Brother Minnie Pearl talks about) was silently gracious about giving me his room. He didn't seem to mind in the least that he had been consigned to the lean-to, which must have been an uncomfortably cold place to sleep that time of year. He was 28, very tall and angular, with dark hair—and appeared seriously undernourished.

We ate supper at the kitchen table. We had corn bread, side meat (also known as salt pork or fatback) and some vegetables she had canned in the fall. I don't remember exactly which vegetables she served, but it was the best she had. She was a true hostess. She didn't have linen or silver, crystal or candles (we ate by the light of a kerosene lamp), but she couldn't have been more hospitable and gracious if she'd been serving a gourmet meal in a mansion.

Before going to bed that night, I asked her what time they normally got up, because I didn't have an alarm clock with me. "Well, we don't get up till daylight," she said, "but we'll get up earlier if you want to," to which I quickly replied, "No, daylight will be early enough, thank you."

The next morning at breakfast she told me she had packed me a lunch to take to school. "Otherwise, you ain't going to have nothing to eat down there at that schoolhouse," she explained.

I was sitting with the teachers at noontime when I opened it up. They brought out ham and cheese sandwiches wrapped in wax paper. I brought out my lunch, wrapped in newspaper. Inside, there were two large biscuits—one with side meat in it and the other with a cold fried egg. There was also a piece of cold, fried peach pie. As all these had been wrapped while they were still hot, the ink from the newspaper had not improved them! The teachers all looked at me, and I looked at them. We didn't laugh. It wasn't funny. They knew what to expect because the children brought the same kind of food in their lunch pails. This woman had given me the best she had, all she had. She didn't have anything like tuna fish or canned ham on her pantry shelf. She didn't even have a pantry. I excused myself and went down to the little country store about a block away and bought some cheese and crackers.

When the principal took me back to her house that afternoon she met me at the door. "Lord have mercy, I've worried about you all day," she said. "You ain't used to them kind of vittles I give you for lunch. I ought to have give you some store-boughten bread, but I didn't have none. I sent Brother to the store today, though, and tomorrow I'll fix you a store-boughten sandwich." Even though she was being paid to take me in, she wanted to treat me like a guest in her house. "I didn't know what you'd like, so I just got some peanut butter to go with some jelly I put up back last summer. Will that be alright?"

I assured her it would be. And for the rest of the time I was there I had a peanut-butter-and-jelly sandwich every day for lunch, and to this day I never see one without thinking of her.

I worked hard on the play—the weather didn't give us much of a break—and at night I'd go back to this woman's house. I enjoyed talking to her and her family. They fascinated me. They were funny people, witty people, who didn't know they were being funny, and didn't try to be. I'm sure they thought I was very peculiar with my "city ways." One thing that disturbed her was the fact that I asked for hot water twice a day for bathing. In freezing weather these mountain people didn't take on too much about frequent bathing. That first morning she said, "You ain't gonna wash and go out in that cold air? Why, you'll catch your death!"

Each morning Pappy would come into my room to wake me up and build a fire in that strange little stove. While he was doing so, I'd put on my heavy robe and hurry across the dogtrot to the bedroom on the other side, where they kept a fire going all night. I'd wait there until my room was warm enough to go back to and dress.

One morning I found Brother already standing by the fire in his parents' bedroom. We had never been alone before, and he certainly had never seen me in a bathrobe with my long red hair falling to the middle of my back. (I wore it braided and wrapped around my head.) As soon as he saw me he was consumed with embarrassment. He had the look of a cornered animal. I saw it immediately, and I was just mean enough to tease him.

"I shouldn't let you see me with my hair down like this," I said. "You know there's an old saying that if a man sees a woman with her hair down he can ask her to marry him."

He just looked at me, mortified. He couldn't even speak.

"And I *certainly* shouldn't let you see me without makeup," I added.

He looked down at the floor and mumbled, "I think you look better without it. I never did care for all that red'nin'."

I let it pass. "I've only heard your family call you Brother," I said. "What's your real name?"

His answer was the longest sentence I ever heard him speak. "Well, they named me Kyle, but I never did care much for Kyle. I'd heap druther they'd a named me Jim."

"Then why don't you change your name to Jim?" I suggested.

"Oh, I got a brother named Jim," he answered.

I just loved it. The whole scene reminded me of the movie *Sergeant York*, even down to Brother standing there in his army uniform. The way these people expressed themselves had an innocence and a wit about it that charmed me.

When I left, the old lady paid me the highest possible compliment. She said, "Lord a'mercy, child, I hate to see you go. You're just like one of us."

In fact, all the residents of that little mountain area made me feel like one of them. The night of the play they called me out on stage when it was over and one of those lanky ole mountain boys walked up and handed me a huge bouquet of red roses. I was so touched I wept. Imagine the trouble, and *expense,* they had to go to in order to get a dozen red roses up on that mountain in the dead of winter!

I thought about that cute old lady for a long time after I left her home. I had been collecting country stories and anecdotes from the time I'd begun on the road, and it was fun to repeat them in dialect. But I had never thought of building a character around them. Nor did I just then. The character evolved slowly, more like pregnancy to birth, until this good ole country girl had emerged to tell these little stories. I named her Minnie Pearl, because both names were country names I had heard and loved all my life.

I began using the character when I had to go into new towns to solicit ads for the play or urge groups to sell tickets to get a big turnout. Minnie Pearl would come out and say, "Howdy," in a soft, shy way—nothing near so bold and brazen as the way she does it now—telling the people how proud she was to be there. Then she'd tell a few stories about her family before doing her little spiel about the play we'd be putting on. It was a lot easier than standing up there as Ophelia Colley, and the people really seemed to enjoy her. She was warm and she genuinely loved them.

I also began doing Minnie Pearl at the coaches' school, mostly to entertain the students and loosen them up. Mr. Sewell loved her and always asked me to do her on graduation night, after the students had gone through their testing in front of Mrs. Sewell and him.

Meanwhile, when I left that little mountain village for my next assignment, I stopped over in Centerville. I sat in front of the fire and told Mama and Daddy about my visit with that family, imitating the old lady as I talked. Mama said, "Why, Ophelia, you sound just like an old mountain woman! You always were a mimic!" And Daddy, with that strange prophetic wisdom he occasionally showed, said, "You'll make a fortune off that some day, Phel, if you keep it kind."

Daddy didn't live to see Minnie Pearl come into her own, but I've always tried to follow his advice and keep her kind.

Chapter Twelve

ON March 17, 1937, I was directing a Sewell production in Seiverville, Tennessee, a small town in the eastern part of the state near Knoxville. It's a date I will never forget.

It was my second day there. I had already rehearsed my cast once, and I was driving around town with the local committeeman to call on merchants about ads for the playbill. Suddenly a car pulled up beside us and the driver motioned for us to stop.

"Are you Miss Ophelia Colley?" he called out when we pulled over.

"Yes, I am."

"Then you must go to the telephone office at once. They have a message for you. A death in your family."

I thought instantly of Daddy. I had been worried about him for some time because he had symptoms of angina pectoris and he was 80 years old. I realized he could go at any time. But I had never actually faced the prospect of his death. The man hadn't intended to give me the message in such a heartless way. In his anxiety to find me, he had simply blurted it out.

I called home immediately and my brother-in-law Wash (Dixie's husband) answered the phone. He confirmed my worst fears. His voice broke as he told me Daddy had died that morning.

"Catch the first bus to Nashville and let us know when you'll be arriving," he said. "We'll send someone there to pick you up."

I went completely to pieces. I couldn't think. I couldn't even check on bus schedules. The committeeman who had been driving me around took charge of everything. He was very kind. He made all the arrangements to get me on a bus to Nashville. I don't remember what happened about the play. I'm not certain if it was canceled or if Mr. Sewell sent another director to take my place, so much of that period remains disjointed in my mind. They say the Lord anesthetizes our minds in times of grief so the suffering won't be so acute, and I believe that's what happened to me.

I do remember that I had to lay over in Knoxville to catch another bus to Nashville and that it was horrible sitting alone in that station. I cried all the way home, even though a close friend of the family met me in Nashville and drove me to Centerville.

When I walked into the house, my whole family was there. Everyone was a wreck but Mama. Typically, she remained in perfect control. It had nothing to do with the way she felt about Daddy. It was her character. None of us had ever seen her break down. Years later she told me she had cried when Daddy died. But we didn't see it. She was still in charge, even in her darkest hour. She wouldn't allow the doctor to give her a sedative, and that was typical, too. To my knowledge she never even took an aspirin in her entire life.

We had Daddy at home that night, with his casket in the library. Friends and relatives sat up with the body all night, as was the custom in those days. People brought food, and I remember them making pot after pot of coffee.

The funeral was held the next afternoon at the house. The rooms were filled to overflowing, and many of the people who had come to pay their respects couldn't get inside. They had to stand out in the cold rain during the service. Later that afternoon we made the two-hour drive to Franklin to bury Daddy in the family plot, but I don't remember the trip. That part is all a merciful blur to me.

There were many touching tributes to Daddy. I especially remember old Mr. Grimes's. He used to come from his farm across the river to sell us butter and poultry, and he had known Daddy for years. "This town lost a fine man when it lost Tom Colley," he told my brother-in-law. "I'd rather have had his word on a money note than the signature of the president of the Chase Manhattan Bank." And Mary's friend Kate Derryberry wrote something we still treasure: "I shall always remember him for his unsentimental kindness, his superb disregard for anything that was small or petty. He was himself—complete, humorous, gallant, courageous. But he would not have liked that last word, which sounds too big. He was too unassuming and had too keen a sense of humor to like that. I am proud to have had my childhood made distinctive by knowing him." Another friend, Emma Tyler, who once visited us from Washington, D.C., wrote: "Mr. Colley reminded me of the tall, stately oaks on the hill across the river. Although I knew him only that brief weekend, I feel that he belonged to my roots rather than my tendrils."

After Daddy's funeral, I stayed home with Mama for a week. I was inconsolable, withdrew into my grief and allowed it to consume me. I don't know how I got through the next few months. The most horrible part was having to put on an act of being up when I had never felt so down in my life. I became hostile, bitter, resentful. It meant nothing to me to be assured that Daddy was in Heaven. I didn't *want* him in Heaven. I wanted him back *here,* on earth with me. I was not willing to let him go. I could not imagine my life without him. *Everything* reminded me of him. I'd be drinking a cup of coffee and I'd think how he used to say he liked coffee "black as night, hot as hell, strong enough to float an iron wedge and sweet as a woman's kiss." I'd see a man on horseback and remember Daddy's handsome figure, riding his stallion through Centerville long after the streets were paved and everyone else was driving a car. I thought about all those wonderful summer afternoons when I was very small, before I started school, when I knew by the long shadows in the front yard that it was near five o'clock—time for Daddy to come home! I'd run down the hill, meeting him halfway as he walked home from the sawmill. He'd swing me between his long, strong, slender legs or pick me up in his arms and carry me back up the hill. I'd be talking all the way, a mile a minute. And he listened. He *listened.* He made me feel he was interested in everything I had to say, no matter how trivial.

If I heard someone mispronounce a name, it would recall Daddy's habit of letting us know when he didn't like someone by refusing to call him by his correct name. My sister Mary used to say that it was always an ordeal introducing a new beau to Daddy because of the surprise of waiting to see if he would repeat the young man's name right. One Christmas I brought home a young man I'd been dating named Walker. There was very little possibility that Daddy could ordinarily have gotten that name mixed up, because his best friend was J. B. Walker. But he managed. Imagine my embarrassment when Daddy persisted in calling him Mr. Walton the entire time he was there!

I remembered all the times Daddy came home from business trips to Nashville with presents for us girls, and always a box of Mitchell's candy for Mama. He would hide the presents in his grip, a bag shaped like a doctor's satchel, only larger. We'd start screaming the minute we heard him come in and go running for his bag as fast as we could. He had always gone to the trouble to find some little surprise for each of us. My favorites were the little glass lanterns filled with candy pellets.

I worried constantly about whether or not I had been a disappointment to him, because I knew he hadn't wanted me to go with the Sewell Company. (Later there were many times when I wished he could have lived long enough to see Minnie Pearl on the Grand Ole Opry so he would have known those years with Sewell weren't wasted. He would have loved Minnie.) I wondered if I'd told him often enough how much I loved him, and if he really knew the depth of my respect.

I was so hurt, so sad and bitter, that I even avoided church. My whole attitude changed. I was angry with God. Nothing mattered anymore. I was careful to put on a show for Mama, just as I put on a show of being up when I was on the road. But it was a brittle performance. It wasn't honest. I was drifting, floating. Even my attitude toward men changed. I became flippant and cynical. I lost my softness and my vulnerability. I didn't *care*. No one was going to hurt me further, because no one was going to get close enough. (Interestingly, during my "hard" period I received 25 proposals of marriage! I guess it proves that playing hard to get— although I wasn't playing—really works.)

I can't say that any one thing snapped me back into the world of reality, where there is always joy to counteract sadness if we only see it. At the time, it seemed that my misery was interminable, but it actually lasted little more than a year. Time, the great healer, saved me in the end. Slowly I was able to make peace with myself, and my God, and get on about the business of living. My recollections of Daddy became warm memories, always accompanied by gratitude that I had been lucky enough to have him for 25 years, rather than bitterness over losing him.

By the spring of 1938 I was at work again on Minnie Pearl. I wasn't sold, by any means, on the idea of merchandising or show-casing her, but the response I got every time I did her gave me a feeling that she might be something worthwhile. Meanwhile, one of my students at the coaches' school in Roscoe proved to be an important influence on Minnie Pearl's development. Her name was Louise Smartt, but for some reason her family called her Jack. She came from Smartt Station, a tiny community near Mc-Minnville, Tennessee, in the foothills of the Smoky Mountains. It was my practice to ask for volunteers from each new class to en-tertain us on Saturday night after supper. We didn't have anything better to do, and some of these girls could sing and play the piano pretty well. Jack was the first one in her class to volunteer. When she sat down at the piano and started singing and playing, we all just fell out. She played only on the black keys, which I had never seen done before, and she sang in a way that was absolutely hilar-ious. She had come up with an adaptation, or takeoff, on some funny old country woman singing straight-faced and serious at the top of her voice, with about the same ability to carry a tune as Edith Bunker had on All in the Family. It turned out that Jack had been entertaining her family with this little act for years, and they thought she was a scream. They called it her country corn. This wasn't real country music at all, but a parody that was so silly you absolutely laughed yourself sick. Jack had seen old country peo-ple singing like that—real loud and off-key, but dead serious about it—and so had I, on my trips to all those small towns in the South. But I had never thought of putting my country girl, Minnie Pearl, to music until I saw Jack do her routines. I remember one song especially:

> *I'm not in your town to stay*
> *Cried a lady old and gray,*
> *to a warden of a pen-i-tent-aray*
> *I'm not in your town to stay,*
> *I'll soon be on my way,*
> *I'm just here to get my baby out of jail. . . .*

It went on and on, a real tear-jerking story of an old lady trying to get her baby out of jail, and we would absolutely die laughing at the way Jack did it.

So I started letting Minnie Pearl sing in that exaggerated, corny way (although I never did learn to play piano all on the black keys, which made Jack's act all the funnier). I picked up songs like "Careless Love" and "Jealous-Hearted Me" to parody, along with using some of her material.

Little by little, I began doing Minnie more and more in my work on the road, and also back at the coaches' school. But at that point it was still me talking like a character named Minnie Pearl. It was not me *becoming* that person.

Another woman who was a big influence on Minnie's development was Carolyn McElveen of Aiken, South Carolina. I went there early in 1939 to put on a play for the Pilots Club, a women's organization comparable to the Business and Professional Women's Club. Carolyn was my contact, in charge of the Sewell Production Committee. While she was taking me around to merchants in Aiken, helping me sell ads for the program, I began lapsing into Minnie Pearl dialect, telling her silly stories the way the character would tell them. Carolyn was the kind of person who truly liked to help others. She was very artistic, energetic and ambitious. She took me over, just as Hot, Dot and Annie had done back at Ward-Belmont. She soon had me doing Minnie Pearl everywhere we went. During my 10-day stay there I think she managed to show me off in front of everyone in town. She promoted me more than she did the play, and I found myself really having fun with Minnie, and people's reaction to her.

Carolyn didn't drop it when I left town. She began writing me letters. She'd say, "Now, we've got to do something about this Minnie Pearl character. She's too good to let slip away. You've got to develop her, *use* her. She's wonderful!"

Then, in March of 1939, about a month after I'd been in Aiken to do the play, Carolyn wrote and asked me if I would come back and do Minnie Pearl for their Pilots Club Convention in April. She said they would pay me $25 for the performance, *plus* my travel expenses. I was thrilled to death! Twenty-five dollars was a lot of money for one show. It was more than I made in two weeks on the road. But the money didn't mean as much as the fact that they wanted *me* up there entertaining them. I had been with Sewell about five years then, and had been responsible for bringing entertainment to thousands of people, but that wasn't the same as being the one on stage *doing* the entertaining.

Carolyn met me when I arrived in Aiken and took me to the convention headquarters at the Highland Park Hotel, where they had a room for me. It struck me, suddenly, that if I was getting paid to do this country girl character she ought to be in costume. I don't believe I'd ever thought of that before, but, then, I'd never been paid to do her before. I had always worn my regular street clothes, effecting her character through dialect and mannerisms. Carolyn agreed that the costume was a good idea, so we set out to find something suitable. On a little side street we came upon a store that displayed its merchandise outside on the sidewalk—a table full of shoes and several clothes racks filled with dresses and skirts. I rummaged through the shoes until I found a pair of white sandals made of imitation leather. Then, on one of the racks, I spotted a pale yellow dress made of sleazy organdy. It had a round collar and a cheap-looking grosgrain bow at the neckline that had been attached with a safety pin. The top was sleeveless, and it had a self-belt that rolled the minute you put it on. I was as thin as a rail, then, and the dress made me look like Olive Oyle in the Popeye cartoon series. I found some white cotten stockings (you never saw country girls wearing silk stockings because they couldn't afford them) and a tacky straw hat, with a brim, that sat flat on the top of my head. I bought some flowers to plop on that, and when everything had been totaled up, the entire outfit, from head to toe, cost less than $10.

There has been a misconception over the years that Minnie Pearl originally wore painted-on freckles and had one front tooth blacked out. This is not so. I never intended her to be a caricature. I dressed her as I thought a young country girl would dress to go to meetin' on Sunday or to come to town on Saturday afternoon to do a little trading and a little flirting. She wore the hat to keep the sun off her face so she wouldn't get freckles. If a country girl came to town with a tan or freckles from the sun it meant she had been working in the fields, and she wouldn't have wanted to give that impression.

I was satisfied with Minnie's first costume, and pleased that I had decided to dress her up, but I had no idea what effect it would have on me.

That night the banquet at which I was to perform was held in the hotel ballroom. Because there was no stage, I decided to make my entrance from the back of the room, walking through the crowd on my way to the podium up front. As I passed among the tables in my costume, speaking to people, smiling and saying Howdy, an incredible thing happened to me. I felt myself moving out of Sarah Ophelia Colley into Minnie Pearl. I felt more uninhibited than I ever had felt doing her before, but it was more than that. I *became* the character. It was the first time I had ever really changed places with her, and it gave me a wonderful sense of freedom I hadn't had before.

Before I left Aiken the next morning I folded that costume very carefully and took it with me. From then on, whenever I did Minnie Pearl, I put it on. I wore it until it wore out. In fact, I was still wearing it when I joined the Grand Ole Opry a year later, except that I had changed the shoes. I had found a pair of black "Mary Janes" with low heels and one strap. They had become my Minnie Pearl shoes, and they still are. I'm more sentimental and superstitious about those shoes than about any other part of my costume. One time I left them in the back of a rented car when we played a park out of Lancaster, Pennsylvania. When I got home and missed them, I frantically called the car rental office in Lancaster. A nice man on the phone agreed to trace the car for me —and found it after a search through the vast parking lot of Dulles Airport near Washington, D.C. The shoes were still on the floor of the back seat, just where I'd left them. I can't describe my relief! The man mailed them to me special delivery, certified *and* registered! I dearly love them. What if those old shoes could talk!

Chapter Thirteen

I went back to the Sewell coaching school in the summer of 1939, but it was apparent by then that my time with them was short. It had become more and more difficult to get bookings for the plays. For one thing, they were hopelessly outdated, both in material and concept. What had been fresh and clever, funny and timely in the late twenties and early thirties, was now corny and silly. Also, home entertainment in the form of radio and recordings was becoming more and more widespread in rural areas, as were motion picture theaters. Communications were changing everything. People were no longer isolated by geography. An era was dying, and the Sewell Company along with it.

In the spring of 1940, I returned to Centerville, not in the triumph I had always envisaged, but in utter defeat. I was 28 years old; I was broke; I had no job, and no promise of one. I wasn't married, and I didn't have a career. I wasn't even qualified to do anything, except teach dancing or dramatics, and not only did I hate that idea, I couldn't have made a living at it anyway because there weren't enough prospective students in my small hometown. I wasn't fit for anything but show business, and there certainly was no call for that in Centerville. I had left home in a burst of optimism, and returned broke, an old maid, a *failure*.

Whenever I hear the expression "darkest before the dawn" I think of that time. I had never felt so depressed, so pessimistic, in my life. What on earth was I going to do with myself? And with Mama, too? By this time she had moved from the big house where we'd all grown up into a little house nearer to town. Her eyesight was so bad she could no longer drive, so she needed to be within easy walking distance of the town square and its shopping facilities. She had rented out the other house and was living off the income from that plus whatever small provision Daddy had left. She had just enough to get by. My other sisters had their own family responsibilities, and none of them could help much. It struck me for the first time that Mama was going to need help and that I was the only one available to provide it.

I don't know which was more depressing and demoralizing, having no money and no job or feeling like such a failure. My pride was hurt and I felt humiliated. I imagined that people in Centerville were whispering, "Poor Ophelia Colley. She's back home no better off than when she left."

Mama and I began scrambling around to find something I could do. There simply were no jobs, at least none I was suited to. I couldn't even have gotten a job as a salesclerk because I was too stupid to make change. (I still am. I've been a mathematical idiot all my life, much to my husband's disgust. He's tuned to figures —mathematical and otherwise!) We managed somehow to struggle through June and July. Then I got wind that the WPA (Works Progress Administration, founded under President Roosevelt to help people get work during the Depression) was sponsoring recreation centers to give children something to do after school and on weekends. I inquired about it at our local WPA office, which was staffed by people who knew me and my family. By rights, I wasn't supposed to be employed by the WPA because we owned our own home, but they knew our situation and felt sorry for me, so they said they would try to get me the job of running the recreation center proposed for Centerville.

The job came through in August with a salary of $50 a month. It wasn't much, but I could live on it and I was grateful to have any job at all. The old Knights of Pythias Hall (originally the Opera House), located above some stores on the town square, was to be used as the recreation center, but I had to get it cleaned up before we could bring in equipment. It was a huge, filthy old hall, and I swept and dusted for what seemed like weeks. Finally we were ready to open, and then the onslaught began.

Every afternoon when school was out you could hear the chil-

dren stampeding up the stairs, screaming at the top of their lungs.
The kids in Centerville had never seen equipment like some we
had, including a badminton-type court on which they played a
form of paddle tennis. They *loved* coming there, and I did everything I could to please them because I wanted to keep my job. I
was their slave. It was the noisiest place I've ever been in my life.
I remember that on Thanksgiving Day that year I had 100 children up there, and it sounded like 1,000.

I'd go every morning to get the place straightened up for the
invasion at 3 p.m. If I had time, I'd write letters while I waited for
school to be out. Monnette Thompson, my best friend from childhood, had married and moved to Buffalo. I wrote her often, and
she says she received the most pitiful letters from me during that
period she'd ever read in her life.

If you worked for the WPA you weren't allowed to have any
other job, but I decided to cheat. I started giving private dance
and drama lessons to a few children. It brought in a little extra
money, and it gave me something else to do. My life was so dull,
so boring. I missed being on the road, having the freedom, the
independence I'd had with Sewell. Mama was as sweet as she
could be, but it's hard to move back home after you've been out
on your own. I hated it, hated being tied down and trapped. I saw
nothing ahead of me . . . no hope for my future. There weren't
even any boys my age left at home. They were all married. I could
see myself ending up as Centerville's old-maid dramatics teacher.
I was miserable.

In October the Lions Club asked me to produce a play for them.
I put on a minstrel show, much like the ones I'd done for Sewell.
For variety I decided to do an olio with Minnie Pearl and three
other characters. I asked Dr. Robert Bailey, our local dentist, to
play Brother, Martha McCord to be my sister and Jess Peeler to
play Minnie's feller, Hezzie. Martha was one of the cutest girls in
town, and she looked great in her Sadie Hawkins costume with a
cut-off skirt and an off-the-shoulder blouse. Our dentist, who was
supposed to be a very sensible man, didn't look like he had sense
enough to come in out of a shower, after he dressed up as Brother.
He wore old overalls with one strap hanging off his shoulder and
a beat-up felt hat, pushed back in front. He was barefoot and
carried a rifle and a jug. Hezzie wore a wonderful suit he'd found
somewhere with a belt in the back, similar to the kind worn by
the Duke of Paducah. (That was the first and only time Minnie

Pearl's family ever appeared with her.) In this little act I wrote for us I did most of the talking, and they just more or less stood around scratching and acting dumb. I told Sister she had to "watch out fer these fellers around here. It ain't safe fer a pretty girl. Why, I had one just now tell me I looked like a breath of spring. Well, he didn't use them words, exactly. He said I looked like the end of a hard winter." I did about 10 minutes of old jokes like that and the audience just ate it up.

One of the men there was Jim Walker, a local banker and close friend of my family. A few weeks later he showed up at the recreation center. "We're having a bankers' convention here in town later this month," he said, "and I was wondering if you would put together a show for us with some of those kids you've been training." I said, "Sure, I'll be glad to do it." He told me the details—time and place and how long he wanted it to run—then he started to leave. He got to the head of the stairs, and stopped. Then he turned back. (I've thought so often how your whole fate can be changed by something so seemingly insignificant you don't even notice it at the time.)

"By the way," he said, "our speaker is flying in from Chicago, which means he'll have to land in Nashville and drive down here, so he might be late. If he is, do you think you could kill time by doing that character you did at the Lions Club?" He didn't even remember the name.

"I'll be glad to," I told him. (It's interesting that he used the phrase *kill time*. I've been killing time ever since!)

The night of the show I lined my students up backstage at the high school auditorium and sent them out to do their little songs and dances. One girl, Marion Carothers, sang a torch song, and I played piano for her. The kids were good, and the men liked the show. When it was over I was a frazzled mess from fooling with all those children, and I had all but forgotten my agreement to kill time if the speaker was late. I hadn't even brought my Minnie Pearl costume. Jim came backstage with an anxious look.

"Our speaker hasn't arrived," he said. "Will you come on out and do that thing?"

"Oh Jim, look at me. I'm a mess," I said. "And I don't have my costume."

"That doesn't matter," he answered. "You've got to entertain these men until the speaker gets here."

Well, I didn't care. The men in the audience were either strangers from out of town whom I didn't know or men I'd known all my life. It wasn't important. I was simply doing a friend a favor. I straightened myself up and walked out there as relaxed as I would have been in my own parlor.

"Howdy, I'm just so proud to be here," I began. Then I told the men I'd like to give them my interpretation of a mountain girl, Minnie Pearl, and I went into my repertoire of country jokes. I had those men in the palm of my hand from the beginning, and I knew it. By that time I'd been doing her long enough to have the material down pretty well, and I felt comfortable in front of this audience because there was no reason to be nervous. After all, I was just killing time. I kept looking over at Jim, and he'd shake his head to signal that the speaker still wasn't there, so I'd do some more jokes. Finally I ran out of material, so I went over to the piano and started playing well-known songs, asking the men to sing along with me. They loved it and I was having a good time when Jim finally motioned that the man had arrived. I got up and thanked them, and they gave me a grand round of applause.

After I got home that night I remember Mama asking, "How was it?" I said, "Oh, alright, I guess. It was fun." It meant nothing to me except that I had helped Jim out of a tight spot. I had absolutely no inkling that I had just passed the most important turning point in my life.

Chapter Fourteen

THE next week I received a call from Harry Stone, general manager of WSM radio in Nashville. He told me that Bob Turner, a Nashville banker who was a friend of my family's, had mentioned seeing me do a country girl character at the convention in Centerville. "He says you ought to be on the Opry. Would you like to come to Nashville and audition for us?"

Would I! I couldn't get there fast enough.

I won't pretend, however, that I wanted to be on the Grand Ole Opry because I had been a fan all my life. Most country music stars dream about being on that revered stage for years before they get there. But I had never thought of it one way or the other, except that I didn't particularly like the music. Daddy liked it. He used to listen to the Opry at home on Saturday nights, but Mama and I didn't care a thing about it. I was into pop music, and I had never even gone to see an Opry broadcast, much less felt a desire to be on the show. What I wanted was a job that would get me out of that noisy recreation hall and back into *show biz! Any* kind of show biz. (I found out later that Bob Turner had gone to Harry Stone and urged him to audition me. "She's really got a great character in that Minnie Pearl thing," he said, "and I know her family well. They need some help, and she could use the work." Bob's kind act, for which fortunately I was able to express my appreciation many times before his death, changed my life.)

My audition took place in the studio at WSM. Jack Stapp, program manager for WSM (and later producer of the Opry network show), Ford Rush, WSM's Artists' Service manager, and Judge George D. Hay, producer, director and head of the Grand Ole Opry, as well as the announcer for the show, were all in the control room watching me. I was very nervous. Auditions are never easy, but this one was made even more difficult by the fact that I wanted the job so desperately. I did my best material, then sang a couple of songs in that country style I had picked up from my friend Jack Smartt. For some reason I auditioned in my street clothes. I still wanted to be Ophelia Colley, future dramatic actress, doing a comedy character part. I wasn't ready to *be* Minnie Pearl.

After the audition Ford Rush took me into his office and explained that they were a little afraid of putting me on, but that they were going to give me a shot at it anyway. He said he knew my background—that I had been raised in the country but had gone to an exclusive girls' school, and that I had traveled as a drama director for six years—and he was afraid the Opry audiences would find that out and suspect I was a phony. He feared they would think I was putting down country people. I explained over and over that I was dead serious about the act and had no intention of making light of country folks, whom I *loved* and of whom I was a part.

I was scheduled to go on on the following Saturday night at 11:05 p.m., which I understood was Mr. Rush's way of hedging his bet. The NBC network portion of the show ran until 8:30 p.m. and, of course, I couldn't go on that segment. Many of the listeners to the local show, which reached a radius of several hundred miles, would have gone to bed by 11, and most of the live audience would have gone home. He figured it wouldn't be too great a catastrophe if I bombed then.

My brother-in-law Wash Shouse drove Mama and me up from Centerville on Saturday. The Opry was broadcast from the War Memorial Auditorium, located downtown right across the street from the WSM studios in the National Life and Accident Insurance Company building. (The Opry didn't move to the old Ryman Auditorium until 1941.) I remember very little about my debut on that November night in 1940 except that I was scared to death.

Judge Hay came up to me beforehand and saw the fright in my

eyes. "You're scared, aren't you, honey?" he said in that gentle voice I grew to love so dearly.

"Yessir, I am," I quavered.

Then he gave me the very best advice any performer can get: "Just love them, honey, and they'll love you right back."

Those words have remained a refrain in my mind ever since.

My act followed a commercial for the Crazy Water Crystals Company (and I don't want any cracks made about that!). I went on in a sort of daze and told the gags in a gentle, soft, country dialect—so different from the confident way I do Minnie now. Then I sat down at the piano and played and sang "Maple on the Hill." I don't really remember what kind of response I got. I had nothing to compare it to. But I distinctly recall asking Mama afterward how she thought it went and her saying encouragingly, "Several people woke up." That was possibly the best one-line review I've ever received. In cold weather, derelicts and drunks in the neighborhood frequently used the auditorium as a warm place for a nap, so her point was well taken. For 25 cents you could come in and stay for hours.

When we left that night to drive back to Centerville I had no idea where I stood, or if I'd ever be asked to come back. On the drive home I felt uncertain and let down.

Then, on the following Wednesday, I received a call from Judge Hay telling me to come in Friday to have my material checked by Mr. Rush for Saturday night's performance. They were going to put me on again!

When I arrived at the WSM offices I walked up to the receptionist, Margaret Frye, and said, "I'm Ophelia Colley from Centerville, and I'm supposed to see Mr. Ford Rush to have my material checked for Saturday night's Opry show."

"What name do you work under?" she asked.

"Minnie Pearl," I said.

She did a double take. "Oh, am I ever glad to see *you!*" She got up from her desk and walked over to the corner, where there was a fat bag of mail. "I've got all this mail here for you and we have no place to keep it. Will you take it with you when you go home?"

I was flabbergasted! The bag looked as if it contained more letters than our post office in Centerville received in a week. (There were more than 300 pieces of mail in it.) Even though I didn't know much about show business, I knew it was pretty good for an unknown to get that much response from a three-minute spot on the air at 11:05 at night, even though fans wrote a lot more letters in those days than they do now. I figured my mail would get me at least a couple more appearances on the show, but I wasn't prepared for what happened when I walked into Ford Rush's office.

"We got a good response from your appearance last Saturday night," he said, "so we want you to become a part of the Grand Ole Opry."

Just like that! Straight to the point.

I was stunned—by the offer and the casual way he made it. But I accepted immediately, before he had time to change his mind. He didn't mention a contract (there were no written agreements with Opry members at that time), and I don't think we even shook hands on it. He told me I'd get $10 a week to do the show. I nodded agreement, and thanked him, and that's all there was to it.

"From what I understand you don't have a backlog of material. Is that correct?" he asked. I told him that it was. "Well, you're going to have to do something about that. You'd better get some-one to help you write up enough stuff so you won't have to repeat the same jokes." I said my sister Virginia would help me. (Imag-ine her surprise when I called her that night and told her what I'd done!) Then he explained that they would check my material each week before the Saturday-night show to make sure it was suitable. Finally he went over my jokes for the next night.

Mama was waiting for me in the lobby, and the moment my material was cleared I rushed out to her, dragging my mailbag behind me. We hurried back to Centerville and sat down together and spent hours reading the letters one by one. The messages were sweet and supportive. I had never written a fan letter my-self, and I didn't realize how many people there are who want to identify with performers they hear and see. These people really felt they knew me, and they considered me a friend. Mama was fascinated by the mail and as proud as I was. I answered every letter. (I still love fan mail and I still answer it. I believe if some-one is kind enough to take the time to write to you, the least you can do is acknowledge it in some way.)

When I went back to perform that second Saturday night, I began to feel more comfortable—comfortable enough at least to look around me and see what was going on. I couldn't get over the atmosphere. I had never seen anything like it, and I still haven't elsewhere! People were milling about everywhere, greeting one another, chit-chatting like cousins at old home week, as casual and relaxed as if they'd been at a family picnic. And this wasn't only backstage, but *on* stage as well. Performers, their families, friends, Opry personnel—all strolled back and forth across the stage throughout the show, oblivious to the performers at the microphone, who themselves were oblivious to them. Because it was radio, it didn't matter to the home listeners, and the live audience loved it. (This intimacy was, and still is, one of the secrets of the Opry's long and unwavering popularity with its fans.)

When I first went on stage I was horrified by this seeming disorganization. I had come from directing plays, which were rehearsed, and everyone knew what to expect. On the Opry, as I soon discovered, it wasn't unusual for the announcer to say, "And now we're proud to present So-and-So," and someone would whisper, "He ain't here. He's gone to get a sandwich," which didn't fluster the emcee, who'd say, "Oh, well, he'll be back in a minute. Meanwhile, let's hear from the Fruit Jar Drinkers." Nobody seemed to mind. The only way you knew when you were supposed to go on was by checking the board backstage.

What I didn't realize was that I was coming on a show that had already been on the air 15 years and whose personnel knew what they were doing. They still keep a board backstage with the name and scheduled time of appearance for each act. We'd come in, check the board, then wander around and talk to our friends until it was time to go on. They even still have seats on the stage so guests can sit right up there with the artists. The overall atmosphere has changed very little through the years, and when we have guest stars on the Opry for the first time their reaction is the same as mine was nearly 40 years ago. They're astonished. Someone called it "organized confusion," and it does look like that to an outsider.

Guest artists also remark on the lack of tension and preshow jitters at an Opry performance. This hasn't changed over the years either. An Opry star walks out completely at ease when it's his or her turn to perform. I noticed this right away and thought these must be the most secure, confident performers in the world. But that isn't it. The lack of tension comes from the total rapport Opry members have with their audience, the absence of barriers. An Opry star will feel the same backstage nervous anticipation in another place, before a Vegas performance, for example, that any

other artist feels. But on the Opry stage, he's at *home*. He's accepted. If he flubs a line or goofs a lyric, it's okay, even though
the show is broadcast live. He just laughs and goes ahead. The
audience understands, because he's one of them. (This doesn't
hold true for guest artists. An Opry audience can be as cold as a
January night in Nome if a non-Opry member does an act they
don't like. I've seen some big names in show business bomb on
the Grand Ole Opry.)

Again, I don't recall exactly what I did on stage that night, but,
judging by the response, it worked again. As far as the audience
was concerned, I was one of them. And, as the weeks went by, I
felt more and more at home. There were about 50 other members
of the Opry cast. They were all very friendly to me, very supportive, and accepted me into the "family" immediately. I might add
that I represented no threat to any of them. I didn't sing and I was
a woman. Men, at that time, *never* figured a woman to be a threat.
That attitude seems to have changed.

I knew nothing at first about the background of the Opry, but
because I was going to be a part of it (temporarily, of course, since
this was just a stepping-stone to other things), I was curious to
learn its history.

National Life and Accident Insurance, a Southern-owned and
-operated company, started WSM radio station in the early 1920s
as a means to advertise and sell insurance on the air. (WSM stands
for We Shield Millions, the motto of the insurance company,
which still has full control of the Opry as well as Opryland Park
and the Opryland Hotel.) In those early years—before 1937, when
WSM acquired network affiliation with NBC—the station ran
whatever programming it could get. Judge Hay, who wasn't a
judge but was a court reporter (for the Memphis *Commercial Appeal*), worked as an announcer at WSM from its inception. He
loved country music!

One night in the fall of 1925, Judge Hay decided to invite a
group of local musicians to come down to the studio to pick and
sing. They sat around playing and singing the old songs familiar
to the rural listeners, and it went over big. The next Saturday
night, Judge Hay invited them back, and the station began to get
enthusiastic letters about this music show. They called it the Saturday-Night Hoedown, and it grew like Topsy. As the years
passed, it became more and more successful.

Then, one Saturday night, right after WSM had gone network,

the station carried a broadcast from the Metropolitan Opera just prior to the local Hoedown. When Judge Hay came on to announce the show, he said, "Now, you've heard the Metropolitan Grand Opera, how about some Grand Ole Opry?" The name stuck, but no one had any idea then that it would become the longest-running radio show in history.

In 1937, NBC decided to carry 30 minutes of the local 4-hour Opry show on the network. It was sponsored by Prince Albert tobacco, a client of the William Esty Advertising Agency in New York. I was to have many dealings with that agency over the years, some of them very interesting.

By 1940 the Opry was a popular, well-established show, but it was not the institution it is today. Those of us who started in the late thirties and early forties feel an almost parental pride, and perhaps a possessiveness too, about the Opry because we worked to make it grow, and we've seen it reach heights far beyond our wildest dreams. This accounts for the unusually strong bond among Opry old-timers.

In those days country music did not enjoy the widespread appeal it does today. It wasn't acceptable in many places, and neither were we. We had problems even in Nashville. Many of the local citizens wanted to sweep us under the rug. They felt the Opry and "that hillbilly music" was a demeaning image for their city, which they were promoting as the "Athens of the South," a seat of culture and higher learning. We used to have a saying at the Opry, "Nobody likes us but the people." And it was true.

I didn't personally begin to get turned on to country music until I'd been working the Opry for several months. But if you're exposed to it long enough it sneaks up on you and I soon found myself as much a fan as the audiences who came to hear it. I still love it. It's by far my favorite type of music. (I don't like *all* country music, but then I don't like all pop or classical either.)

At the risk of sounding immodest, Minnie's popularity on the Opry grew very rapidly. This was due mainly to two things—I was the only comedienne on the show, and WSM went to great lengths to push and promote me. Harry Stone and Jack Stapp and all the other people at the Opry were wonderful about seeing to it that I was put on other weekly shows in addition to my regular Saturday-night appearance. I was lucky to come on the Opry when I did, because after a while it became so crowded they didn't have the time to push new acts the way they did for me.

Also, I was the first newcomer they'd had in several years, and Opry audiences at that time trusted Judge Hay so much they accepted anyone he brought on. Very little happened on that stage in those days that the audience didn't love. Just being up there was a mark of distinction, like "Sterling" on silver. Nowadays, the audiences don't feel the least big obligated to like someone simply because he's performing from the Opry stage. Television has made them more independent, less naive.

Another positive factor was the galvanizing influence of Judge Hay. I can't say enough about the marvelous effect he had on my career, and my life. In the first place, he was a Christian gentleman, strongly motivated. He used to remind us all, "The Opry was started and built on brotherly love," and he convinced us, by his own example. And the country people around Nashville, for whom he initially put on the Hoedown, adored him. It is characteristic—and sad—that he never shared in the monetary rewards.

At first I kept my job with the WPA, coming to Nashville only on weekends to do the Opry. But there was a rule that you couldn't have other work while employed by the WPA, so I soon had to give up the WPA job. As I began doing more and more radio shows at WSM, I was in and out of the station frequently. The atmosphere there was a lot like the Opry. Everyone came to the station to pick up his pay, and most of those pickers had vague addresses. Dr. Lew Childre, one of my best friends on the Opry in the old days, was typical of the "addressless" acts. When anyone asked Lew where he lived he'd say, "Under the Woodland Street Bridge." Nobody seemed to have roots in Nashville. It was all very friendly and relaxed. The old-timers were still alive then. They had colorful names like the Gully Jumpers, the Possum Hunters and the Fruit Jar Drinkers. Many of them performed only part-time, supporting their families with regular jobs in and around Nashville during the week. A few did personal appearances out of town, but the only two who were really out there hitting the road six days a week were Roy and Bill.

Roy Acuff and Bill Monroe were the only two *stars* on the Opry in 1940. I met them both during my first few weeks on the show. (I didn't meet them the first night because all the Opry performers aren't there during the entire show. The show ran four hours then, and many performers came in only for the segment they were scheduled to work.) Bill had had a number of hit records and was already well known for his bluegrass music, which was big at that time. He was the leading exponent then, and at the time of this writing is still king of bluegrass music. Roy Acuff, in turn, was king of the Grand Ole Opry. His hit records, such as "Great Speckled Bird" and "Wabash Cannon Ball," had already sold millions. Both Roy and Bill were attractive men. Roy was the smaller of the two, but he was strong and wiry, a virile young man. We used to make bets backstage about "who could whip who" if he and Bill ever got into it. (Not that they were in any way adversaries. It was just typical of the kind of nonsense we talked.)

Roy and Bill would come back in on Saturday in time to do the Opry, then head out again Saturday night after the show. They traveled in big, long Cadillacs with their names painted on the sides: Roy Acuff and the Smoky Mountain Boys and Bill Monroe and His Blue Grass Boys.

Now, the most coveted position in country music at that time was to appear on the network portion of the Grand Ole Opry show. This made your personal-appearance range so much wider. At that time NBC had two networks—the red and the blue—and the Opry was carried on the blue network, going out to about 50 stations. (Later, the networks merged and the Opry picked up another 100 stations.) As the star of the Prince Albert Grand Ole Opry network show, Roy was well known enough to get bookings wherever he wanted them, within a radius close enough to allow him to get back into Nashville on Saturday night for the broadcast show at 8:30 p.m. (Later, it changed to 9 p.m.)

Toward the end of December 1940, after I'd been on the Opry about a month, Roy came to me and asked if I'd be interested in going on the road with him and his group. "I've had a pretty long run here," he said in a classic understatement. (Three or four years in one place was a *very* long run for a country music artist in those days.) "I'd like to have you join my act."

Roy told me he would pay me $50 a week, plus expenses. As I was already making $10 a week on the Opry every Saturday night, Roy's offer would bring my weekly income up to $60. It was an enormous amount of money to me, and I accepted gratefully. He told me our first date was in Evansville, Indiana, on New Year's Day.

I had no way of knowing *that* booking was the beginning of 27 *consecutive years* of one-nighters. If I had known I might not have rushed home so enthusiastically to tell Mama the good news!

Chapter Fifteen

T HAT first trip out with Roy marked my introduction to The Road, a way of life indigenous to country music, and one that has an unmistakable effect on anyone who stays out there very long. I've seen what it can do, good and bad. I've seen it make poor men into millionaires and nice men into drug addicts. I've seen it break up marriages and increase the birth rate in small towns. I've seen fat men get skinny, skinny men get fat and young men get old before their time. I've seen broken heads and broken hearts and men who were broken, period. But make no mistake about it, I also saw some of the very best times of my life. (Thank God Henry Cannon came into my life 7 years after I went on the road so that I was able to spend the next 21 years traveling with a stable, dependable, loving husband. If I had lived the road life alone for 27 years, I doubt seriously that I would be here to write this book!)

When I look back on those early road years, a montage of pictures flashes through my mind—endless stages, from schoolhouse gymnasiums to tents to huge, municipal auditoriums, even to Carnegie Hall and Madison Square Garden; thousands of towns that merge and become indistinguishable in my memory; countless drab, smelly hotel rooms, lumpy beds with chenille spreads; all-night diners with grease-stained menus and indigestible food. I remember the indescribable discomfort of riding all day in the hot summertime in cars with no air conditioning (sometimes four to the back seat, three to the front), arriving for a show with my clothes stuck to my back and every bone in my body aching. There was nothing to do about it but cry or be silly. We were silly. Nobody cried.

I remember the first time I saw whiskey passed around a car with a Coke to chase it. I thought, "Oh, if Mama saw this she'd die." I remember countless nights driving through the darkness with maybe only one or two of us awake, when someone would get serious and introspective and share his deepest feelings and fears. The road makes you a member of a very exclusive clique. There is the occasional abrasion—personalities clash in close quarters, to put it mildly. But the camaraderie is strong and sweet.

I didn't learn all this until later. When I went out with Roy, I was so dumb I thought I already knew about life on the road. Hadn't I spent six years traveling for Mr. Sewell? But like the feller said, I didn't know nuthin'. I didn't even suspect nuthin'!

On New Year's Eve, Roy, his band, myself and a young girl in his show named Rachel all piled into a big long Cadillac to head out for Evansville. The instruments had been tied on top of the car. We looked like high-class gypsies. I was thrilled and excited, but nervous too. I felt very honored that Roy had asked me to be on his show because I had been around the Opry long enough to know that everyone looked up to him. I wanted to impress him, and I wasn't spilling over with confidence about being able to do that. After all, this was my first *professional* Opry road appearance as Minnie Pearl, and I was uncertain about how I would be received.

We were showing at the Evansville Coliseum. Eddy Arnold and Pee Wee King and his Golden West Cowboys and some other acts were meeting us there for a big New Year's Day package show. (I continued to do package shows for the next 27 years. During the week, we would work small houses with just one group, but on Sundays, acts would join for package shows in big auditoriums.)

We arrived at the coliseum well before time for the matinee, and as I had never rehearsed singing with Roy's band, he suggested I do so. I put Minnie's costume in one of the little cubbyhole dressing rooms in the basement of the building, then went outside in the hall to rehearse with the band. I had never sung with a hillbilly band before. On the Opry I always accompanied myself on the piano. Now, I am well aware that I can't sing. (The nice part is that I play comedy and don't have to sing. I know people who can't sing and don't play comedy, either.) That old expression "She don't sing good, but she sings loud" could have been coined for me. The boys tuned up and I let go singing "Maple on the Hill" with everything I had. It can be a pretty song when it's done right, but I sing it like killing snakes. Just about that time Eddy and Pee Wee walked down the steps. They saw this well-turned-out young woman in a smart suit (I had a good figure in those days) standing there as straight-faced as could be, going at it tooth and toenail at the top of her lungs. They both stopped dead in their tracks and stared at me. Eddy was horrified. He thought Roy had hired a new girl singer. He whispered to Pee Wee, "Has Roy gone crazy? If he puts that girl on the show they'll boo her off the stage. She can't *sing!*" Pee Wee said, "No, I think that's that new comic on the Opry, Minnie Pearl."

Eddy breathed a sigh of relief. "Thank God," he said. "I thought she was *serious!*"

We had a lot of laughs over that. In fact, Eddy hasn't stopped teasing me about my singing to this day.

After my first show that afternoon I knew I hadn't gotten as big a response as I'd been getting on the Opry, but I wasn't sure why, and I didn't know what to do about it. I didn't have sense enough to know that doing 3 minutes and 15 seconds on the air is nothing like standing in front of an audience for 20 minutes pounding out gags. I didn't have a show, but that wasn't all. I was holding back. I still wasn't ready to divest myself completely of my own personality and become a silly character. I wasn't ready to give up sex appeal and a feminine image to be a clown.

Roy had every right to be disappointed. From hearing me on the Opry he thought I had a personal-appearance act together. He didn't say anything, and I was so dumb I wasn't sure if he realized I hadn't done too well, but I felt like I had let both of us down. It wasn't that I did anything wrong. It was just that I didn't do it right. I didn't *sell.*

I tried to rake together some more material for the evening show, but it wasn't all that funny, and I've no doubt that Roy realized immediately he'd made a mistake.

We rocked along from town to town during the week, back into Nashville on Saturday, and out again Saturday night after the Opry. Saturday was absolute madness. It was the only day we had at home, so I ran around, nonstop, doing my laundry, picking up cleaning, washing my hair, unpacking and repacking, getting to the bank, doing any necessary shopping, making it to the Opry on time, and all this by bus or taxi. Youth saved me.

On the road I was being exposed to a new breed of people, both on stage and in the audiences. I couldn't get over the way some of the fans responded to these performers. One woman got so carried away she almost let her baby drown. We were playing an outdoor date at Sneeds Grove in Halls, Tennessee, when a sudden summer shower came up. I was watching the Daniels Quartet from the stage, which was covered, when I noticed this woman standing down front. She was looking up, absolutely mesmerized by these singers and oblivious to the downpour. Then, to my horror I saw she was holding a tiny baby in her arms, with its little face turned up to the rain. The baby was gasping for breath, literally drowning. The woman was in another world, totally unaware of what was happening. I rushed to the edge of the stage and motioned frantically to her, pointing to the baby. She caught on quickly and got him out of the rain and breathing normally again. But it had been a close call, and I thought about it for weeks. This was an early indication to me of the intensity of the participation of the country music fan.

As for my fellow performers, I soon learned that these hillbilly pickers had a jargon and lifestyle all their own. Some of them used racy language and were very explicit with their terms. I wasn't offended by it. It was just the way they talked, and I had enough sense to know if I was going to be living in a man's world, in *their* world, I would have to accept it. But I didn't know what to talk to them about. My background was Centerville, Ward-Belmont and Mr. Sewell's amateur plays. They weren't interested in any of that. They were talking about Cleveland, Atlanta, Ft. Pierce, the shows, the box office, the different acts that were coming along in the business. It was all foreign to me. Rachel, whom I grew to love dearly, had been traveling with Roy's group for a couple of years, playing great banjo and guitar, and also doing an act with Bashful Brother Oswald (Pete Kirby, who is still with Roy today). She tried to be as helpful as she could, answering any questions I asked about road life, but I knew I wasn't fitting in.

The more I got to know Roy, the more I appreciated being with his show. He was a professional, a first-class showman who gave his audiences everything he had every time he walked on stage.

He was also a gentleman and a fine Christian. I was impressed by his consideration for people and his integrity. I remember we played some little old schoolhouse back up in the hills one night not long after I went on the road with him. We were late getting there, so the principal had let the people go on inside, without paying, to get out of the freezing-cold weather. When we arrived, the principal explained what he had done, then said, "I'll run them all out and let them come in again so you can sell them a ticket. It won't take long." (In those days acts carried their own tickets for the smaller shows, and one of the band members sold them at the door while the others were setting up.)

"Why, there's no use in your doing that," Roy told the principal. "Let them stay where they are. After we do our little show, we'll put a cigar box out by the door and they can drop their money in it as they go out."

That night, after we left, Roy said, "I'll bet I didn't lose a dime. I'll bet every one of those folks put their money in that box." And I'm sure he was right.

By the time I had been with Roy for about three months, I knew I wasn't cutting it. He never criticized me, but he did make occasional suggestions. He kept telling me to *relax.*

One night we stopped at an old truckers' joint to eat. No one was in the place but our group. One of the boys put some money in the jukebox and I got up and started dancing by myself, doing this old-fashioned clog, a type of square dance. Roy watched me awhile. Then he said, "Now why don't you do that on the stage?"

I said, "Oh, that's too silly. I couldn't do that."

"Minnie, you have to realize that you *must* be silly," he answered. "Don't ever be embarrassed to give them a good show."

He was trying to help me, but I was too stupid to listen. You can't feel embarrassed and be a comic. There's a certain kind of embarrassment that comes when you don't get a laugh, but that's not what I mean. You can't be embarrassed at *being* a comic, and, even though I may not have been fully aware of it then, I *was* embarrassed about what I was doing. I was 29 years old, a mature young woman, and I just couldn't see my way clear to cut loose and act a fool. I had still not given up the other dream of being a dramatic actress.

Not long after that incident in the truck stop, Roy came up to me backstage on a Friday night. "Minnie, you're just not fitting into our little act," he said gently.

I started crying. "I *know* I'm not, and I'm so sorry. But I can't help it."

"I know you can't," he said. "It's going to take a little more experience. But I can't keep you because it's an expense to me and I'm not making all that much money."

We were still coming out of the Depression, and people did not have much money to spend on entertainment. We played many dates where the admission was 50 cents for adults, 25 cents for children. I knew Roy was right and I was broken-hearted. Again, in my life, I felt like a *failure*. Also, I was desperate for the $50 a week. I had given up my WPA job months before, and I knew I couldn't pay my room and board in Nashville (I had moved there to a boardinghouse when I went on the road), help Mama out and take care of my own expenses on the $10 a week I was getting from the Opry.

It may seem an odd basis for a lifelong friendship, but Roy Acuff couldn't possibly have done a better thing for my career than fire me from my first job. It forced me to take a good long look at myself and my act. Roy has been my best friend for more than forty years now, and he doesn't like to remember that he once fired me. But he doesn't realize what an important turning point it was in my career. Now, every time we work together he makes me feel good. When he sees me backstage, he always says, "Minnie, I'm glad you're here. When I put you on I always know you're going to give the folks a good show." I love it because I *never* fail to remember the early days when I didn't "give 'em a good show." It makes me think of that night in the truck stop, and how much I learned from Roy.

For the next five months I conscientiously worked on letting Minnie Pearl come out. I put the dance in my act; I wrote new material with Virginia; I loosened up and acted sillier. I realize now I came on the Opry unprepared for comedy. I had done the act before small groups for several years, but the approach to comedy on a large scale had never occurred to me. Getting up and doing a gentle interpretation of "the mountain girl, Minnie Pearl," in front of a luncheon group of 25 or 30 men is a far cry from walking out on a cold stage in front of four or five hundred (now tens of thousands at times) *paying* customers who demand a hard-sell show of talent. I've often said my risk element is four or five times that of a singer. A singer dies once, at the end of a 2½- or 3-minute number. I can die every 15 seconds. It took years of constant work to build up the veneer it takes to walk out, do the show and not let anyone know you care if they laugh or not. You'll always care, but you must never let them know. That's what I call the "rhinoceros hide" of the professional comic.

I was afraid word would get around that Roy had had to fire me and I wouldn't get work with any other road shows. But it never did. Roy didn't tell anyone what had happened, and he asked his men not to talk about it. They agreed that if anyone asked they would say I had wanted to get off the road at that particular time. All of his men are dear friends of mine and gentlemen of a very special school. (I cannot say enough about the musicians in our business who accompany the so-called stars. Many of these musicians are stars in their own right, and several have been lucky enough to go ahead and prove it. Just two examples—Chet Atkins backed up Red Foley when Red went on the road after he joined the Opry, and Willie Nelson used to back up Ray Price. But the backup musicians—I refuse to call them sidemen because I hate that term—have always been marvelous to me. I have a very special affection for them. I sing at the close of my act, and it takes a long-suffering musician to put up with my so-called singing. The band at the Opry now is made up of men I've known since their teens, and their support when I start to "rip off here with a few sweet spasms of comfort and joy," as I always say, is heart-warming. They even pretend they like it.)

I was living in a boardinghouse on Sixteenth Avenue when I got fired by Roy, and had been paying practically nothing in rent, but I still couldn't make ends meet. The lean times with the WPA were nothing compared to this. I had no collateral to borrow money from a bank, and I couldn't ask Mama to mortgage her house because it was all she had. So I borrowed from friends. Hardly a week went by when I didn't borrow from somebody, usually the same two or three friends, and it was the most demeaning thing I've ever had to do. Jack Smartt, my friend from Sewell days, had moved to Nashville and was dancing with a square dance group on the Opry, in addition to her regular job during the week with the Agricultural Extension Service. I often borrowed from her. I'd get on the streetcar and ride out to her office and borrow $5 to live on for the week; then, when I got paid on Monday, I'd call her and say, "I've got your $5. You want to come get it or shall I bring it?" We've laughed about that often . . . how I was perfectly willing to ride the streetcar out to *her* to borrow the money, but wanted her to come to *me* to get it back! Mary Watkins, a friend who worked at a local department store, Cain-Sloan, was another one who lent me money. These gals saved my life and I am eternally grateful.

In those days the WSM Artists' Service booked everybody. There were no agents or personal managers. The Artists' Service took a commission, just like agents do, unless you worked for an act; then the leader paid the fee for the entire show. I began free-lancing through WSM, and started getting quite a few bookings. People were interested in using me because I was a novelty. There was no girl comic on the road working as a single. But all the shows had their own units, so the only time I was used was when someone was sick or couldn't go out for some reason. I averaged two or three jobs a month at $25 a job. It certainly wasn't enough to live on, but it helped.

I worked a few dates with Bill Monroe. There was a wonderful story going around the Opry then about Bill and his brother. They said if Bill had to travel east to get to a booking, he would go out of his way to go by his brother's house in Kentucky and get him out of bed in the middle of the night just so they could have a fight. Rumor had it that Bill loved to fight and could handle himself well if the going got rough.

One night we were working one of those mining towns up in West Virginia and I learned that it was more than a rumor. There was one little guy in his band who had a drinking problem and was constantly getting into fights. He reminded me of a man back home, a man Daddy used to talk about who invariably got beat up every time he had too much to drink. Daddy would say, "Mitch, why in the world do you always pick a fight when you're drinking? You know you're gonna lose." Mitch would say, "Tom, I could whip half a dozen if I could stand up!" This little guy in Bill's band was like that. Right after the show that night he went to a beer joint across the street from the auditorium. A little while later someone came running over to tell us that two big guys were beating up on this little guy in the band. The rest of the band members were packing up their instruments. They stopped, ready to go over and rescue their buddy. But Bill told them not to bother. He said he didn't need them. He went over there alone, grabbed the two big guys off his musician, butted their heads together, knocked them cold, then dropped them to the floor. Then he said, "Come on, boy," and walked out leaving the two guys lying there unconscious.

We just loved stories like that. They would make the rounds backstage at the Opry, and we all got the biggest kick out of hearing about one another's adventures on the road.

In the summer of 1941, Pee Wee King moved back to Nashville and joined the Opry again. He had been a member back in 1936, but had decided to move to Louisville, which was his wife's hometown. Joe Frank, Pee Wee's father-in-law, was promoting and managing him. Joe holds a revered place in the Country Music Hall of Fame because he was one of the first promoters who saw the potential of country music shows. He thought Opry stars could play big houses and fill them up. He used to say, "Get out of those Monday-night schoolhouse dates and up there where the big money is." People made fun of him, but he had vision, and he stuck to his beliefs. He lived to see his dreams come true, but not on the scale of country music now.

That August, Mr. Frank called me and asked if I'd like to go on the road with Pee Wee King and the Golden West Cowboys. "I'll pay you $50 a week," he said. He barely had time to get "dollars" out before I had accepted.

I went on the road with Pee Wee the following Monday. In addition to his other musicians, Eddy Arnold was singing and playing lead guitar for him. He also had a girl singer, San Antonio Rose. She was a great gal, and the boys in the band loved to tease her. When she came out to do her songs, they'd sing behind her, just loud enough so she could hear it, but the audience couldn't: "Sanitary Rose, everybody knows, when she blows her nose on her hose, her petticoat shows!" They were all crazy. I had liked Pee Wee instinctively that first time I met him in Evansville. I fell in with his group easier than I had with Roy's because I'd had more time out. I was beginning to feel comfortable around these hillbillies and they, around me.

I'd better explain about the term *hillbilly*. At some point during the middle forties some of the people in country music decided we should stop calling ourselves hillbillies. I don't know where it started. They thought the term was demeaning. It certainly didn't matter to me. But they felt "country and western music" sounded better than "hillbilly music." It's funny, but now that we've all become accustomed to country and western, we don't like to hear other people say hillbilly, even though we still use the word when talking about one another. Among us, it's a term of endearment. We'll say, "Now isn't that just like an old hillbilly." But let an outsider say the same thing and we're insulted. It's like you can cuss your brother, but you don't want to hear anyone else cussing him.

The hillbillies I worked with became my brothers, my close friends. Over the years, I sensed that I had earned their respect by the way I was able to take the road life. In those days, before luxury buses and air travel had become the preferred modes of transportation, it was rough, physically. I didn't complain or whine or ask for any favors or special treatment because I was a woman. I took the rigors and changes just like the men. I came from hardy stock, and I think my heritage of the rugged ancestors on my father's side served me well during those years. Also, I had six years of grueling preparation on the road for Mr. Sewell.

I was older than these boys, and they brought out my maternal instincts. I was their confidante, their mother confessor. Without meaning to, I became involved in their lives. We traveled in such close quarters that they just naturally shared their thoughts with me, and I worried about them. For one thing, I worried because they didn't save their money. That was really ironic, since *I* hadn't saved a dime. But I didn't have a family or a lot of responsibilities the way most of them did. I only had Mama. Let's just say the expression "He saved his money" is used by hillbillies, but not often. That line became a favorite joke of mine and Henry's after an incident backstage at a park date after we were married. At these fairs we would start at around 2 p.m. and work four or five shows a day in sweltering heat, and it was *tough!* Most of the parks had makeshift dressing rooms, no more than cubbyholes really, with walls that didn't go all the way to the ceiling. At the end of one very long, hot day Henry was with me in one of these little dressing rooms and an old-time baggy-pants comic was in the stall next to us. He knew we could hear him. He was changing his wardrobe and said, "Thank God I don't *have* to do this. I *saved* my money." Henry and I just loved it. The man was obviously down on his luck, but he hadn't lost his sense of humor.

Chapter Sixteen

I N August of 1941, after I'd been with Pee Wee a couple of weeks, we were offered a unique job that turned out to be one of the most exciting experiences of my life.

Europe was at war, but the United States was not yet involved in the conflict, and most Americans didn't think we ever would be. Nevertheless, the U.S. Defense Department had begun what they called Selective Service. Young men were required to serve in some branch of the service—army, navy, air force or marines —for a period of one year. Bases had sprung up all over the country to train these young men, and the GIs were hungry for entertainment.

At that time the R. J. Reynolds Tobacco Company sponsored a very popular radio show called the Camel Caravan, starring Vaughn Monroe. (They also sponsored the network portion of the Grand Ole Opry on Saturday night.) Someone got the idea of putting the Camel Caravan on the road, as well as on the air, with three units of the show traveling around the country entertaining servicemen at their bases. They organized a troupe from Hollywood, one from New York and one from Nashville featuring members of the Grand Ole Opry. Mr. Frank went to New York and sold the William Esty Agency on using Pee Wee's show for the Opry Camel Caravan. It was a fabulous opportunity for all of us because it broadened our personal-appearance contact considerably. The young men on these bases came from all over the country, many from places too far from Nashville for Opry stars to perform live because we always had to be back home for the Saturday broadcast. But for me it was absolutely invaluable because it gave me the stage experience I needed to get Minnie Pearl in shape. For 19 months, I worked almost every day, sometimes three shows a day, and these soldiers were not the easiest audiences because they weren't on those military bases by choice. They hadn't gone down and bought a ticket in their hometown to see a country music show. They had gone to a free base show because there was nothing else to do. You had to be quick and punchy to get through to them, and that gave me the guts and brass to let Minnie kick up her heels and have fun.

There is only one thing that will season an act, and that is show hours, which I was sorely lacking before the Camel Caravan. You either bring it on the stage with you, or you don't. You don't get it after you get out there. And once you've accumulated those show hours, no one can take them away from you. It's what separates the pros from the amateurs.

We had a great troupe on the Opry Camel Caravan. In addition to Pee Wee and his band, and Eddy Arnold and San Antonio Rose, the producers added a girl trio, the Camelettes, a dancer, Dainty Dolly Dearman, and a glamorous pop singer, Kay Carlisle.

Kay would have been at home in a sophisticated New York supper club. She wouldn't have been caught dead singing a country song, and at first she took a dim view of us hillbillies. But she was *fun*, and we were soon like one big crazy family. Ford Rush, a striking man with hair like Charlie Rich's, went along as our emcee. He had been a radio performer in Chicago in his younger days, and he was more or less the coordinator for our show. He sang, too.

In addition to my regular $50 a week from Pee Wee, the William Esty Agency offered me an additional $50 if I would act as chaperone to the cigarette girls we took along to all our shows. These were very pretty young girls who walked through the audience before each show, passing out sample packets of Camels to the servicemen. Well, I would have agreed to chaperone King Kong for $50 a week (with my Opry money, this brought my total weekly income to $110, practically *millionaire* status compared to my poverty a few months earlier), but I had no idea what I was getting into. I might as well have been trying to keep a bunch of guineas together. (You'd have to come from the country to know about guineas. They're wild. They're like mercury, impossible to hold in one place.) We had a big turnover in the cigarette-girl department. They'd come running to me in tears, wanting to go home because some soldier had pinched them as they passed down the aisles with their cigarette trays. The boys couldn't resist. The girls had darling figures, and they wore cute little majorette costumes with skirts so short they barely covered their bloomers.

Our show was aimed at pleasing servicemen, men who were away from home and not happy about it. (That's when Minnie began getting a little racy with her gags.) Eddy Arnold opened with "I'll Be Back in a Year, Little Darlin'," and the boys loved it because they all thought they would be back home in a year.

That fall we traveled as far as our radius would allow, to get back into Nashville on Saturday night, hitting four and five bases each week. We rode in five red vehicles, all bearing the Prince Albert logo painted on the side. The lead car had a little horn that beeped out, "The Camels are coming, da *da*, da *da*." Pee Wee's car pulled a trailer/dressing room for outdoor shows. The instruments were hauled in a truck, with sides that let down to make a stage. When our red caravan drove onto a base it was exciting. We got a lot of attention. Those boys we were entertaining may not have been happy about *their* situation, but we were having the time of our lives. Most of us were single and we didn't have a care in the world. I roomed with Dainty Dolly, who is still one of my best friends, and we thought we were just too much for words. I loved playing the camps. It was the only time in my life I was popular, but then all the girls were. It was a matter of supply and demand—lots of men and very few gals. We had absolutely no thought of war. We were having too much fun to worry about what was going on in Europe, or anywhere else in the world.

On the morning of December 7, 1941, the Caravan pulled into San Antonio. We had the day off, so Dolly and I decided to hop over to Dallas, where I wanted to visit my college friend Betty Binyon and Dolly wanted to see relatives.

Betty and I went out sightseeing early, and when we got back to her house we found her husband sitting by the radio. We took one look at his face and knew something terrible had happened. Betty thought one of her parents had died. "The Japs have bombed Pearl Harbor," he told us in a stricken voice. We said, "Where in the world is Pearl Harbor?" Neither of us had ever heard of it. "Honolulu," he explained. It still seemed very far away.

We hovered by the radio. Announcers kept repeating the story of the bombing in excited voices, with all the gory details about so many of our ships going down and thousands of young men killed. I called Dolly and we hustled back to San Antonio.

When we got there, the members of our troupe were huddled in their rooms talking about what this would mean to us. We thought the Camel Caravan would end instantly. We didn't realize there would be more need for it than ever. We were all in a complete panic, like children.

The next day we were scheduled to play both Randolph Field and Kelly Field. It was gloomy and overcast. About noon word came on the radio that President Roosevelt had declared war on Japan. We were all frightened to death. My impulse was to go home immediately. We didn't know where the Japanese would strike next and we were right in the middle of a prime target—Ft. Sam Houston, Kelly Field and Randolph Field. A precision bombing raid could have wiped out all three.

That afternoon we got our first taste of what it was like to be at war. We were accustomed to breezing onto these bases in our caravan of red cars without being stopped. They would wave us on through the gates as they saw us coming. But this time we were not only stopped at the guard gate; we were checked by MPs for individual identification. Then they searched our vehicles before they let us through. This became standard practice, of course, and I made a great gag out of it, which I used throughout the war, every time I played a military base. Minnie would say, "I felt so at home when I got here. In fact, one feller told me I was the homeliest girl he'd ever seen. They were so cordial and pleasant when we got to the gate. Why, they even had fellers out there with my initials on their sleeve—M.P.—Minnie Pearl. Them fellers even got in the cars to look for me. They searched ever' one till they found *me!*" With boys transferring back and forth from one base to another, that joke became so well known they'd call out from the audience "Tell us about the MPs" before I got to it. Sometimes MPs would run on stage when I pulled the gag and grab me. The boys loved it.

On the bases we always visited the hospitals first. That afternoon on December 8 we walked the wards at Randolph Field base hospital and tried to be lively and cheerful. It was awful.

The sick boys had gotten sicker. We struggled through a show for them. We began to see the seriousness of the situation our country faced and the real danger we were in. Americans were totally unprepared for war, and these military men knew it. That night we realized that being entertainers didn't give us special privileges. Ford Rush's son, who traveled with us as a sort of road manager, went off ahead of the others while the boys were unloading their instruments. They had told us to stick together as a unit, but he had gone to check the stage. The MPs grabbed him and took him into custody. He didn't have proper identification, and Ford had to go all the way to the base commander to get him released. After that we were all issued special ID cards as members of the Camel Caravan.

Professionally, that night was a momentous occasion for me because it was the first time I was ever heckled, and I learned an invaluable lesson from it.

Quite a few boys in the audience had tried to drown their sorrows in drink. They were scared, uncertain about the future and miserable because their Christmas leaves had been canceled. It was a terrible time to put on a show. You can be sure Eddy Arnold didn't open with "I'll Be Back in a Year, Little Darlin' " that night, or any night thereafter. (He found out what a "no-no" song it had become when he forgot and opened with it one night shortly after Pearl Harbor and got booed all the way through the number.)

The boys who'd had too much to drink on this particular evening were not happily boisterous. They were hostile drunk, and one of them decided to take it out on me. The audience had responded well to the Camelettes, who were all attractive, and to Dolly, who was a cute little redhead. When I came on I didn't exactly stop the show; but I sure slowed it down. They didn't want to hear comedy or see a funny-looking country girl in a silly hat. They wanted to get back to the pretty girls. This guy started hollering at me. Every time I'd pull a gag, he would step on my punch line, or answer it, and he was getting bigger laughs than I was. The more they laughed the louder he got. I hadn't had enough experience to cope with this and I really let it get to me. I began stumbling over my lines, which gave him more time. He began imitating me in a grotesque voice. It just destroyed me. I did an inexcusable thing. I left the stage in a shambles without finishing my act. I ran backstage bawling my eyes out. Ford Rush put the next act on, then he came over to me.

"You shut up that crying right now," he said sternly. I just cried harder. I was frightened, anyway. I thought the world was falling to pieces. I wanted to go home and by this time I didn't care if they fired me. But Ford Rush went on.

"You listen to me. To begin with, the first time you walked out on a stage, particularly as a woman, and said, 'Here I am. Look at me; laugh at me,' you were letting yourself in for just what you got tonight. If you are going to say, 'I'm funny; laugh at me,' you automatically become a target. The sooner you learn that the better. It's even worse for a woman because it puts her out of her natural habitat. You wear a silly costume and go out there acting silly and you have to be prepared to take whatever comes. If you're not experienced enough to handle a heckler, then ride over him. Get louder than he is. You've got a microphone and he hasn't. Don't worry about your timing. Do your act. Pull your gags the best you can and get off. Don't acknowledge him at all. He *wants* attention, and if you don't notice him he can't have any fun."

It was great advice and he was right. My feminine ego was hurt, and you can't play comedy and worry about that. I can truthfully say I've never since let a heckler bother me. We go on stage to entertain and make a living, hopefully in that order, and one person out of a whole audience could never disturb my evening now. I haven't been heckled often in my career, but on the rare occasions when I have, I've had fun with it, played with the person or persons and sometimes invited them on stage. That shuts them up fast because they don't want to be up there where you are. They want to be down in the audience being a smart aleck. It's no fun for the heckler if he sees you don't care.

Our Caravan was more in demand than ever after war was declared, and we were hitting bases all week and back to Nashville on Saturday nights for the Opry.

Then, in February 1942, a momentous thing happened. Word came that we were going overseas. Nobody in that bunch had ever been out of the United States and we were thrilled. They were sending us to Panama. The Canal had become the most heavily guarded spot on this side of the world because our supply lines would have been cut off without it, so many new bases had been established there. We were to play them all.

We shopped frantically in Nashville for new clothes for the trip. We'd been told that it would be hot in Panama in March, but to us

hot meant Mobile in the summertime. We had never been exposed to the real tropics. Besides, it was difficult to think of *summer* clothes when there was snow on the ground in Nashville, so
we packed what looked good rather than what would be practical.
I'll never forget one outfit I took. I just loved it. It was a turquoise
wool suit with a pink cashmere sweater. Pee Wee had a new
wardrobe made for his boys that consisted of white wool cowboy
pants and a change of shirts—heavy blue satin and heavy pink
satin. Kay Carlisle bought a trunkload of glamorous new gowns.

We waited at the Roosevelt Hotel in New Orleans to receive
word on the time of our departure. The officials didn't issue the
information ahead for security reasons. We were to sail to Panama
on the *Veragua,* a beautiful ship owned by the United Fruit Company. It had been converted to a troop ship. We settled in at the
Roosevelt to wait, and had a marvelous time sightseeing. Finally
word came that we would be leaving at eight in the morning. I
was beside myself with excitement. The ship surpassed my expectations. It turned out to be the romantic ship of my childhood
fantasies with Monnette. It was a real luxury liner, and Dolly and
I shared an elegant stateroom. The girls in our show were the only
females aboard. All the other passengers were military personnel.
Talk about being in Heaven! We had a *terrible* time each night
deciding which attractive officer to date. At night the ship was
under blackout orders, which was wonderful because it meant
you could stroll the deck in darkness. Inside the ballroom, where
blackout curtains covered the portholes, we sang and played
piano and danced and partied until dawn. The ship had the same
personnel it had carried as a luxury liner, so the food and service
were excellent and it was all *free.* We ate ourselves sick. For five
days and nights we had a ball. Then we hit Pamama and the party
was over.

The minute we stepped off that ship the heat hit us like a con-
crete wall. It was around 100 degrees and the humidity was murder. It was like stepping into a furnace. And there I was in my
turquoise wool suit!

They loaded us into a Panamanian bus, called a *chiva.* It was
the worst piece of junk we'd ever seen, and the native driver
thought he was Mario Andretti. After five days and nights of solid
partying and very little sleep, none of us was in any condition to
bounce up and down on rough roads in a bus with no springs
while suffocating with the heat. When we arrived in Cristóbal we

were all as limp as dishrags, and we had a show to do that after-noon. They checked us into the Washington Hotel. It was the most magnificent place I had ever stayed. The lobby was enor-mous, with beautiful terrazzo floors and lush potted plants every-where. One end opened onto a terrace with a breathtaking view of the ocean. People from all over the world walked through that lobby—Australians, with their unmistakable accents, Scots wear-ing kilts, handsome English naval officers. It was so *cosmopoli-tan.* We hillbillies looked around in wide-eyed wonder.

Our tour began that afternoon with an incident I will never forget. By the time we had arrived on the base, the musicians had already set up their instruments and were ready to go. (Those satin shirts were wet with perspiration even before the poor boys got on stage.) Pee Wee opened, then Eddy sang, and we went on down the line to Kay Carlisle. Glamorous Kay always wore beau-tiful gowns, but she had on a knockout that day. It was chiffon, cut on the bias, with spaghetti straps. The top was flesh-colored; then the color shaded gradually darker down the skirt to the bottom, where it was vivid tangerine. It resembled the type of show gowns Bob Mackie designs today, and it was perfect for her act because she opened with a song called "Tangerine," which was a big hit at that time. Kay was one of the most popular acts on the show, and quite a character. She was super glamorous, but she made fun of herself beautifully. She called herself Miss Magnolia Blossom, affecting this Southern drawl that would make us fall out laughing. She was also gutsy and ahead of her time in many ways. This was a quarter of a century before bra burning became fashionable, but Kay Carlisle never thought of wearing one. She had a beautiful bustline and she knew it. She pranced out on that stage in her gorgeous gown and jumped right into "Tangerine," swaying and twisting her body to the Latin beat, really giving them a show. The fact was, she was giving them more of a show than she knew. Chiffon doesn't breathe, and she had perspired enough to dampen the top of her dress. A hot wind had come up and gusts of it would hit her, plastering that flesh-colored fabric to her bosom like a second skin. If she'd been out there topless those boys wouldn't have seen a bit more.

None of us backstage knew what was going on, and neither did Pee Wee and the boys in the band because her back was to them. All we knew was that Kay was getting an *incredible* response from that audience. She was always a hit with the men, but the sound

coming from those boys was different—like the roar of a bull—
and it was getting louder by the minute.

Suddenly the commanding officer came storming backstage. He
was puffed up like a bullfrog, snapping a swagger stick against his
leg. "Get her off; get her *off*," he yelled. I didn't know what he
was talking about. "Isn't there a chaperone with this show?" he
bellowed. Someone pointed to me. "Don't you realize these men
have been down here without a white woman for months? If you
don't get her off that stage *this minute*," he shook the stick in my
face, "this tour will be canceled."

I was scared to death. I could not *imagine* what Kay had done
to get him so irate. I rushed to the side of the stage to try to get
her attention, and then I saw the front of her dress. I knew *exactly*
why he was disturbed! Kay looked nude from the waist up! The
roar from the audience was getting louder. I expected them to
storm the stage at any second. I couldn't get Kay's attention, but
Pee Wee finally looked my way. I motioned him over and told
him what was happening. As soon as Kay finished "Tangerine"—
to thunderous applause and wild cheers—he told her she had to
leave the stage *right that minute*. She didn't want to go. She'd
never had a response like that in her life. They stood there for a
moment, having a confrontation about it. Then Pee Wee told her
to look down. When she saw what he saw, she came off.

We stuffed handkerchiefs, Kleenex, anything we could get,
down into the top of her dress. When she walked back out there
with all that padding in front, you could hear this long
"Ohhhhhhhhhhhhhhhh!" of disappointment. But she killed them
anyway. She put on a terrific show and they loved her.

Kay was the only one among us who was *not* embarrassed by
the topless incident. She thought it was hilarious, and suggested
we keep it in the show. It was exactly like the old story of the
comic who falls off the stage and breaks his leg in the middle of
his vaudeville act. The crowd roars with laughter, and the stage
manager runs down the aisle yelling, "Keep it in the show, keep
it in the show!"

We stayed in Panama about two weeks, playing every base
there. Many of these camps had been set up hastily after Pearl
Harbor, and some were located miles into the jungle. One morning we were en route to Rio Hata, a particularly remote encampment. We were bouncing along on a narrow dirt road in a caravan
of open jeeps when we suddenly came to a clearing where there

was a thatched-roof hut that served as a little store for the natives. We screamed when we saw the sign outside—Coca-Cola! Just like *home*. We all jumped out of the jeeps and rushed inside to get a Coke. They didn't have any. Hadn't ever had any as far as we could tell. All they had was the sign.

One of our shows was on Taboga Island. This is an island a few miles from Panama. An antiaircraft installation had been put there, and it was heavily guarded by our troops. They took us over on a navy launch. We had to walk up a path cut through the jungle to get to the installation, which was by an old hotel that looked like a movie set for *Sadie Thompson*. It had a big porch all the way around it, slowly rotating ceiling fans and half doors leading into the bar. We did our show on the porch. The officers had invited us for lunch—we were fed every place we worked, no matter what time it was, night or day—and the main course was something that looked like chicken. We began eating, then looked at each other. Some of those old hillbillies started shaking their heads. "Is this chicken?" someone asked. They said it was. These country boys had been eating chicken all their lives, and they knew it didn't taste like any chicken they'd ever had before. We'd been told about this lizard thing they had in Panama called an iguana. It looked like a possum in front and an alligator in back. We knew the natives ate it, and compared it with chicken. Some of us started turning a little green. It was a while before I got a taste for chicken again!

My little cigarette girls had forgotten to bring their costumes that day and I was upset with them. Considering that was the only responsibility they had, I figured they ought to be able to handle it. Then I turned around and did something just as dumb. In addition to chaperoning the girls, I was also in charge of the cigarettes. It was my duty to see that the large packing cases of Camels got loaded and unloaded at every stop, and that none of them disappeared. Cigarettes were a precious commodity during the war. When we were getting ready to leave that day I told our band members I needed help in getting those big boxes down that steep hill to the launch. Two fresh-faced little servicemen in camouflage uniforms were standing nearby. They jumped forward and volunteered to carry the cases. I thought that was real sweet of them. Naive me! They set off into the jungle ahead of us. Of course, I never saw them or the cigarettes again. Ford Rush was most displeased. "You ought to have better sense than to let any of these servicemen handle those cigarettes. They're just like gold out here," he scolded. He threatened to take the loss out of my salary. Those boys must have been the most popular guys in camp that night. I never let anyone in uniform near my cigarettes again, even though I secretly hoped they made lots of money on their "commandeered" merchandise.

About halfway through the tour we changed headquarters from Cristóbal to Panama City. I had a friend there from Nashville who worked for the United Fruit Company. He'd been living in Panama City long enough to know his way around the native hangouts. We'd been seeing the tourist sights and we adored Panamanian music, but we hadn't been to any real native clubs. He offered to take a group of us to the most popular one in town. It was the wildest place I'd ever been in my life. The floor show featured a couple doing a scarf dance. She put a scarf around his hips and he put one around hers. Then they danced around facing each other, using the most sensual body movements imaginable. It would be very tame today, but it was the most erotic thing I had ever seen and I was shocked out of my mind. By then I considered myself *very* sophisticated, a real woman of the world, but the minute I saw that, I reverted right back to Centerville and the Methodist church. I kept thinking, "What would Mama say?"

By the time we were ready to leave Panama we were really looking forward to getting back to the good-old U.S.A., where there was plenty of hot water and modern laundry service. We had a terrible time doing our laundry in hotel rooms because things wouldn't dry in that humidity (this was long before the days of wash-n'-wear fabrics), and if you sent things out to be cleaned it took days and they washed them anyway. Washing our hair was another problem. We never had time, except very late at night. By then all the hot water was gone and the electricity had been turned off to enforce blackout regulations. So we shampooed our hair in cold water and set it on rollers in the dark. Thanks to the humidity, it was usually still damp when we took it down the next morning. You can imagine how we looked. Even glamorous Kay wilted a bit.

The navy decided to fly us home because they thought the Caribbean had become too dangerous for ships. I had never been in an airplane in my life and neither had most of the others. We were all terrified, especially when they loaded us onto an old DC-3 troop plane. It had bucket seats, with parachutes lined up down the middle of the aisle. The parachutes were a joke. We didn't have the slightest idea how to use them. Some of the boys played pinochle on them, and some slept on them, but nobody wore one.

On the way, we stopped in Guatemala City for what we thought would be a one-night layover. We did a show at the base there, but the next morning when we were packing up to leave they told us there had been a delay. We ended up staying there a week, more or less confined to our hotel, crowded up four to a room, not knowing when we were leaving or why we were being kept there. It was Easter Week and there were parades in the streets every day, but we were asked not to wander about, so we watched from our hotel room windows.

By this time we were really a mess and had just about given up trying to do laundry or wash our hair. We were being entertained by some Guatemalan government officials, and one of them had become smitten with glamorous Kay. He sent her *armloads* of flowers every day, and our bare, conventlike room soon resembled a funeral-parlor slumber room when a very popular person had passed away. Kay helped alleviate our boredom by regaling us with stories of this Guatemalan's amorous attempts.

One night he invited her to dinner and she insisted her roommates go along. While we were dressing, Kay complained bitterly about the fact that she had to wear a soiled sweater and, worse, that her hair was so dirty. She wore it in one of the most popular war-years styles—curls on the top, sides swept back into a pompadour and more curls hanging to her shoulders. Normally her curls were bouncy and fluffy, but with the grime and grease accumulated from our travels her blonde ringlets looked like they'd been dipped in olive oil. Every time she glanced in a mirror she cringed. Imagine our reaction, then, when, during our romantic candlelight dinner, her Latin lover seductively picked up a curl from her shoulders and gently touched it to his lips. The expression on Kay's face was priceless. She made a brave effort to keep a straight face, but she couldn't look across the table at us because we were choking with laughter. The Guatemalan was murmuring tender endearments in Spanish while she was trying desperately to get that dirty curl away from his mouth. We absolutely dissolved, and finally so did she. I'm sure that poor man thought American women were the most unromantic lot he'd ever seen.

Our families had been notified through WSM that we were on

our way home, and we were anxious and nervous because we knew they would be concerned about the delay. We found out later that WSM was issuing daily bulletins as though we were on the battlefront. Finally we were loaded onto another plane—this time a commercial Guatemalan airliner—and flown to Brownsville, Texas. When we got off that plane we were so happy to be back on American soil we got down and kissed the ground. Then we all rushed into the airport and lined up at the pay phones to call home. When we got back to the Opry the next Saturday night we were welcomed like war heroes. We thought that was fitting, considering some of the action we'd seen.

Chapter Seventeen

I N those days the dream of every member of the Grand Ole Opry was to become a regular on the network portion of the Saturday-night radio show. I was no exception. But I had about given up hope of being included in that select number (there were only three or four regulars on the 30-minute show, with different guests each week) because I had once been turned down.

It had happened in the spring of 1941, when I was still working the road with Roy. WSM had told the William Esty Agency they had a girl on the local show who was network material. So the agency sent the account executive for Prince Albert tobacco (sponsors of the network show) down from New York to look me over. I was introduced to him backstage before I changed into Minnie's costume. I didn't know why he was there. Agency men were always coming down from New York to check on the Opry for one reason or another, and it wasn't unusual to run into one of them. I had on a smart suit (I've always loved good-looking clothes, and I wore them well when I was young and slim), and I carried on a brief conversation with this man outside the dressing room. I didn't talk like Minnie Pearl; I talked like Sarah Ophelia Colley. After all, my parents had spent a good deal of time and money teaching me to speak properly. (I read without moving my lips, and I can carry on a relatively intelligent conversation when

I want to.) I talked to this man a few minutes, then went into the dressing room to change. He went out front to watch me work. Later he had dinner with Jack Stapp, producer of the network portion of the show.

"I don't want this girl on the Prince Albert show," he told Jack. "She's not authentic. Sooner or later the listeners will see that. She's no country girl. She's a sophisticated young woman, and the audience will get that. She won't last."

(I've thought of that statement many times. The devil in me has wanted to look him up and say, "So, she didn't last. Poor old thing, she's only lasted 40 years!")

I was crushed when Jack told me I had been auditioned and rejected on the grounds that I wasn't authentic. I was creating a character, playing a part. If he'd said I wasn't funny, I could have accepted that more easily. But being turned down for not being authentic really stung, especially since I'd heard the same misgivings expressed by Ford Rush a year earlier. I told Jack I felt it was an unfair judgment. "Why can't the people be the judge?" I asked. He said, "I'm sorry, Minnie, but we have no authority over who they put on the network show. All we can do is suggest."

There was nothing anyone could do, so I tried to swallow my disappointment and put it out of my mind.

Then, about 10 months later, Harry Stone came down to a show I was working in Florida with the Camel Caravan. He had exciting news to tell me. The account executive who had turned me down was no longer handling the Prince Albert account, and the new man had agreed to put me on the network! I wasn't being offered a contract, or even a promise they would keep me for a trial period, but they were at least going to give me a shot at it the following Saturday night to see how the network audience responded to Minnie.

I fretted and worried the rest of the week about my material. Virginia was still writing for me and I had bought gags from a couple of Nashville writers from time to time, but I had never had top professional writers who could turn out good material in volume. They were very difficult to find, and much too expensive for my pocketbook. But I knew New York would expect my material to be as good as other comedians of the day, people like Jack Benny and Eddie Cantor, who had dozens of writers at their disposal.

I called Virginia and she and I both worked frantically to put together the best gags we could come up with for my 3 minutes and 15 seconds on the air. We only had a couple of days. When Saturday night came I was a nervous wreck. I so desperately wanted to be good on my first network exposure. I was backstage, still worrying about my material, running it over and over in my mind, when suddenly I heard the Prince Albert theme song that opened the show:

> *Howdy all you friends and neighbors*
> *Join us in our Prince Albert show*
> *Tune up the five-string banjo*
> *Take down the fiddle and bow*
> *Roll back the rug on the floor*
> *Light up the old cob pipe*
> *Everyone will have some fun*
> *At the Grand Ole Opry tonight*

I panicked and darted toward the side of the stage, not paying any attention whatever to my surroundings. The stagehands were hurriedly changing backdrops from the sponsor of the previous segment to Prince Albert. They still used the old-fashioned method of lifting and lowering the scenery by hoisting or dropping heavy sandbags. In my nervous rush I didn't hear them call out, "Watch the scenery." The next thing I knew I felt a heavy blow on the top of my head that almost knocked me down. My vision blurred, then I saw stars. I staggered back, dazed and dizzy, totally disoriented for a moment. Then I realized I had run smack under one of those falling sandbags. Now my head was spinning and I couldn't even think straight. I just knew I would never remember my new material. I heard them announcing me. I have never gone on stage in such a state. I don't know how I got through my 3 minutes, 15 seconds. I think I was less than sensational.

I thought, "How typical. Everything happens to me. Nothing comes off without some flaw. Buy a suit with two pair of pants, you burn a hole in the coat"—the hillbillies' comment on luck. (That's why I wear a price tag on my hat—another accident. I put some dime-store flowers on my hat for the Opry one night and mistakenly left the price tag on them. As I moved my head around during my act, the tag dangled down off the brim. Someone laughed at it, so I left it there, and Minnie has worn a price tag on her hat ever since. Anything for a laugh, I always say.)

I knew that night that I was being taped for playbacks the following Monday. That was a rule for every network show. Each Monday afternoon the regulars would meet at WSM and listen to the tapes of the previous Saturday-night show. At the same time the William Esty people were listening to a copy of the same tape in New York. Then they would call Nashville and give each performer a critical rundown of what they liked and didn't like. I had a miserable weekend worrying about what they would say to me in Monday's session. (I also had a headache.)

As it turned out, they didn't say much. Maybe they sensed that "nobody liked me but the people." Anyway, they let me stay on the network, and they said they would find writers for me, which relieved me and Virginia.

New writers meant a new routine for me. When I got in off the road on Saturday mornings I had to go by WSM and pick up my material that had been sent down from New York, in addition to all the personal errands and chores I had to take care of on my one day in town. Then I had to study the material and get it down by that night. It wasn't mandatory for me to memorize my lines, since it was radio, but you can't read comedy from a script and get the timing down to perfection. You have to know it in order to flow with it.

I was usually not happy with the material the agency sent. I didn't feel comfortable with it. This was no reflection on the writers. They simply weren't into country humor. I was allowed to make changes if I got them approved, but I was hesitant about doing so because I knew they didn't like it. I would have done most anything to stay on that network show because it meant so much to my overall career. It gave me a much wider range of bookings because it reached the entire country, whereas the rest of the show, carried locally on WSM, reached a radius only of about 500 miles. It also meant an immediate increase in my personal-appearance price.

The main difference between the material New York sent down and the material Virginia and I had been writing was the tone. We went for chuckles; they went for belly laughs. Ours was gentler. And sometimes their gags didn't mean much to country folks. I remember once they had me talking about Brother's clothes and saying, "They were enough to take the heart out of Hart Schaffner & Marx." That was a line of men's suits. We didn't know anything about Hart Schaffner & Marx labels. In the country all we knew about was Duck Head overalls and Buster Brown shoes.

Something like this would be typical of Virginia's material:

"My feller and me went to a weddin' the other night, and, oh, it was so pretty and so sad. I cried and cried and had the best time. The bride, she come down the aisle in the prettiest white dress. It'us short in front, but it sagged somethin awful down the back. Two little younguns had to come along behind and tote it fer 'er. Why, if she'd a had to git away from there in a hurry with that long dress a swingin' out behind her, she'd a fell and broke her leg, they'd a had to shoot her. She looked so happy. I don't blame her. I know how long she'd been after him. We started about the same time, but she outrun me. The groom was a'waitin' fer her at the h'alter, and that's what it was, too. He didn't know it, but he found out in a couple of days. He was a'waitin' there fer her, and everyone said the bride looked stunnin' but the groom, he jus' looked stunned. He looked like another clean shirt would do him. And the lady at the organ was playing Meddlesome's wedding march and it was so pretty, and they had flow'rs, they had nasty-tursuns and peetunyas and beegonyas; well, h'it smelt jus lak a funereal. The groom stood there in front a'all them folks and told that girl he'd give her all his wordly goods, and his pappy was a'settin' there in front a'me and he said, 'Uh, oh! There goes Jed's slingshot!' "

The agency material ran more like this:

"I seen two fellers and one of them said to the other one, 'I believe that's the ugliest girl I ever seen,' and the other one said, 'Oh, she might be a pretty good old girl. You know beauty is only skin deep,' and the first one said, 'Well, let's skin her.' "

Minnie didn't care much for that, but she was desperate. I was having problems with more than the material. I wasn't delivering. I was too uptight, too conscious of being under close scrutiny by the agency. You have to be relaxed to play comedy, because the minute you tighten up, your timing gets thrown off. I was going out on the road every week and putting on good shows, but back on the Opry on Saturday I wasn't selling. I have Jack Stapp to thank for Minnie's survival on the network those first few months. I'm confident that it was due to his support that I was kept on. In fact, the people at WSM were supportive in every way.

In 1942, I was hospitalized with peritonitis, and it was touch and go for a few days. The doctor had called my family to my bedside. Most of the time I was delirious from the high fever, but in one of my lucid moments I overheard two doctors discussing my case as though they didn't expect me to live. It was terrifying. WSM was releasing daily bulletins on my condition. And the people from the station went out of their way to be helpful and comforting to Mama and my sisters. Then, when I had passed the crisis (it took me two months to get back on my feet), Harry Stone, the president of WSM, came to the hospital and talked to me like a father. He inquired about my financial situation and gave me the money to pay my hospital bill, which I paid back in installments. (To show how close the Opry audiences felt to their regular performers, WSM received a barrage of letters and phone calls inquiring about my condition. The incident stirred up so much concern that in 1950, when I was hospitalized again for surgery, WSM *taped* me ahead of time so they could put me on the air in my scheduled spot. It was absolutely unheard of to have anything on the Opry network that wasn't live, and to my knowledge no one has been taped for the show since. But they didn't want to panic the listeners, so they kept me on the air.)

In 1943, a year after my network debut, NBC's red and blue networks merged and the Opry picked up another 100 stations. From that point on no other radio show could touch us for coverage. We had 150 channels all across the dial. We got complaints from couples out courting on Saturday night because they couldn't get anything on their car radio during that half hour except the Grand ole Opry.

When the show first went full network, something happened that we old-timers still laugh about. With 150 channels carrying the Opry, the William Esty Agency was more anxious than ever to make certain that everything went smoothly for their client, Prince Albert tobacco. They sent a man down to sit in on our rehearsals. We all looked at one another. "What rehearsals?"

"You mean you don't rehearse a network radio show?"

You should have seen the look on that man's face. He was horrified. He went straight to the WSM officials. Well, by that time the Opry had been going along for 19 years, 7 of them on the 50-station red network, and no one had disgraced himself yet, so they didn't see any reason to rehearse. Roy, who was the star of the show, talked to the agency man.

"I'll tell you how we handle it," he said. "We have a fiddle chaser. If we run short, we just let the fiddler play till time's up. If we run long, we don't use the fiddler."

Well, this guy just went to pieces.

"You *will* have a rehearsal," he ordered.

We explained that we were on the road all week and had no time for rehearsal.

That didn't faze him.

"Everyone on the network show will be here by 11 a.m. Saturday for rehearsals." He said there would be no exceptions.

That really threw us because it meant revising bookings so we wouldn't be too far away on Friday night to make it back into Nashville very early Saturday morning. On some weekends we didn't get back till midday, or even early afternoon. So that had to change. They tightened up on us for a while, but we soon got back to our natural, more relaxed ways. To this day, the show still isn't rehearsed. We don't even rehearse live TV broadcasts of the Opry. That's why the people love it so much. It's *real*.

One suggestion that came from the William Esty Agency during this period was very beneficial to me. One of their men came down to see the show and suggested I change the opening of my act. Minnie had always gone out on stage and opened with "Howdy," in a gentle, friendly voice. I thought a country girl would greet strangers that way. He wanted me to holler "How-*dee*" in a brash, bold voice and let the audience answer back. He said, "Before you go on I'll tell the announcer to ask the audience to yell 'Howdee' back when you greet them." I didn't like the idea at all, but he was already running out there to tell the announcer.

When I yelled "How*dee*" that night, the audience response was tremendous. They loved the participation. It was to become Minnie's trademark, along with the price tag on her hat.

The routine of being on the road all week and back in Nashville on Saturday was becoming second nature to me by the time the Camel Caravan ended in 1942. The fact that we had to come back each Saturday night to do the Opry was the reason the Caravan couldn't continue. It was simply too expensive to get us all the way back into Nashville once a week, and travel was becoming more and more difficult with gasoline rationing and all the rubber available for tires going into the war effort.

When the Caravan disbanded Eddy Arnold left Pee Wee and went out on his own. He began having hit records with RCA Victor and went on to become one of the biggest-selling recording artists of all time. San Antonio Rose left the act and was replaced by Becky Barfield. Then the following summer a tall, lanky man joined our act in Texas. His name was Ernest Tubb, and he had a hit record called "I'm Walking the Floor Over You." After a few tours with us, Tubb went out on his own as a single. Pee Wee used to consider himself a star maker, and he was. Many acts got their start with him. He also brought Grandpa Jones and Cowboy Copas to the Opry. Pee Wee always had a good road show because he had a flair for making it look good, like it was really big time. He gave his acts the biggest buildup imaginable when he brought them on stage, saying things that weren't necessarily true. But to him they were all the greatest.

Traveling the road during the war years was the kind of experience that either kills you or cures you. If you made it through that without cracking up, you knew you could take anything they threw at you on the road. There was no way Pee Wee could keep two vehicles going with gasoline limited and no tires available, so he bought an old, elongated limousine, like an airline limo, except this one had been a funeral car. (Believe me, there were many times, when we were half dead with fatigue, that it seemed very appropriate to be traveling in a funeral car.) There had once been three or four rows of seats in this limo, but Pee Wee had taken out the back ones to make room for the instruments, so eight or nine of us crowded in a space that would have been uncomfortable even for six on long distances. There was absolutely no way to get comfortable. You couldn't stretch out. You could barely move. There were no headrests on the backs of the seats, so you sat straight up with your hands in your lap, stuffed in like sardines.

Gasoline and tires were our biggest problems. We schemed every way imaginable to get gasoline ration stamps. And our re-treads had been retreaded so many times the original rubber began to rot from the rim out. On one 500-mile trip into Nashville we had 13 flat tires! I thought Pee Wee was going to explode. We had the thirteenth on a bridge in Henderson, Kentucky. He jumped out of the limo, fuming, and yelled, "Everybody out of the car!" He was waving a tire iron, threatening to throw it through the windshield, cussing a blue streak in Polish. His brother-in-law was along on that trip, and since they both grew up in Polish families in Milwaukee, they spoke the language as fluently as English. Pee Wee's brother-in-law was embarrassed at the string of Polish curse words, which sounded like gibberish to us. We piled out of the car. Pee Wee was still raving in Polish and his brother-in-law was blushing and holding his head, saying, "Oh, Pee Wee, not that. Don't say *that*, Pee Wee."

Pee Wee was so funny. He had a set of rules for his band members: (1) Don't date in your wardrobe, (2) Don't take a girl across a state line, (3) Don't pick your nose on stage and (4)*Always* laugh at Minnie when she's doing her act.

I'll never forget the night Becky Barfield had to go to the ladies' room when we were on a desolate mountain road in Pennsylvania. She had begged Pee Wee to find her a filling station for hours, but we hadn't passed any. Those guys hated to make stops once we were rolling, anyway. They would make you wait until the last possible minute. Well, Becky had already waited past her last minute when we hit this steep winding road. Finally she told Pee Wee she couldn't wait another second. Rest room or no rest room he was going to have to pull off the road. It was pitch black out. She got out on the passenger side and disappeared. We assumed she'd gone around to the back of the car so the headlights wouldn't hit her. We all sat in the car, waiting for Becky to return . . . waiting, waiting, waiting. Five minutes went by. Still no Becky. Pee Wee told one of the guys to go find her. The guy got out on the driver's side. When he got around to the other side of the car he saw that our rear wheels were parked on the very edge of a 20-foot drop off the mountainside. Poor Becky had stepped out of the back door into thin air! It's a wonder she didn't break something. We hauled her up, brushed her off and started off again. Then she realized she'd been so scared she'd forgotten to go to the bathroom!

Chapter Eighteen

URING this period someone got the bright idea of putting tent shows on the road. One of the first to do this was a blackface act, Jam-Up and Honey. I went with them for a couple of years—first with Pee Woo, then later with Eddy Arnold's show. That was when Eddy and I became such close friends. He and I had to come back to the Opry each Saturday night, but most of the time he left his band out on the road. So we'd drive all Friday night in that funny old Ford car he had, with me trying to stay awake to help him stay awake. I remember we were on the tent-show circuit when his wife, Sally, had their first child, JoAnn. And I remember how Eddy was such a proud papa.

Tent shows were a tradition which is now gone forever. But then they were a new and fascinating experience for us—the Opry under canvas. The tents seated about a thousand people, many times the capacity of some of the small auditoriums and schoolhouses we played.

Through the tent shows we were exposed to a way of life we hadn't known existed—the world of the roustabouts. These were a group of workmen who traveled with us to put up and take down the tent. They had come from circus backgrounds. They had a lingo all their own, which we copied. They called the tent the "rag," and taking it down and putting it up was "striking the rag" and "raising the rag." After each show the performers drove on to

177

the next stop, which meant we traveled at night, while it was cool.
Because there was no air conditioning in those old cars, this was
a blessing, but it also meant arriving in the wee hours of the
morning to check in to some pretty awful small-town hotels,
which wasn't always a blessing. The roustabouts would stay behind and strike the rag, which took several hours. The tent had to
be folded just so, and all the chairs loaded onto trucks. Then they
would camp out for the night on the tent grounds and drive on to
the next show place early the next morning. It also took several
hours to put the tent up once they arrived in a town, so we could
go only 40 or 50 miles between dates. We inched our way across
the South this way, hitting rural areas where people might not
otherwise have been able to see an Opry show.

We learned a lot from these roustabouts. They taught us that
tent-show people—circus people—feared three things: fire, hail
or sleet, and a high wind, or, as they called it, a blow. A high wind
could pull the tent away from its moorings, causing it to fall on
people and smother them. I can remember many times being in
the middle of my act and hearing the wind start to come up.
Immediately that *ping—ping—ping* sound of the sledgehammers
pounding the metal stakes, driving them deeper into the ground,
would be heard over the wind. It was frightening. Once during
our first season we were hit by a hailstorm during a show, and it
tore holes in the top of the tent. Jam-Up and Honey had to order
a new one, and they complained that it cost so much it ate up their
profits for that season.

The roustabouts taught us how to lead people out of the tent in
case of fire. They were very conscious of that possibility because
of a recent tragic Ringling Brothers Circus fire in Hartford, Con-
necticut. We were also taught to get underneath the wooden platform stage in case of a big blow, or a "Hey, Rube!" We didn't
know what the latter was until they explained it. The roustabouts
would sometimes take up with girls in these little towns, and the
local young men would band together and come out to the tent to
fight it out. Back in the circus days the performers would warn
one another by hollering, "Hey, Rube!" The expression came
about because the circus people called country boys rubes. I
imagine that's where *rube comic* originated. Country comics were
always called baggy pants or rube comics in those days. (We had
only one "Hey, Rube!" alert during my two years with tent shows.
One night we could sense restlessness among the roustabouts,

and one of them finally told us one of their men had picked up a local girl and the boys downtown were threatening to come get him. They said they would keep a lookout while we worked, and if we heard them holler "Hey, Rube!" we were to get under the stage immediately. It made us pretty nervous while we were doing the show, but we got out of town without an incident. I've often wondered how the roustabouts found time to pick up local girls, as they were in and out of a town so quickly, but I guess they made time.)

I have some wonderfully nostalgic memories of the tent-show days. We would get up and have breakfast around noon. Then we'd stroll around the town before packing up and loading the cars and heading on out to the tent grounds. The roustabouts would have just finished raising the rag. Uncle Dave Macon was with the show and I adored him. While the musicians rehearsed we'd sit out on the tent grounds and talk. He was an absolute cornerstone of the Grand Ole Opry and one of the first to be put in the Country Music Hall of Fame. He had many wonderful stories. It would be just about dusk, or "along about of an eve-nin'," as they say in the country, when it was cooling off and pleasant outside. I remember the different topographies of all those little towns. Sometimes we'd be out in the middle of a field, or somebody's pastureland. The roustabouts would be lazing around on quilts, resting after their hard work of putting up the tent, and Uncle Dave and I would have these long, leisurely con-versations. He was a marvelous banjo player and an exciting per-former. The audiences loved him. I've been asked many times by journalists if I thought an act like his—really old-timey country—could kill an audience today, the way it did then. Or was he just a freak success because he was so old and colorful-looking? He had a little goatee and wore big wing-collar shirts, called gates-a-jar collars, with a stickpin in his tie, a vest and a little black hat. He told jokes and sang those old, old songs. He had that flair, the kind of showmanship that is ageless. He was a pro and in my opinion would be as much of a character now as he was then.

The tent shows helped season my professionalism consider-ably, and it was beginning to show on my network broadcasts. Those invaluable show hours were mounting up, and it was be-coming easier all the time for me to let Minnie take over com-pletely when I worked. I was beginning to feel comfortable and at home in her personality.

It wasn't until the war was over that I fully realized how much our servicemen had done to help establish my career. They had been responsible for widening the scope of country music. They took their guitars and their hillbilly songs wherever they went, and they spread the word—from battlefront foxholes to South Pacific beachheads; from remote jungle stations to the most celebrated cities of the world—London, Paris, Rome, even Berlin. The Grand Ole Opry was one of the most popular shows carried on the Armed Forces Radio Network, and our boys all over the world became familiar with Minnie Pearl, who was just a rank newcomer when they left home to fight the war. She came to symbolize a part of all the good things they had left behind, and it was an invaluable boost for me because I didn't have recordings to carry me along. My success depended on personal appearances, which depended on my popularity as an Opry star, and the fact that these boys considered Minnie an old friend by the time they came home gave me a foundation for my career I might not have had otherwise.

I had a little sideline project going during the war years that I thoroughly enjoyed. It was a four-page tabloid called the *Grinder's Switch Gazette,* which I published once a month. My subscription list grew to 1,200 before I had to give it up. It was too time-consuming because I wrote most of it myself. The features included business gossip and news—who was leaving or joining what shows, what Opry stars had joined or returned from the service, new recording contracts, etc. Then there was always an editorial signed by Minnie and usually written by my sister Virginia. It contained little wisdoms and homilies, like Minnie quoting Uncle Nabob as saying, "I always wonder why people think we can get along with our neighbors across in foreign lands if we don't first learn to get along with the folks who live across the hollow." Or it might contain an observation on anything from the war effort to the season. I have one from November 1945 that reads in part:

> I always love the Fall. One reason, I reckon, is because I was born in the Fall (I ain't sayin' *which* Fall). But I love the crispy days when you got to bring in a couple of logs and start a fire in the settin' room fireplace . . . that sharp, tangy scent of the wood smoke a'smartin' your eyes and leavin' that unmistakable smell on all yore clothes and in yore hair. That's a country smell—I

guess city folks wouldn't care for it; but when you been born and bred in the country, it's perfume to yore nose.

There's smells outside that's just as enjoyable . . . the sweet fragrance of the apple that comes up from the cider mill. . . . the sharp, bitter scent of green walnut hulls crushed in the back lot. And hoverin' over it all that mingled odor of burnin' grass, jimson weeds, leaves and sumac bushes.

Headlines in that particular issue included "Tent Shows Close for the Season," "Roy Acuff Leaves for Hollywood" (he went to make the movie *Night Train to Memphis*) and "Jimmy Wakely Guest-Stars on the Opry."

I always used some crazy picture for the cover. When Roy and Mildred Acuff's son Roy Neal was born, I ran a picture of the three of them on a sofa with the baby's foot in Roy's mouth. The caption read, "Roy Acuff's Mouth Grows Another Foot." Pee Wee's wife had twins during that time, so we ran a cover picture of Pee Wee in his cowboy outfit inside a playpen with the twins on the outside. The caption read, "Don't Fence Me In," which was a popular song of the day.

Fans and fellow performers alike loved the *Gazette*, and I've often thought that it might have become a country music trade paper, considering the growth of the Opry, had I kept it up.

The Opry was still very pure in those days. The old-timers wanted to keep the music as authentic as possible, which of course meant no amplified instruments. They didn't allow drums or horns, either. They still won't allow an artist to come on and sing to his record, but they have loosened up considerably on the instruments that are permissible. You still are not likely to find a Moog synthesizer on the Opry stage, however.

I remember one of the very first times we had amplified instruments of any kind on the Opry. Our guest for the network show that night was Bob Wills, the king of Western swing. We were all excited about seeing him because he was a big star from Texas. He had a million-selling record out called "San Antonio Rose" (not to be confused with Pee Wee's singer by the same name). Tommy Duncan, Bob's lead singer, did the vocal. I had never heard a real Western band from Texas before. There's as much difference between that sound and country music as there is between boogie-woogie and bluegrass. We were all very impressed with Bob. He was way ahead of his time. He pulled up into the crowd in front of the old Ryman Auditorium in a sleek, custom-designed bus like country music stars use now. The people were awestruck. His men got off the bus dressed in an all-white Western wardrobe—no sequins or flashy studs, just exquisitely tailored gabardine, cut in the Western style. I adore it. It's the sexiest thing in the world to me. And they all wore white Stetsons.

They came on the Opry stage to thunderous applause. When Tommy stepped up to the microphone to sing "San Antonio Rose," the crowd screamed and carried on the way they did over Elvis years later. Bob's fiddles were amplified, unheard of on the Opry stage, and he threw the audience into a panic. Women went wild over him. In fact, one of them went over the balcony. He was playing double fiddle with another band member, and I was standing to the side of the stage watching, fascinated. In the Ryman, the balcony sloped down so far around on one side you could see it from backstage. I noticed a woman leaning over the railing with her arms outstretched toward Bob, an expression of desperate yearning on her face. Suddenly she tumbled right out of the balcony. She let out a scream and landed, *splat,* on the stage. I don't think it hurt her much. It probably didn't help her, either, but at least she got a close look at Bob.

Along about 1946, Roy Acuff decided to leave the Opry for a time to take advantage of some lucrative personal-appearance of-fers he'd been getting in California and other Western states—places too far away to make it back to Nashville on Saturday night. Red Foley, who had been in Chicago on the WLS Barn Dance, was hired to replace Roy as the star and host of the 30-minute network show. Red had made a name for himself both on the Barn Dance and another radio show, the Plantation Party. He was an excellent performer with a marvelous baritone voice that sounded more pop than country. He could sing anything, and he could change pace without effort, going from a dramatic hymn like "Peace in the Valley" to a kicky swing number like "Chattanooga Shoeshine Boy" to a love song like "Jealous Heart," keeping the audience in the palm of his hand the whole time. They loved him, and he loved performing for them. Red wore clothes better than anyone I ever saw. He always had a well-put-together look, even when he dressed casually. He had beautiful red hair, which he wore brushed back on the sides, and he had that same casual, relaxed approach to performing that Dean Martin has. Although I missed seeing Roy every Saturday night, Red was fun to work with and the most easygoing artist I've ever known. I never saw him get uptight about a show. We used to laugh that Red Foley was so relaxed he'd fall asleep on stage if they dimmed the lights for a minute.

An incident took place not long after Henry and I married that was typical of Red's laid-back manner. The American Medical Association was having a convention in St. Louis, and the R. J. Reynolds Tobacco Company brought in all their stars to entertain the members. Vaughn Monroe and Jimmy Durante, who were both on Camel-sponsored radio shows, came in from New York, and some of us from the Opry went up from Nashville. (It's incredible, now, to look back and recall the strong tie the AMA had at that time with the tobacco industry. R. J. Reynolds was running full-page ads in national magazines picturing a doctor wearing a white coat with a reflector around his head, the caption reading, "More Doctors Smoke Camels Than Any Other Cigarette." Incredible now, but not so much had been made then of a possible connection between smoking and cancer.)

Henry flew us to St. Louis in our plane. After we got there we went right to Keil Auditorium to rehearse. We were sitting out front, watching Vaughn Monroe run through his numbers, when Red said, "You know, I forgot to bring my wardrobe for the show." He was dressed very casually, and this was long before the days when stars went on stage in street clothes. "All I've got with me is what I've got on." He turned to Henry. "Do you think you could fly back to Nashville and get my stage clothes?" Show time was only a couple of hours away. Henry explained that it would be impossible for him to return to Nashville and get back before Red went on. It was almost an hour's drive just to get to the airport. "Is that a fact?" Red commented casually. "Well, I'll just wear what I got on, then." And he slumped down in his seat and went immediately to sleep, as unconcerned as he could be. (I'd like to note that Red went on stage that night and literally stopped the show. He finally bowed off after several encores, so, with him, the wardrobe was incidental.)

One Saturday night, not long after Red came on the network show, I was getting dressed backstage when I heard the audience absolutely going wild over someone. They were roaring with laughter. Several other performers had come out of their dressing rooms as well. (It was always a sign of big success on the Opry if you aroused an audience enough to bring the other acts to the wings to watch.)

I recognized the performer instantly, even though I hadn't seen him in 20 years. His name was Rod Brasfield, and I had idolized him as a teenager. He had come to Centerville every year with a repertory group called Bisbees Comedians, which was a tent show. But in those days Rod played a leading man, and his brother, Boob, did the comedy. Each time they came to town they stayed a week, putting on a different show every night, and I didn't miss a one. They had drawing-room sets that had possibly once been elegant, but had long since lost their luster. The men wore tuxedos with frayed collars. Rod's hair was parted in the middle and slicked back like a real dandy. Boob's wife, Eva, always played a duchess or a wealthy socialite. She wore a crepe dress, blotched with sequins that had lost most of their iridescence, and a tacky feather boa. I thought they were all elegant beyond words. Boob played the irreverent butler, constantly making wisecracks about these rich people. He used reddish makeup so his face looked flushed, as though he'd been imbibing freely, which (rest his soul) I think he did from time to time. The audiences absolutely adored him because he was the smart aleck everybody wants to be. He didn't stick too closely to the script. I remember when an actor was lying dead on the stage in a dramatic scene and he turned to the audience and said, "It ain't so serious; he'll be back tomorrow night." The audience went to pieces. Even the dead actor broke up. Boob would ad-lib off-color lines that no one else on earth could have gotten away with in front of those prim and proper Christian ladies. I thought he was absolutely hilarious. Mama wasn't so sure. But she let us go, anyway. Everybody went. There was nowhere else to go.

I got to know Rod, Eva and Boob because I hung out backstage in absolute awe of them. I would have left home in a minute to join them if Mama and Daddy would have let me. I'd rave about their shows, their costumes, their sets, their talent, and Daddy would say, "Can't you see there is absolutely no money in that. They are operating on a shoestring." But all I saw was the magic of being up there in that wonderful make-believe world.

When I would tell Rod and the other players about my dreams of being in show business their response was just as negative as Daddy's. They would tell me the same thing I tell young people who come to me with stars in their eyes: "Stay out of it!" Of course I didn't listen to them any more than the kids listen to me.

(It might seem strange that professional entertainers, who couldn't imagine making a living any way except show business, discourage aspiring performers. It's because we see all the brokenhearted ones who don't make it. The public sees only the stars. The percentage of success is so terribly small that the odds are against you from the start. And if you are lucky enough to make it, you have to work doubly hard to stay there. Nothing is sadder than a performer who's had a taste of the top, then fallen to the bottom again. As Edna St. Vincent Millay said, "When you have drunk from the spring at the top of the mountain, there's nowhere to go but down, my darling, down.")

I was surprised and delighted to see Rod Brasfield doing comedy on the Opry that night. He had picked up a lot of tricks from his brother, Boob, and he was hilarious. He was rail thin and wearing a stage suit that must have been tailored for a man weighing 350 pounds. The pants were held up with suspenders and the coat absolutely swallowed him. He also wore a very small hat that sat square on the top of his head. (He left me the hat when he died. It's now in the Country Music Hall of Fame in Nashville.)

As soon as he came off the stage, I ran up to him and told him I was Ophelia Colley from Centerville, reminding him of the times I had pestered him backstage about getting into show business. He pretended to remember me. I'm not sure that he did, but he was too kind to let on if he didn't. He was one of the kindest men I ever knew.

Within a few months Rod had become a regular on the network show, and we began doing double comedy in addition to our solo parts. For the next 10 years I had some of my happiest times on radio working with him every Saturday night. The audiences never knew when he was going to pop up toward the end of my act. I'd say something like, "Then, this little old weasel stuck his head out and said . . ." and before I could finish, Rod would interrupt, "Howdy, Minnie," and we'd go from there. We never knew exactly what the other was going to say. We played off one another by "worrying" a gag, or "pointing" it to the audience. For example, if he'd say, "I bought myself a new car and the first thing I done was grease it all over," I'd point it with, "Grease it all over? Why'd you do that . . . Why'd ya grease it all over?"

"So the finance company can't get a'holt of it," he'd say, clacking his false teeth.

Rod's false teeth didn't quite fit, and he used them beautifully by clacking them when the timing was perfect in a joke. The effect was hilarious. His favorite expression was "By Ned, buddy," and it became his trademark, as "Howdee" became Minnie's. He'd say, "By Ned, buddy—Miss Minnie, I sure do wanna walk you home tonight." Then he'd clack his teeth. "I always wanted to walk home with an experienced girl."

"But Rod, I'm not experienced," Minnie would answer innocently.

"Yes, and you ain't home yet, neither," *clack, clack*. The audiences loved him, and so did I.

Chapter Nineteen

MARRIAGE was the last thing on my mind when I met
Henry Cannon in 1946.

I was having a *real* good time. Even with its hardships and
disadvantages, I loved life on the road. The hillbilly pickers
whom I had felt uncomfortable around in the beginning were now
my family, my best buddies, and I felt secure in the knowledge
that I had been accepted as one of them. Saturday nights in Nashville were fun, too. If we weren't heading right back out on the
road after the Opry, I could count on having a date, because my
roommate, Orra Williams, loved arranging dates for me. Also, I
had gotten to know several men in Nashville.

Orra was secretary to Jack Stapp, program director at WSM, and
we had been sharing a room at a large boardinghouse on West
End Avenue, across from the Vanderbilt Gym, since 1941. It was
a once fashionable old brick home owned by a lovely widow, Mrs.
Effie Long. Miss Ef, as we called her, rented out five bedrooms to
career girls. The place was like a college dormitory, absolute madness most of the time, with 10 girls running in and out. Orra and
I had a funny little room upstairs in the back of the house that,
oddly enough, we entered by going through a closet. There was
an old call box in the kitchen with buttons that rang in rooms
which had once been servants' quarters, and since one of them
was connected to our room we deduced that we were living in the

upstairs maid's room. But we didn't care. We loved to joke about it. Besides, these were the war years and rooms were hard to come by.

There were three military installations near Nashville, and servicemen swarmed down on the town every weekend like locusts invading a wheat field. It wasn't a matter of whether a girl *had* a date, but with whom. It was wonderful! By the time I'd get in off the road during the wee hours of Saturday morning the girls at Miss Ef's would already have their dates lined up for the weekend. Orra was determined that my being gone all week was not going to impede my social life for a minute, so whenever she accepted a date for herself she made one for me also. She didn't care whether I *wanted* a date or not. I'd get back in town worn out, with a million things to do before the Opry on Saturday night, and she'd already have me fixed up with a date for after the broadcast. Some of these guys were real duds (I wasn't like Minnie, who always said she didn't care for blind dates but maybe she *would* have better luck with one who didn't see *too* well).

On some of those nights, Orra would be waiting for me backstage at the Opry with her date and mine. If the guy wasn't attractive, she'd have this Laverne-to-Shirley look on her face that said, "Yeeuuck!" Other times my date would be real cute and Orra would be beaming from ear to ear. Since I never asked her to get me dates, I didn't feel obligated to keep them, so there were occasions when I just walked out the back door of the Opry, got in a cab and left my roommate with two dates. This is significant because it shows what being on the road will do to you. It would never have occurred to me to walk off and leave a date before I'd spent time on the road, but being out there isolates you from social mores and makes you more apt to break the rules. Whenever I skipped out on a date, Orra would come in late and wake me up, complaining, "Pearl, if you ever do that to me again I'll never get you another date!" I'd say, "Well, I didn't ask you to get me a date in the first place." I was awful. I just didn't care. Unfortunately, at that time my life on the road was more important to me than my life off the road. I say unfortunately because, as I have pointed out, the road is a very unreal existence.

When we did go out together, though, we always had fun. Even if the guys weren't too much it was okay because Orra and I thought we were so hilarious, we'd fall out over each other. Orra and I had a lot in common. She had studied dramatics in New York and Chicago and loved the theater as much as I did. But it was her sense of humor that endeared her to me. There was a dance every Saturday night at the Commodore Room at the Andrew Jackson Hotel, and we'd close the place, then go somewhere to have breakfast before going back to Miss Ef's. Sometimes I had to leave for the road early Sunday morning and I'd be like a zombie.

We kept this routine up until Miss Ef closed the boardinghouse. Then, because Orra didn't want to be alone during the week, she moved into a basement apartment with another friend, Harriet Ayres, and I moved in with the Seaton family out off Harding Road. I still spent a lot of time at Orra and Harriet's, however, because their place became the hangout. The apartment was a riot. It was exactly like the basement apartment setting for the play *My Sister Eileen*. There were always people coming and going. We learned to recognize everybody by their shoes, because that's all you could see from the street-level windows as people walked down the steps to the front door.

I came in one weekend to find Orra floating in the clouds. She was engaged! His name was Bill Pitner, and he was from Franklin, Tennessee. They had been dating long enough for Orra to know it was the *real* thing, and Bill had asked her to marry him as soon as he got out of the navy.

From that moment on, all I heard from Bill and Orra was the name Henry Cannon. Bill had decided I'd be perfect for his friend Henry, whom he had grown up with in Franklin. They had gone all through Battleground Academy together, and had played tennis together since they were kids. Bill couldn't wait for Henry to get home from Japan, where he was finishing up a four-year stint in the air corps, so he could introduce us.

Meanwhile Bill and Orra got married in February of 1946. I was the maid of honor, and we had a whirlwind of parties that went on for several weekends. Harriet moved out of the basement apartment and Bill moved in, but it was still our weekend hangout because everyone gathered there to party.

While Bill kept selling me on his friend Cannon, he had begun writing Henry letters about me, saying they were going to set us up as soon as he got home. Henry was no more interested in meeting me than I was in meeting him. I was perfectly satisfied with my social life, and I was tired of friends trying to marry me off. I was having the time of my life! If some people saw me as an old maid at 34, I figured that was their problem.

Also, I had become thoroughly disillusioned with marriage—or perhaps I should say with married men. After being on the road for nearly thirteen years I had seen too much—enough to make me very wary of marriage. (In defense of the men I've known in show business I must say that I seldom saw a performer chasing after a woman. They don't have to. The women come to them and make it very obvious they are not only available, but eager. That's not easy for a man to ignore.)

Then, one night in May of 1946, I called Orra to find her so excited she couldn't talk fast enough. "Guess *what?* He's home, he's *home!*" she exclaimed.

"Who's home?"

"Cannon, *Henry Cannon!* He's back from the air corps and he'll be here next Saturday night and you've just *got* to come! Wait till you *see* him."

Well, that can kill anything.

The next Saturday night, after the Opry, I showed up at Bill and Orra's with a date. I have a faint recollection of being introduced to Henry and of us squaring off and looking at one another, but I can assure you that no sparks flew on either side. He was with a date also and I remember we were all dancing but I don't recall dancing with him. Bill and Orra were very disappointed. They wanted us to fall into one another's arms right on the spot.

All that summer, I continued seeing Henry occasionally at Orra and Bill's. But we were both always with someone else. The girls Henry dated were very different from me. They were beautiful and quiet and very elegant. I do remember that Henry always seemed glad to see me when I'd drop by the apartment after the Opry because I always ended up at the piano, playing the popular songs of the day—"Don't Take Your Love from Me," Henry's favorite; "I'll Get By"; "The One I Love Belongs to Somebody Else"; "Don't Get Around Much Anymore" and on and on. I've always played by ear, which is great for sing-alongs, though not much good for straight listening. Things would always liven up when the music got going.

Whenever they could, Orra and Bill would get me away from my date and say, "Don't you think Henry Cannon is great?" I'm sure they were doing the same thing to Henry. They weren't about to give up, even though it was obvious no great explosion had taken place between us. He *was* attractive, and the more time I spent around him the more I realized that he was one of the funniest men I'd ever met, but I still didn't think of him as a prospective beau. My mind was on the road and my life out there. That's where I lived. Nashville was a place I visited on Saturday nights.

My most vivid memories of Henry that summer and autumn revolve around music. He is not musically inclined, but he loves it, and he was a big fan of both Roy Acuff and Bill Monroe. Whenever I came into the apartment, which is the only place I ever saw him, he'd always ask me to play the latest popular country songs from the Opry. He had heard me on the radio, especially on the Armed Forces Network when he was overseas, but he'd never seen Minnie Pearl perform. I didn't sing like Minnie when I played at the apartment. I sang as straight as I knew how (although that's not too straight). They would all gather around the piano and join in, just like a scene from one of those early MGM Hollywood musicals.

On a Friday night in December of 1946, I went down to Orra and Bill's with a date to have dinner. I was on the road with Ernest Tubb at that time, and it was unusual for us to have Friday night off.

We were sitting around talking after dinner when the phone rang. It was Henry, calling Bill to see if anything was going on at the apartment. He said he and his cousin, Newt Cannon, had been to a wedding reception and they were in the mood to party. Bill told them to come on over. When they arrived we could see their feet coming down the steps. I opened the door. It was a cold night and the two of them were standing there dressed in good-looking suits, shivering, with no overcoats. Henry Cannon without a woman! I hadn't seen that before. He looked *very* handsome.

The party picked up immediately. Henry and Newt had been toasting the bride and groom for some time and they were in great shape. I thought they were the cutest things I'd ever seen. Newt and my date and Bill and Orra went into the kitchen for something, leaving Henry and me standing by the fireplace, talking. All of a sudden he put his hands on my shoulders and turned me around and kissed me very soundly! It was a kiss I liked mighty well. Then he said, "Go get your coat and tell your date to take you home. I'll follow and pick you up and bring you back here."

"I can't do that!" I protested. "I don't go on late dates, and I'm not going to do that."

"Get your coat and tell your date to take you home and I'll pick you up," Henry repeated. This was Henry, the air-corps captain speaking. It sounded like an order. I had never run up against anyone before who just flat out *told* me what to do. I went and got my coat.

When I walked into the kitchen wearing my coat, my date looked at me and said, "Where are you going?" I said, "I have to go home." He knew me well enough to know I seldom left a party at 10 o'clock. "Are you sick?" he asked. I couldn't think of an excuse. I knew Henry was standing right behind me. So I said, "No, but I have to go home now."

My date drove me home and walked me to the door. I was so anxious to get rid of him I'm sure he suspected something. But I didn't care. I just wanted to see Henry again. (Something had happened. And I liked the feeling!) I made all the motions of unlocking the door and going inside. Then I waited until I heard my date's car drive off before I went outside again. Henry was just pulling up. I jumped in his car and he drove me back to Orra and Bill's.

When we got to the top of the stairs that led down to their apartment, Henry stopped. There was a full moon that night, and I remember it all so vividly—the cold, crisp moonlit December night and the excitement of the moment "engraved on time." Henry kissed me again. Then he looked at me and said, "Baby, after the Lord made you he sure must have buffed his nails." That did it. I was hooked!

He said, "You're going to have to get off the road." I said, "*What?* What do you mean?" He said, "Well, we're going to get married, and you can't be out there on the road."

I looked at him like he was crazy, and he stared back at me as sober as a judge. Then he led me down the stairs.

When we walked into the apartment together Bill and Orra both looked like the cat that swallowed the canary. They had yellow feathers sticking out of their mouths. Orra had a strong maternal instinct about Henry. She called him son. She was as proud as the mother of the groom.

Henry said, "We just made up our minds we're going to get married."

Orra screamed and Bill cheered.

I hadn't made up my mind to anything.

"*Wait a minute!* This is all moving too fast for me!" I protested.

I didn't believe what was happening. I thought Henry might be kidding. I had heard of being swept off your feet, but this was ridiculous. He was the one doing all the talking. I hadn't agreed to anything. Henry had taken complete charge, which was a delightfully new experience for me, and I loved it. I was sitting there dumbfounded.

When he took me home that night, I said, "Look, let's not kid around about this getting married business. I don't know what to think. Let's agree to meet at Bill and Orra's tomorrow at 5 p.m., and if we still feel the same way then, we'll know it's real."

He agreed.

Henry tells people that he never had any doubt from the first kiss that we were going to marry and that it was going to last. I was not so certain. I spent a restless night wondering what on earth was happening to me. I had always thought falling in love was a slow, gradual process. And here I was talking marriage to a man I'd never even had a real date with! My mind told me I had gone stark raving mad. But my heart kept saying, "This is it!"

The next day I dressed to go down to Orra and Bill's with the care of a bride on her wedding day. I got there first, and I was a nervous wreck. But when Henry walked through the door, I knew for certain that the previous night hadn't been a wild fantasy. He looked better than I had ever seen him. He had come from work —he was a pilot who owned half interest in a charter service— and he had on his leather air-corps flying jacket and a pair of casual slacks. Every time I had seen him before he'd been dressed in a suit and tie. He was a hundred times more glamorous this way. He looked like a *real* pilot, and during World War II all the girls had become enamored of the image of the pilot—brave and steady in the air, rough and ready on the ground, *sexy!* I just melted.

We didn't say a whole lot because Orra and Bill were there, but we must have been glowing because we both knew it was definitely *on!* Afterward, I went on down to do the Opry and Henry made arrangements to pick me up after work. I was leaving early Sunday morning to go back out on the road. We sat up half the night planning a huge wedding that never came about.

We made our plans just before Christmas, and I didn't have a day off until Sunday, February 23. I was under contract to Ernest Tubb and a promoter, Oscar Davis, until that time. Still, we set the date. But we soon realized we had to give up our plans for a big wedding. With me on the road, there was simply no way to make all the necessary arrangements in time. And we didn't want to wait any longer than we had to. As it was, those 2½ months seemed to crawl by. The only time we had together was when I'd come in to do the Opry on Saturday. The road wasn't nearly so much fun after I fell in love. I resented the time it kept me away from Henry. My friends at the Opry and the troupe I traveled with thought I had made a very hasty decision. They had never heard me speak of dating anyone named Henry Cannon, and suddenly I announced I was going to marry him.

But their reaction was *nothing* compared to Mama's. She thought I'd lost my mind.

Chapter Twenty

THE plain truth is Mama didn't want me to get married to anyone. It had nothing to do with Henry. She was well acquainted with his background because his family and her family had known one another in Franklin since Civil War days. Henry's father and Mama's brother, Uncle Sam, were close friends. It was marriage, not the man, that she opposed.

From the time I began making good money, I loved spoiling Mama just the way Daddy spoiled her when he was alive. In addition to supplementing her small income so that she was able to live comfortably, I loved indulging her with stylish, expensive clothes and hats. Mama adored hats. When I was growing up one of the jokes around our house was Mama's habit of wearing a hat to the supper table. At one point after Dixie was born she went to the doctor for a checkup, and he told her she ought to get out more. She'd been tied down for years having babies and taking care of toddlers, and he thought it would be good for her to turn some of that responsibility over to the reliable help we had at home so she could pursue her own interests. That's all Mama needed to hear. From then on there was no holding her back. She became involved in a constant whirlwind of activities—religious, cultural, civic and social. The reason she sometimes wore her hat at the supper table was because she had either just gotten home from some event in time to sit down to eat or she had plans to rush out right after she ate.

Mama's hats had always been something of a conversation piece in Centerville, and after I began buying them from the smart millinery shops in Nashville she became even more noted for her elegant chapeaus. Mama liked expensive things and had an eye for quality, even after her eyesight failed. I'll never forget the time I tried to fool her with an inexpensive hat. I'd found it on sale at a department store in Nashville, so I bought it, along with another, a very expensive model from a millinery shop. My sisters were going down to visit Mama with me, so I told them to say the cheaper hat looked better on her. When I arrived with two hat-boxes she was as excited as a child. It was always such fun to buy presents for Mama because she took on so. She opened the box with the $15 hat first. She tried it on and we oooohhhed and aaaahhhed and told her it looked wonderful. She couldn't see well enough to know exactly how it looked, but she kept feeling it. She said, "Daughter, I just don't think this hat does much for me." We said, "Oh, Mama, it looks beautiful." But she was ready to see the other one. When her hands touched the $40 hat, her face lit up like a Christmas tree. She put it on and felt the way it sat on her head. Then she smiled and said, "Now, daughter, this hat is more *me!*" We just died laughing. Then we told her what we'd done. She said, "I knew that was a cheap hat. Don't you think I know a $15 hat from a $40 one? You can't fool your old mother."

Mama was almost totally blind when she died, and her sight had been greatly impaired from cataracts for 20 years prior to that. She'd had two operations, but they were only partially successful. Yet her pride and her spirit kept her as independent as ever. She made very few concessions to her blindness. One thing that was an embarrassment to her in her last years was the fact that she couldn't see well enough to know if a dress was stained. But she had lovely neighbors in Centerville who would come over and check her clothes to see which ones needed to go to the cleaners. Everyone knew her problem, and she had the run of the town. She knew her way around by instinct, and she thought nothing of walking down to the town square for lunch or to get her hair done at the beauty parlor. After they put a state highway through Centerville several people took me aside and said they were worried about her because she would just prance across Highway 100 as though it was still a dirt road. When I spoke to her about it she said, "Oh, daughter, anybody going by would stop for *me*." I said, "Mama, everybody who travels that road is *not* from Centerville. They don't know you." But she put my concern aside with a wave of her hand.

We weren't allowed to move any furniture in her house, so she felt completely comfortable and safe there, but she was ill at ease in strange places because she didn't want anyone to know that she couldn't see. Whenever we'd go into a restaurant, she would hand me her menu and say to the other guests, "Ophelia always orders for me. She knows what I like." She wanted absolutely no sympathy or pity.

By the time I met Henry, Minnie Pearl was well known and popular on the Opry. I think Mama would have liked Minnie anyway, but she certainly liked the fact that this "country girl" had brought us the means to live more comfortably than we ever could have otherwise. Also, Mama got attention, which she loved, vicariously through Minnie. If any of my Opry buddies were passing through Centerville going to or coming from a date they would always stop by and pay their respects, unless it was in the middle of the night. Those hillbilly pickers flattered her to death, and she ate it up. And it wasn't in the least unusual for fans of Minnie's who were complete strangers to stop by Centerville and visit Mama.

I'd go down there and she'd say, "Daughter, the most charming couple from South Carolina stopped by to see me the other day."

"Mama, I don't like the idea of you inviting strangers into your home," I'd tell her.

She'd say, "Don't be silly, daughter. They're nice people who love you, and of course they're welcome here."

So Mama had two concerns when I told her I was getting married: (1) Would this mean an end to the expensive clothes and little indulgences I showered on her? and (2) Would I give up my career, thereby making Minnie, and the attention she brought Mama, a thing of the past?

Her concerns were only normal. She knew her other daughters wouldn't let her starve. But they were all married with obligations of their own, and she enjoyed the little luxuries I was able to give her. And at her age, with the physical handicap of her blindness, the idea of changes or disruption in her life was frightening.

Knowing all this, it was with great trepidation that I invited Henry down to Centerville to meet Mama. The only advice I could give him was, "If you've ever been charming in your life, pour it on."

I went on ahead of him and spent the day with her, hoping that I might be able to soften her up. I had no idea what her reaction to him would be. I knew she'd be cordial, because she was a Southern lady with impeccable manners. But Mama could be *cold* cordial in a way that was more devastating than if she'd been overtly rude. Henry was nervous about meeting his future mother-in-law, but I don't think he was half as scared as I was. I wanted Mama to love Henry the way I did.

All that day she kept voicing her disapproval of our plans to marry so quickly. It simply wasn't socially acceptable in the South to rush into these things. Couples remained formally engaged for at least six months. She said, "Ophelia I don't see how you can possibly be sure after just a few weeks."

"But Mama, I saw him all summer," I said.

"Yes, but you didn't date him," she protested.

That evening she dressed with meticulous care. She was still a handsome woman, and she'd had her hair done just so. She also put a little rouge on her cheeks.

Henry was supposed to arrive at seven o'clock and I prayed he wouldn't be late. Mama was very punctual and didn't approve of tardiness. Henry tends to want to leave the house at the time the party starts. But this time he walked up the steps right at the stroke of seven.

Mama had positioned herself in a regal pose by the fireplace. I'll never forget the look on her face. She knew her last daughter was about to go, and she was about to meet the man who was taking her "baby" away. She stood very straight, with her chin thrust out, steeled against the invader.

My stomach was churning as I went to the door. I don't remember how I greeted Henry, but I can assure you I didn't kiss him. I think we shook hands. I said, "Mama, this is Henry Cannon." She walked forward gracefully to meet him, and he took her hand.

"Mrs. Colley, I have heard all my life that you were one of the most beautiful ladies who ever came out of Franklin," he said in a voice as smooth as oil. "I know now that they were right."

My mother melted right there before my eyes. She suddenly looked 16 years old!

"Well, how nice," she said, flushing.

"Yes, ma'am." Henry wasn't going to stop there. "I've heard my family speak of you often, and they always say that you were one of the most popular belles in Franklin in your day."

"Well, I did have a few beaus." Mama was absolutely at his mercy by this time. He had won her over just as easily as he had me with his line about the Lord buffing his nails! I don't remember the conversation after that because I saw that he had her in the palm of his hand. But poor Henry left that night without knowing if he'd passed or failed the test.

She didn't say much after he was gone, but the next morning when I got up I found her rummaging around in the bottom of the old sideboard.

"Mama, what are you doing?" I asked.

"I'm getting out the pearl-handled knives," she said.

That was the clincher. There was no doubt left how she felt about Henry as she went after the pearl-handled knives. They were her most prized possession. She had received them from her family when she married, and I knew if she wanted me to have them she approved of Henry 100 percent.

The approval was mutual. Henry and Mama came to love each other so much that he wouldn't even allow anyone to tell mother-in-law jokes in his presence. He bought her presents and courted her and treated her exactly like the belle of Franklin, which of course is how she still saw herself. In fact, Henry spoiled Mama worse than I did.

She loved bridge and continued to play as long as she could see even vague shapes on the cards. Henry and I would go down to see her, and Dixie would come in from her farm just outside Centerville. Mama would already have the cards dealt when we got there. She didn't want to wait a minute to get started. She always insisted on having me as her partner. She had gotten very childish in her old age about winning. She wanted to win every hand. And Henry saw to it that she did. No matter what suit she named trump, she made her bid because he'd swap cards with me until I had what I needed to fill in her hand. Mama couldn't see well enough to know what was going on. All she knew was that she always had better cards and more fun when Henry was there.

One time Frances and Virginia and I went down there without Henry. Frances and Virginia wouldn't cheat for Mama the way Henry and Dixie and I did, so she was losing. Then Dixie came in and Mama associated that with Henry. So she said, "You come sit here and be my partner, Dixie." Frances, who was playing with Mama at the time, said, "What about me?" Mama waved her off. "I'll play with you later." When Dixie sat down, Mama said, "Now we'll have some fun." Frances said it certainly made her feel loved and cherished!

Mama's pet name for Henry was "the old man." She was always disappointed if I showed up in Centerville without "the old man." Virginia would say, "I think it's perfectly terrible the way you all spoil Mama," and Dixie would say, "That's why she likes to play with us and not with you and Frances." We had the best time.

After I left Mama's that morning, knowing the pearl-handled knives were mine—which meant Henry had been accepted—I began frantically making lists of all the things I needed to do to plan a wedding. We had already accepted that a big formal ceremony was out of the question, but, with me on the road, it soon became apparent that I didn't have enough time in town to plan even a small one. I didn't have any sisters living in Nashville at that time, and there just wasn't anyone around who could take on that responsibility for me. Then I began thinking about my family and Henry's family. If we limited our invitation list to blood relatives only, we would have had to invite half of Franklin, not to mention Centerville. The only solution was not to invite any of them.

I'm sure at this point Henry's family wondered what on earth he'd gotten himself into. He came from old, aristocratic stock in which everything was done *in the proper manner.*

Henry's great-great-grandfather, Newton Cannon, was the governor of Tennessee during Andrew Jackson's presidency. The two men were archenemies, and until the day she died, Henry's Aunt Cynthia always referred to Jackson as poor white trash. She said Jackson had doped Grandfather Cannon's horse at a race at Cloverbottom. She said even his cockfights were fixed. I don't think Aunt Cynthia much approved of her favorite nephew marrying "show business," but I doubt that she let anyone know. She adored Henry and went along with anything he wanted to do. She and I became very close, and I loved her like a second mother. (Aunt Cynthia lived to be 92, and during the hippie/love scene of the sixties she once said to me, "They throw the word *love* around today until it hasn't any meaning anymore. I say, don't *tell* me you love me. Treat me right!") And I know others in Henry's family must have had their doubts. My *family* was acceptable, but I'd been away from home for 13 years and I was an unknown entity at that point. The Grand Ole Opry, country music (or hillbilly, as it was still called, then) and Minnie Pearl, were not what you might call impeccable credentials. But they never let me know if they thought their Henry was making a mistake, and in the end it was his sister Jennie who picked up the announcements and mailed them out for me. (We didn't send invitations because the wedding was so small.) This was very bad form on my part, but I had no choice, and I was extremely grateful for her help. His sisters were staunch supporters of mine right from the start. No one has been more fortunate than I in choosing in-laws.

We were married in the Scales Chapel at the West End Methodist Church on February 23, 1947. The only people in attendance were Jennie and Tom West, the man she eventually married; Katye and Oscar Rose, two of my best friends; and Bill and Orra, of course. Bill was Henry's best man and Orra was my matron of honor.

I didn't wear a traditional wedding gown because we had decided to keep the ceremony simple and informal. Instead I got married in a beige gabardine suit. It had a three-quarters-length double-breasted jacket—the new fashion that season—and a slim skirt. With it I wore brown accessories—hat, gloves, alligator shoes and bag—and a green orchid. Henry still sends me a green orchid on our anniversary, when he can get one. (They haven't been in some of the places we've been when February 23 rolls around.)

Orra and Bill had vacated their small basement apartment to move to Pulaski, Tennessee, so Henry and I moved in. We couldn't have found a more sentimental and romantic setting in which to start our life together because we had met and fallen in love in that little apartment. I settled happily into married life with my handsome pilot.

Henry was already a pilot when he joined the air corps the day Pearl Harbor was bombed. He'd been fascinated with flying since childhood, so he had taken lessons from a local instructor and gotten his license. Then he and his best friend, Vance Burke, had gone in together and bought a plane for $300. Imagine the plane they got for *three hundred dollars!* Henry says he wouldn't taxi down a runway in one like it, now. Vance had a farm near Henry's home in Franklin, and they used one of his fields for a landing strip. They were real hotshots with that plane. On Sunday afternoons they'd often fly down to Columbia or Murfreesboro or some other little town to see Opry matinees, which showed in those places at that time.

Henry was working for Genesco then (he had gone to Vanderbilt to study engineering, but he says he quit when they informed him his dormitory was not a "rest home"), and from what some of his friends revealed he had led a pretty lively bachelor life. (Not many young men could offer to fly their dates off into the wild blue yonder, even if it was in a $300 plane.) Then, after he got out of the service, he went into partnership with another fine pilot to form Capitol Airways, a nonscheduled charter service which is still in existence. He was flying DC-3s and many other types of aircraft, and I thought it was the most glamorous thing in the world.

There had been several love affairs in my life—naturally—before I met Henry. He would be the first to say that a woman who didn't marry until she was nearly 35 was bound to have had some romances. I did, and I'm glad that I did. I profited from all of them. I cried some, but that helps me appreciate "the good life." Only by comparison can you come to a point where you can say, "This is *the one!*" I'm glad I felt deeply for one of the musicians who joined Pee Wee in 1943. He taught me to truly appreciate this beautiful, pure country music, most aptly interpreted by the fiddle. The sound of the fiddle as it traces the beauty of the mountains and their call, as opposed to the city and its frenetic tempo, still sends me. As Tennyson said, "I am a part of all that I have met." How well I know.

Chapter Twenty-One

I was 34 years old when I got married, and I had been on my own for a long time and had already become set in my ways. I was also as stubborn and independent as the dickens. Considering all this, it's amazing to me that there was never any question as to who wore the pants in our family. I think it started the first time Henry kissed me and told me I was going to have to get off the road. He was the first man who had ever *told* me what to do, and I liked it. I am headstrong, and the type of woman who will dominate if given half a chance. And because Henry is quieter than I am in social situations, I'm sure there are people who meet us casually and think, "Aha, I'll bet she runs that show!" Nothing could be further from the truth. He was from the beginning and is to this day the unchallenged head of our household. Anyone who really wants to find out the inside scoop need only talk to Mary Cannon, who has been our housekeeper and my confidante/secretary for 33 years. Mary absolutely hoots if anyone suggests that I run our marriage.

Henry is not a dictator, but he is the boss, and I wouldn't have it any other way. Any man I could override wouldn't hold my interest for long. And the fact that Henry is one of the funniest men I have ever met makes him even more attractive. He *thinks* funny. He has a dry wit and his timing is absolutely perfect. It's incredible that he can still surprise me after all these years, but he does. We'll be having a discussion about something and he'll make one of his wry observations and I will absolutely *fall out.* He's not trying to be funny. I'm very conscious of people who try to make me laugh, and Henry has never done that. It's just his natural way of expressing himself—and has been since the day I met him.

I had fulfilled my last road commitment the night before our wedding, and I had no intention of going back. I had planned to continue working the Opry network show on Saturday nights, but had decided to leave the road completely, which absolutely dumbfounded my Opry buddies. They couldn't believe their favorite trouper would forsake the glamor(?) of the one-nighters, but I was ready to give it up. I didn't think I'd miss it. Counting my Sewell days, I'd been traveling for the better part of 12 years, and that should have been enough for anybody. Besides, I was *in love,* and my priorities had shifted accordingly. I was going to lead the life of the suburban matron.

When I look back on the first months of my married life I can't help chuckling. What ambitious moves I made toward being a "young married." I was stupid enough to think I could drop out of the exciting, frenetic, fast-paced world of show business into the calm, normal civilian world of ladies' clubs and civic activities.

I joined *everything!* I went to meetings—coffees, luncheons, teas. I worked on committees. I was up to my ears in "concerned citizenship."

I worked at being a wife and homemaker for almost a year. I tried to cook, to do all the household duties (which did, and still do, bore me to death), but there wasn't that much to do in that little apartment. Then Mary Cannon, whose family had worked for my family back in Centerville when she was a little girl, came to work for us and took all the household responsibilities off my shoulders.

I wanted children, but they were not forthcoming. Even though I had always loved my career, I had never thought it would be a substitute for marriage, home and children. I wanted both a career and family life. I really envy women, like Carol Burnett, who have been able to combine the two successfully.

Henry wanted children, too. We had talked about it a great deal during our dating period, and continued to plan in that direction after we were married.

As months passed, I grew more and more desperate. Every time I saw a pregnant woman, I envied her so much it was an actual physical pain, a longing I could literally *feel*.

Whenever there was a christening at church, I'd have to stifle tears, and any time I saw a mother with a small child, I ached with longing. I didn't talk about it with Henry because I felt he was as disappointed as I was and it hurt me so to think I had let him down.

One night after we'd gone to bed I couldn't hold it back any longer. I broke down and cried, sobbing like a little child, over my disappointment and my fear that Henry would somehow love me less if I didn't give him a baby.

I found out a lot about my husband's character that night. He couldn't possibly have been more comforting, more understanding or more reassuring. His attitude was, "If God means for us to have children, we will have them. If He doesn't, we won't." And he continued to remind me of that all the years I worried over it.

If facing the fact that we were never going to have a child depressed or saddened Henry at that time, he never let me know. His concern was for my health, both physical and emotional, and not for any disappointment he may have suffered. His attitude and his unwavering support saved me. I was able to accept God's will in this matter because my husband was so accepting. (And that's just one of a million reasons why I adore him.)

We'd been married less than a year when the itch to hit the road again started nagging at me. Henry was flying charter trips for Capitol, and he would dash off and come back with the aura of far places, which made me miss it even more. Working the Opry on Saturday nights was my undoing. I'd make out pretty well with the solid-citizen routine all week, but the time spent in that other atmosphere on Saturday night destroyed me. I was hungry for the camaraderie of my buddies on the road, and I missed the transient life. I wanted to *go*. I must have been born with wanderlust. My sisters tell me that when I was still in my crib I'd stand up at three or four in the morning and grab my little bonnet hanging on the foot of Mama's bed, where they'd leave it after taking me for a walk. I'd swing the bonnet in one hand and shake the sides of the crib with the other, yelling, "Bye-bye, bye-bye," until someone got up and gave me some attention. At 35, the old urge to go bye-bye was still as strong as ever.

Finally, I told Henry I *believed* I'd take a date or two. (That was like a man dying of thirst after crossing the Sahara saying, "I believe I'll have just a sip of water.")

Henry was marvelous. He said, "Of course, you miss it, just as I would miss flying."

So I went back. I "unjoined" all my social and civic groups, packed up the old comedy grip and hit the road.

During this same period, Henry began interesting the Opry stars in using charter flights with his company. He made friends easily with the performers and inspired confidence in a mode of travel which was new to them. Henry was really an innovator. Looking back on it, I can see that it was personal confidence in Henry that prompted these hillbillies to take to the air. He became popular with them immediately. Although he'd never before been around show people, he fit in perfectly. He was, and is, low-key, and he has a natural, spontaneous sense of humor. (All my friends thought he was much funnier than me, and still do!) They admired his honesty and his kindness and the fact that he wasn't impressed by celebrities.

I didn't fully realize how unimpressed Henry is by show biz stars until several years later on a trip to New York. We'd been wined and dined by NBC and the William Esty Agency all week and they had gotten us front-and-center seats for that season's biggest Broadway hit, *Guys and Dolls.* Henry was seated on the aisle. Just as the overture started, I heard whispering all around me. I knew someone famous had arrived. Being from the country, I turned to look. There stood Elizabeth Taylor at her most devastatingly beautiful. She had just married Michael Wilding and she was absolutely glowing. I said, "Henry, Henry, here comes *Elizabeth Taylor!*" "Oh, mercy," he mumbled, and turned around and stood up to say hello. He thought it was someone he had met and was supposed to know! He had never been (and still isn't) a fan of movies and had no idea who Elizabeth Taylor was. I tugged on his coat and said, "Henry, *sit down!* She's a *movie star,* the most beautiful woman in the world!" He said, "Well, she does look pretty good," and then went right back to his program.

I think another reason why Henry fell in with my Opry crowd so easily was because pilots and performers have a lot in common. I didn't become aware of this until Henry and I had been married a while. It has to do with the work style. Unlike the "normal" person, whose attention to the job is spread out over an eight-hour day, a pilot's work, like a performer's, is concentrated into a shorter period of time, which, however, demands *total* concentration. This concentration is so intense while it's happening that everything else is blocked out of the mind. Then when it's over and they're ready to relax—when the pressure and the responsibilities are off—they usually play with as much intensity as they work.

Promoters started using Henry's DC-3s to take package shows of six or seven acts to the Far West, a territory virtually untouched in our business. We loved it! We'd pile on the plane after the Opry on Saturday night and head for Dallas or Denver for a Sunday matinee and night show, then start toward Seattle or Portland with shows in all the large towns en route. It opened new vistas for all of us.

But Henry and I were still working separately on many dates —he'd be flying a show to one part of the country while I was booked in another—and we didn't like being apart. So Henry worked out an arrangement with his partner in Capitol Airways to sell him his half interest and keep a Beechcraft, so he could continue his private charter business with the Opry stars. Thus began our years of flying to dates in our own plane.

About this time we bought our first little house. We were so excited! The best thing about it was our new neighbors. By coincidence, we moved next door to a girl I'd known at Ward-Belmont, Jane Craig. She and her husband, John, and their children are still our best friends. Jane gives me many hours of fun on the tennis court and at the bridge table. I have never taken my friends lightly. I couldn't live without the laughter, warmth and companionship of girlfriends.

As soon as Henry sold his interest in Capitol Airways, he began flying me to all my dates, working the charter trips in between. Eventually he dropped the charter service altogether because my career had picked up to the point that it took all of his time to get me back and forth. By then Henry had taken over all my business management (and not a moment too soon). When we first married and he learned how much I'd been earning, he was appalled to discover I had no savings account and had never set up any kind of financial plan for my future. I didn't know anything about money—still don't—except that I could always spend a little more than I made. I'll never forget the first time I ever saw a $1,000 bill. I couldn't wait to spend it! After a week of shows in Detroit the promoter paid me in cash, which is the custom in country music, and one of the bills was a thousand-dollar denomination. The next day I walked into a smart store and bought a leopard coat with that bill. I thought I was really something. (That leopard coat provoked a small incident in our first year of marriage. I loved the coat, but Henry despised it. He never let me know until the fall following our marriage in February. I had put the leopard coat in storage. When I mentioned getting it out he suggested I swap the coat for a conservative beaver coat. I was aghast. My *beautiful, flashy* leopard coat. I'd seen Esther Williams wear one just like in in *Sun Valley Serenade;* But I meekly exchanged the leopard coat for a conservative beaver coat. I was a dutiful wife—completely out of character!)

Henry is a remarkable businessman. Business is as natural to him as it is unnatural to me. From the time he took over my management in 1947, I have left literally every detail of my career up to him and he's handled it perfectly. Whatever financial security we enjoy today is due entirely to his business talent. We've had an agreement all these years that has worked beautifully—he doesn't tell me what to do on stage, and I don't tell him what to do in business. In money matters and business dealings I trust his judgment implicitly, and he feels the same way about my ability to handle Minnie's performances.

Henry loves Minnie. He always did, right from the start. In fact, I've often accused him of loving Minnie more than he loves me. He answers that he told me he loved me when he married me and if he ever changes his mind he'll let me know. Minnie's career has never been a threat to Henry either. His confidence in himself is too great for that. I'll never forget the time a man sidled up to him backstage and asked, "How does it feel to play second fiddle to your wife?" Henry looked at him with that blank expression he can assume. "I don't play a musical instrument," he said dryly. We've had our ups and downs, as any marriage does, but none of our downs has been over my career, and having him there has made it all worth it. As I once told an interviewer, "Henry's what's kept me on an even keel all these years. After the lights die down, the greasepaint's off and the applause and laughter is over, you've got to have somewhere and someone to go to. Your name up in lights is nothing but lightbulbs, and they can go out quick."

Henry thoroughly enjoyed his charter work with the Opry stars, and I was sorry when he had to give it up to fly me exclusively. He flew charters for Carl Smith, Elvis Presley, Webb Pierce,

Hank Williams and dozens of others who preferred short hops in the plane to the long hours in cars. This was before the days of jets, so Henry's Beechcraft was almost as fast as the commercial planes used then. Also, Henry could put performers closer to their fair dates than the larger commercial planes could, because he could land on small rural airfields.

Henry was genuinely fond of almost all of the country music stars he flew, but one of his special favorites was Hank Williams.

Chapter Twenty-Two

I had first met Hank Williams during World War II. It wasn't long after the Camel Caravan, when I was still with Pee Wee King. We were playing Dothan, Alabama, and Pee Wee had asked us to go down to the local radio station that afternoon to do a promotion spot. I had a severe sore throat. I was hoarse and had no business being there, but we never thought of not working because we were sick. That was true of everyone, even if you felt terrible and had a high temperature. It was an unspoken rule that was never challenged. It wasn't smart, but it went along with the show-must-go-on tradition.

When we walked into the lobby of the radio station, which was upstairs in an old building, I noticed a couple sitting there. The man looked like he was down on his luck. He was wearing a tan suit, boots and a cowboy hat that was slightly soiled. He was tall, thin—terribly thin—and hollow-eyed. He appeared to be in his early twenties. The woman was a very attractive blonde with beautiful skin and a good figure. Pee Wee introduced them as Hank and Audrey Williams. I had never heard of Hank Williams, but Pee Wee had. He had negotiated with him to buy a song for Becky Barfield called "I Am Praying for the Day That Peace Will Come." Pee Wee gave him $20 for the song.

Many people have asked me if I experienced a prescience of his greatness when I met Hank. I didn't feel anything. When I met Brenda Lee I felt it. I knew instantly that that child had something very special. But I haven't felt it often, and I didn't feel it with Hank. Of course, I hadn't seen him perform. He was living in Montgomery then, working clubs locally, and he had come to Dothan just to see Pee Wee and sell his song. I do remember being touched by the sight of him because he was so pitifully thin.

I mentioned to Audrey that I was sick, and she offered to take me to a doctor, saying she knew one in Dothan. She was very kind. She and I went alone, leaving the others at the radio station. When we went out to get into their car, I noticed the fender was smashed.

She said, "We had an accident recently, and we've been so busy we just haven't had time to put the car in the shop and get it fixed."

It didn't appear to be a recent dent, and I surmised they simply didn't have the money to fix the fender. But she was too proud to say so. Audrey was a very proud woman, and I think this time she was showing wifely pride to cover for Hank. I believe she was terribly in love with him then, although people said later that she wasn't. Thinking back on the looks she gave him and the manner in which she tried to protect him, I think she loved him deeply, and there was no doubt about his love for her.

It was one of the tragedies of our business that Audrey and Hank had such a star-crossed romance. Their marriage ended bitterly in a divorce about a year before he died, and a number of people in country music were critical of her. They thought she aggravated Hank's alcohol problem. But I think his sickness went way back to childhood, long before Audrey came into his life. I always liked her, and I mourned her death, just as I mourned his.

It wasn't long before we were all hearing a great deal about Hank Williams. When he hit, he exploded. He was the biggest thing country music had ever seen, and the fans absolutely adored him. His charisma on stage was unsurpassed. Elvis later had that effect on an audience, but in the beginning most of his fans were teenage girls who responded to his gyrations as much as to his music. Hank appealed to all ages, and both sexes, and he didn't have to move a finger.

The first time I actually saw him work was on a tour in 1948 when Henry and one of his pilots flew us out West in a DC-3. Hank had not joined the Opry then, but was working on Louisiana

Hayride, a popular country show from Shreveport. I recognized him as being the man I'd met in Dothan, but he was a different person. He was alert and bright-eyed, with a fine wardrobe and a clean white hat. He was on his way.

Oscar Davis, the promoter of the tour, had set Hank to go on just before I did. As I said, I'd never seen him perform, although I had heard him sing on the radio. His song "Lovesick Blues" was already on the charts.

When the time came for him to work, I went to the wings to watch him. He ambled out on stage with his guitar and started singing. An excitement seemed to spread through the crowd, continuing to grow as he sang several songs. By the time he got to his last number the excitement had grown to a fever pitch. The crowd would not let him leave the stage. The rest of us on the show might as well have stayed at the airport—especially me, who had to follow him.

After umpteen encores they finally got Hank off and me on. It was not one of my better shows. They still wanted more of Hank! And I didn't blame them. The man had something indefinable, something that made an audience crave more.

I told Oscar after the show—and every other promoter after that —"*Never* put me on after Hank Williams!" And I never followed him again.

Bob Hope had a similar experience with Hank when we were in Louisville working the Hadacol Tour. Bob had been brought in especially for that show. As a superstar of radio and movies, they naturally set him to close. Everyone was amazed (everyone except us hillbillies) when Hope had to wait, and wait, and wait, and wait, while Hank took encore after encore. Hank finally walked out on stage without his guitar and said very simply, "Folks, I thank you a lot, but we've got a mighty big act waitin' to come on, so I'd better leave."

After Hank joined the Opry in 1949, he and I worked together frequently and we became close friends. I adored him. Then Henry began flying him and they became very close. I think he considered Henry one of the few people he could trust implicitly. They had some great times together, and they also had some serious moments when Hank would open up and be uncharacteristically revealing about himself. He wrote "Jambalaya" on one of his flights with Henry.

Hank once made the most incredible remark I ever heard anyone make about their mother. He told us he used to get into a lot of honky-tonk brawls when he was still a kid living at home. One night a guy beat him up so badly he was left for dead in a roadhouse parking lot. A cab driver had been called by someone else, and when he pulled in to pick up his fare the headlights hit Hank, lying there unconscious in a pool of blood. The cabbie recognized him and took him home to his mother. She looked at his wounds, then said, "First we get you sewed up; then we go get him." Hank said, "Minnie, there ain't nobody in the world I'd rather have alongside me in a fight than my mama with a broken beer bottle in her hand." He said it as though it was nothing out of the ordinary at all.

Through his songs of heartbreak and loneliness, and his tragic personal life, Hank's image became one of a sad, hopeless man. But he was actually one of the funniest men I ever knew. He had a wry sense of humor, much like Henry's (which might be one of the reasons they took to one another so readily), and he loved to tell stories on people. He never played the star. He was always close to his band members, and they were very fond of him.

I like to remember Hank as he was at his peak—with a twinkle in his eyes, his wardrobe immaculate, and *killing* them with his show and his unforgettable songs. But something he said to me the last time we were alone will always stick in my mind. It was a horrible day.

Hank, Ernest Tubb and I were booked to play San Diego. I had flown out alone after the Opry Saturday night because Henry had a charter flight. I went over to the auditorium about 2:30, and the people were already coming in for the three o'clock matinee. Ernest and Hank were arriving from Bakersfield, where they had played the night before. I was surprised they weren't in yet, because their musicians had to set up. (In the early days setting up didn't take long. When I first started on the road the pickers tuned up in the car half the time, then walked on stage and plugged in. Later they became more sophisticated and spent a half hour or so setting up. Now they come in *hours* ahead with a separate sound truck and a board for all sorts of electronic equipment, equivalent to what they have in a recording studio, and sometimes it takes them longer to get their sound balanced than it does to put on a show.) The promoter was already walking the floor. Then word came that Tubb had had car trouble and that Hank was in really bad shape physically. But they were on their way. The promoter waited as long as he could—the crowd was growing more restless by the minute—then asked me if I'd go on and open. I had never opened a show, but I felt sorry for the man so I agreed. I told the audience that car trouble had delayed the others, then I started telling gags with one ear tuned to backstage so I could hear them come in. Finally, after about 15 minutes, I heard the musicians arrive, so I told the crowd I'd let Ernest Tubb reopen the show and I'd be back later.

I got off just in time to see this pathetic, emaciated, haunted-looking, tragic figure of a man being assisted through the stage door—not too gently—by a male nurse. The male nurse had undoubtedly had enough problems with Hank to warrant being impatient with him, but it upset me to see my friend handled that way. When you love a child you don't want the child to be treated roughly, even if he's being a brat, and that's the way I felt about Hank. He was like a pitiful lost child to me, and I had never seen him in as bad shape as he was that day. I ran to him and hugged him. He threw his arms around me and clung to me, crying. I tried to comfort him, to tell him that everything was going to be all right, just as you would try to comfort a child crying in the dark. No one will ever know what tortured dreams he had. Perhaps all of life was a bad dream to Hank. By this time he was killing himself with drugs and alcohol, and his mind had undoubtedly been severely affected.

It broke my heart to see this incredibly talented, sweet man in the depths of despair and pain, and I begged the promoter not to put him on. It was so *cruel*. They wouldn't have put a man dying of cancer out there on stage for people to gawk at. Nowadays a star of that caliber would have a manager, or someone in authority, who wouldn't allow him to be seen in that condition. But in those days management and career guidance as it is known in Hollywood hadn't reached country music, and the hillbillies were on their own.

The promoter was determined Hank Williams was going to perform that day if he had to carry him out there on a stretcher. They started pouring coffee down him. They walked him back and forth. They dunked his face in cold water. Finally they somehow got him into his wardrobe and steered him toward the stage. It was pathetic. It tore me apart to see him out there trying to sing, his voice cracking, hanging on to the microphone for dear life, a sickening caricature of the superb, magnetic performer he had been at the height of his career.

The audience was not kind. I could understand their disappointment and sympathize with them. They had paid to see *Hank Williams,* not this sad, sick man who belonged in a hospital. But I was angry with them, too. I wanted them to show more empathy for him in his condition, even if the illness was self-inflicted.

After the show the promoter told me he wanted me and his wife to drive Hank around town until the next performance at 8 p.m. to keep an eye on him. Hopefully, he would sober up in that time. "He'll do what you tell him to do," the man said. He obviously hadn't had much experience with anyone strung out on pills and whiskey. In the state Hank was in, he wouldn't have listened to his own mother. But I went along because I didn't want him left alone with these people who didn't love him, who saw him as a piece of merchandise they'd bought for the day.

That was the longest automobile ride I've ever had in my life. We actually drove around for only a couple of hours, but it seemed like an eternity. Hank was *really* hurting by then. They had already kept him off the stuff for four or five hours and his body was craving help. He kept asking us to stop the car, trying to come up with every excuse he could think of to get us to pull over. He was all bent over in the front seat, his hair in disarray, hunched forward with his thin arms crossed tightly over his abdomen.

I was trying to think of *anything* that would take his mind off whiskey, so I said, "Come on, Hank. Let's sing." I started singing "I Saw the Light," a gospel song he had written several years earlier. He joined in, his voice cracking and off-key, then suddenly he stopped and looked at me. He put his hand on mine and said, *"That's just it, Minnie. There ain't no light. It's all dark."*

It was the pitiful cry of a man alone at his road's end. He lived about six months after that, and no one knows how much more suffering and hell he went through before he died on New Year's Eve, 1953. The autopsy said he died of an overdose of pills and alcohol, but I think those were the instruments of his death, not the cause. The cause lay somewhere deep in his psyche, and only God knows what went on there.

It's difficult to realize he was only 29 years old when he died, because his body was so worn from all the abuse he'd given it. There's no telling what heights he could have reached had he been able to straighten himself out and enjoy a normal lifespan. He was one of the most prolific songwriters ever born, and there is little doubt that he had many many more hit songs left in his mind and heart when he died.

Henry and I feel privileged that we were around him during his happy times and saw more of that side than we did the other. It's odd, but neither of us ever saw Hank take a drink. Nor did we ever see him use drugs of any kind. We were around him many times when we knew he was under the influence of something, but we never knew what. Over the years he has been immortalized and is now considered a legend in our business. He would have found that amusing. He was just a regular funny ole boy raised in Alabama, as down to earth as dirt. But he had that awesome talent. We've never seen another like him in country music, and I doubt we ever will.

Chapter Twenty-Three

BY 1947 the barriers were really beginning to come down for country music. Word came that we were going to play Carnegie Hall.

I was thrilled. Believe it or not, I still had delusions about being a great actress, and even though I wasn't going to stand on the stage of Carnegie Hall in that capacity, just being asked to perform in that hallowed auditorium was a magnificent honor. The bill featured Ernest Tubb, Minnie Pearl and another act, Dot and Smokey. We were booked for two nights and we packed 'em in! We played to SRO (standing room only) crowds on both shows, and it was really exciting.

I think that was the first time I realized how far-flung country music had become. The boys had come home from the service, and many who had never been exposed to country music before they left had now become fans. Later that same year we played Constitution Hall in Washington, D.C., another first for the hillbillies. It's hard for some of the new country music artists to realize how limited we were in the early days as to where we played. In the twenties and thirties and through the middle forties country music performers didn't play the big halls or the class houses. We showed in high school auditoriums, one-room schoolhouses, beer joints and at fairs.

But once the music began spreading there was no stopping it, and it is absolutely incredible to me to realize that now, more than thirty years later, it is still growing in popularity. Lucky for me, Minnie Pearl's acceptance grew along with country music's in the late forties. I was particularly honored in 1948 when Minnie was mentioned in a vice-presidential election acceptance speech.

I was at home the morning Harry Truman and Alben Barkley were to make their official acceptance speeches, but I didn't have the radio on. All of a sudden my phone started ringing off the wall. Friends from everywhere were calling to tell me that Barkley had stepped up to the microphone and said, "Well, as Minnie Pearl would say, 'I'm just so *proud* to be here!' "

I wired him immediately and thanked him for honoring Minnie that way, and assured him that Grinder's Switch was in an absolute uproar.

He wrote back and said he had listened to the Opry for years and that Minnie was one of his special favorites. The letter was kind and warm and I felt an instant friendship. Later he invited me to come to the inauguration as his guest, and also to attend a special Kentucky party to be held in his honor prior to the swearing-in ceremonies.

I went wild over what to wear, the typical female response to an exciting invitation. Having never before been to an inauguration, I was thrilled at the prospect of being so close to a historically significant event.

Henry was flying a charter trip that day, so I went to Washington with the Nashville group on the Tennessee Train. We had a wonderful time, and the party atmosphere continued throughout the two fun-filled days I was there. The party for Vice-President Barkley was celebrity-studded. I had never been on the Washington scene before, and I was struck by its similarity to our show business atmosphere.

Vice-President Barkley was a charming man. He was a down-to-earth grass-roots politician-turned-statesman who really loved people and knew how to mix with them. He was a marvelous storyteller, and most of his were country stories, so he and I hit it off fine. I grieved when he died. America lost a great champion.

Toward the end of 1949, I had one of the most exciting and memorable experiences of my career. Word came in November that the William Esty Agency had decided to send a show to Europe (under the auspices of their Prince Albert tobacco account) to entertain our men in the U.S.–occupied zones there.

Imagine, my first trip to Europe, VIP treatment, all expenses paid and getting to go with my best friends! They had selected Red Foley, Rod Brasfield and me, the three regulars on the NBC Grand Ole Opry, plus Roy Acuff, Hank Williams and Little Jimmy Dickens. They also invited all the wives, and Henry. They even put the wives in the show. They outfitted them in cute gingham costumes and taught them a little square dance. Red's wife, Eva, also sang on the show, first solo, then in some darling duets with Red. The only spouse they didn't put to work was Henry, and we loved teasing him about that.

Spirits were high and we anticipated a great time, even though some of the members of the troupe were nervous about flying across the Atlantic. None of us had been to Europe before. We were to be flown by the U.S. Air Force in a DC-4. The guys kept telling Henry how glad they were to have him along, as if he could walk right up into the cockpit if something went wrong and take over.

We all nearly fainted when we saw the inside of the plane. I had expected something like the DC-3 troop carrier that had brought us back from Panama. But this looked more like Air Force One. The custom-designed interior featured spacious, luxurious seats, with an extra large galley, where an accommodating steward served us delicious snacks, meals and drinks. We even had a special compartment just for our costumes.

Before leaving the United States, we touched down in Washington to clear last-minute military red tape, since we were going under government orders. Then we took off for our first show in Stephenville, Newfoundland. That same night, after our performance, we flew to Wiesbaden, Germany, where we were quartered most of the time.

We went all over Germany, and even to Vienna, where we showed at the beautiful Opera House. (Our trip through Bavaria was marked by a chilling visit to Dachau Prison Camp, which I wish I had not seen. The evidence of suffering and death was still overwhelming, and the MP who showed us through the camp made his commentary painfully detailed and explicit.) We arrived in Vienna on a Sunday afternoon and checked into the old, elegant Bristol Hotel. Henry and I felt we were on a real honeymoon as we luxuriated in what could easily have been the bridal suite, judging from its splendor. We didn't have a show that night, so we went to the famous club Maxim's and had a party. We were so happy—and so young! I look back on it with vast pleasure. Everyone was in a festive mood. Hank and Audrey were happy then, and we were all gay and carefree for the entire evening, almost. One of the tall, sexy strippers at the club tried to run off with Henry during the partying, and I became terribly jealous. It was good for him, and for me too, since it was just a brief flare-up. It convinced me all over again that I certainly had better watch my handsome, brown-eyed pilot more carefully. (And I still feel that way!)

I love to remember that trip on the rare occasions when I feel show business has been a long hard grind of dull one-nighters. I like to recall it all: the enchanting strains of the Strauss waltzes that were played continually in the background as we lunched and dined on scrumptious food in restaurants laden with old-world charm, the hilarious language mishaps you might expect with hillbillies trying to communicate in German; the awareness of being surrounded by so much history and the excitement of foreign sights and smells.

On the way back we stopped at the Azores and performed at our air base there, and then on to Bermuda, where we landed long enough to enjoy a bit of its balmy atmosphere.

We had one terrifying moment on the return trip. While we were still over the Atlantic, we hit an air pocket and the plane dropped about 500 feet. We'd all bought armloads of souvenirs in Europe, and junk came flying out of the overhead racks, scattering everywhere. The aisle was littered with cuckoo clocks! When we finally recovered, one of the boys said, "Now ya' see, Henry, if you'd been up there flyin' this thing that would'a never happened." Henry loved it . . . as untrue as it was.

I keep going back to the fun we had. It was sheer Heaven to have so many beloved friends along. The shows were enough to spoil a performer for life—packed houses, screaming responses and always that wonderful sense of fun. The servicemen couldn't do or say enough to convince us of how much they loved having us there. They were so homesick, and in our country show we brought home to them. We were entertained as well, until we were embarrassed by the hospitality. But it was the camaraderie of our troupe that made the trip so memorable. Little did we know that it would be the last time we would all be together on one plane. Red and Eva, Rod and Hank and Audrey are all gone now. When I think of them, I like to remember that trip, and how we all acted like kids on a picnic, playing hooky from school.

In those days I was riding high. As Henry says, I couldn't get over myself. It's a good thing incidents cropped up now and then to put me in my place or I might have had to start buying Minnie's hats in a larger size.

One such incident involved June Carter.

I had first met the Carter family very early in my career. I was playing Birmingham and they were on the same bill. I had heard of them for years, because the original Carter Family—Maybelle, Sara and A.P. had been around since the late twenties. But the original trio had disbanded and Mother Maybelle had gone on the road with her daughters, Helen, Anita and June. June was about 11 years old then, and as cute as she could be.

Maybelle came to me backstage before the show and introduced herself. She had the most soulful eyes I had ever seen, and a beautiful speaking voice. She said, "I want you to see June do her imitation of you." Then June pranced up, not in the least bit shy, and went right into "Howdee, I'm just so proud to be here." She told a couple of jokes and did sound *exactly* like Minnie. Coming from a child, it was really funny. It didn't take any great insight to see that this girl had enormous talent as a comic. (This is one of those times when I *did* have the prescience of stardom standing there before me.) I watched her on their portion of the show that afternoon and saw that she was a born actress, a natural performer. Mother Maybelle asked me if I thought they ought to let June put her imitation of Minnie in the show. I said, "No, the child is too good to go into a career doing imitations of someone else. She ought to be encouraged to get up her own act." And she did. And she never copied me.

Years passed and, as I said, I was riding high. I was the only female comic on the Opry, and I thought I was funnier than a crutch.

One night I was listening to the Opry on the car radio on my way to a fair date in Nebraska. I heard June doing this character she had created, which she later called Aunt Polly. She was hilarious, and the audience obviously loved her. She was knockin' 'em in the aisles. I said to myself, "Uh-oh! You'd better watch yourself, ole girl, and start paying attention. This gal is *good!*"

I remembered how my father used to say, "Everyone can be replaced. No matter what you're doing in life, don't ever get the idea that you can't be replaced." We have a saying in show business: "Watch it, or you can be replaced with live talent."

June subsequently performed on the Opry for many years, and

although there was never any sense of competition between us, and certainly no jealousy, she kept me on my toes without knowing it. I've always said the world lost a great comic when she married Johnny Cash. She's a lovely lady, and one of my dear friends.

Chapter Twenty-Four

THERE have been so many times in my life when something seemingly insignificant has led to something momentous that I can't help believing in God's Plan for all of us.

One of those times was in 1956 when I met Ralph Edwards at the General Conference of the Methodist Church in Minneapolis. Mama had always wanted to go to this annual gathering, which is the largest event held by the Methodist church each year, so I took her and my sister Frances along with me.

Mama was 80 years old at the time, and had not been out of the state of Tennessee in 50 years. She had never been in an airplane in her life. The morning we left she was all dressed up in her mink cape and a pretty new hat, and she stepped on the plane with the air of a world traveler. After we were aloft, the pilot, who knew Henry, came back to speak to her.

"Are you enjoying your trip, Mrs. Colley?" he asked.

"It is delightful," she told him. "I never intend to travel any other way."

Frances and I just loved it.

Anyway, as entertainment for the conference, Ralph Edwards, whose television show, This Is Your Life, was then one of the most popular in the country, did a closed-circuit TV show with that format on some of us there. Minnie made her appearance before 15,000 young people who had come from all over the country to attend the conference, and they seemed to love her.

Then, by coincidence, Ralph Edwards flew back on the same plane with us as far as Chicago. He started talking to Mama and fell in love with her. He was a big Methodist, like she was, so they hit it off great. She didn't watch television, so she didn't think of him as a celebrity (which wouldn't have impressed her anyway), but she liked him as a man, and he thought she was as bright and funny as she could be.

I didn't think any more about meeting Ralph Edwards, except that he was very nice and I appreciated his paying so much attention to Mama.

Then, in 1957, I was asked to go to Hollywood to do some promotional film clips for NBC-TV, commemorating WSM's twentieth year with the network. I considered it an honor to be asked, and I was excited about my first appearance on network television, but I had no idea it was all a hoax to get me there.

Henry was flying us in the Beechcraft, and we left a day or two ahead of time, but that wasn't unusual. Along the way he stopped at the most remote little airstrips imaginable, places like Lloydsburg, New Mexico, where they didn't even have a phone in the hotel room. I didn't think much about it. I never knew where we were going to stop, anyway.

We finally arrived in Hollywood on Tuesday. Ted Switzer from NBC met us at the airport and took us to this nice old hotel in Los Angeles called the Town House. He insisted on taking us to dinner immediately. I wanted to call Mama first. I kept in close touch with her by telephone as she got older and I was traveling constantly. But the man rushed us on out, and by the time we got back that night it was too late to call her.

The next morning Ted was at the hotel room practically before I'd finished breakfast. I wasn't scheduled to do my filming until that evening, but Ted had my whole day mapped out. I said I had to call my mother first, but he wouldn't let me, and Henry had already left for the day on the pretext of some sort of business.

I knew that I was being picked up at 6:30 p.m. for my filming, and I wanted to get back to the hotel early so I could rest and get myself together. I had never appeared on network television, and I was anxious about it. But Ted, who was as cute as he could be, kept me out until past 4:30. He didn't seem to pick up on any of the strong hints I was dropping about returning to the hotel.

When I got back Henry wasn't there, and he hadn't left a note. That was odd because he always leaves me a note (signed: *Re-*

gards, Henry) whenever we're traveling and he's not going to be in the room when I return. But I didn't think much about it, I was so concerned about calling Mama. I got the switchboard and the operator contacted long distance, but then said, for the *umpteenth* time, that all the circuits to Tennessee were busy. I was *very* annoyed. I couldn't understand it. It wasn't Mother's Day or any other holiday, and by this time it had been three days since I'd talked to Mama and I wanted to check on her.

I was still holding the phone, debating what to do, when Henry walked in.

"What are you *doing?*" he demanded frantically.

"I'm trying to get Mama," I said, "but all the circuits are busy."

"Hand me that phone," he said. "I have to order you a sandwich right now, so they'll have time to get it up here from room service before they pick us up at six."

I gave him the phone and went on to start getting ready. He didn't give me another chance to use it before Ted arrived to pick us up.

We immediately took off down the freeway toward the NBC studios in Burbank. Henry was still smoking then, and by this time he was so nervous he cut his hand on the car ashtray trying to put out a cigarette. Blood was spurting from the wound. I told Ted to stop and he said, "No, no, we don't have time; we're running late." Henry kept saying, "It's alright. Don't worry about it." But one handkerchief was already soaked and he was bleeding all over a second. He still had that blood-soaked handkerchief bound tightly around his hand when we arrived at the studio. I felt this terrible urgency all around, but I didn't relate it to anything except the normal atmosphere of television. I noticed a crowd lined up out front waiting to get in. I asked Ted which show was about to go on. He named one I'd seen once or twice.

The minute we were inside the artists' entrance Ted propelled me along the hallway to a dressing room. He had told me earlier that they'd been lucky enough to get Claude Thompson, the best makeup man in Hollywood, to do my face for the film clips. (Claude is now with Dinah Shore, and we get a kick out of talking about this whenever I do her show.) I was told to hurry into my costume.

As soon as I was dressed, they hustled me down to makeup. I sat in the chair and put my head back. Claude told me to close my eyes as he started working on me. He made me keep my eyes closed so long I thought he must be a fanatic about eye makeup.

How much could you do to two eyes? (All the while cameras were silently being rolled up behind me.)

I was still lying there with my eyes closed when I heard my mother's voice say, "Daughter, where are you?"

It scared me to death. I thought I was either hallucinating, or I'd died and Mama was calling me. It didn't occur to me for a second that it *was* Mama, actually *there*. I had seen her in Centerville the week before, and, as far as I was concerned, that's where she was still. I came out of that chair like I'd been shot, and the shocked look on my face that the camera picked up was *not* acting!

Then I heard Ralph Edwards' voice say, "Sarah Ophelia Colley Cannon, THIS IS YOUR LIFE."

I screamed bloody murder and grabbed my face and started crying. I turned around and there they all stood—Mama, Frances, Virginia, Mary and Dixie. I screamed again, "Oh, nooooo!"

Fortunately they cut to a commercial immediately. Claude dabbed my tears away, and I had a minute to compose myself as they hurried us onto the set. They put me on the sofa, with Mama beside me, and my sisters all around.

As uncanny as it may seem, right in the middle of all this confusion, fever-pitch excitement and mental bedlam, one thought sprang into my consciousness, flashing like a neon sign: *"Hey, ole girl. This is it. Here's your chance to pitch yourself on national television. You couldn't buy a chance like this. Now take this show and run with it."*

That's what years of experience on a stage does for you—it teaches you to think on your feet. There are countless things that can come up at the last minute before a show or during one, so you have to learn to shift gears quickly, to *recover* in any situation, and that's exactly what I did that night.

The producer, the director, even members of the crew told me many times later they remembered that night as a shambles after I got going. At one point Ralph said to the director in the booth, "Where are we?" He had lost his place in the book. The director said, "Never mind. Let her go and we'll ride it out." I've never had more fun in my life! And it opened up new vistas for me. I did a lot of network television during the next few years as a result of being seen on This Is Your Life. (It's hard for people now to realize how big that show was in 1957. It was in the top ten.)

Mama was hilarious on the show. And all my sisters were funny, too. NBC gave me a film of the show, and we watched it together many times after that and teased one another unmercifully. My sisters had been given the Hollywood treatment—new hairstyles, makeup and wardrobe—and they looked like mannequins of themselves. Mama was the only one who looked and acted natural. When my sisters wanted to buy Mama a dress to wear before they left home, she said, "No, I only wear dresses Ophelia picks for me. I have a very pretty new one and I'll wear that."

Since Mama couldn't see well enough to read, my sisters had taught her her lines, and she knew them verbatim. When I started cutting up and acting silly with Ralph, we got ahead of Mama and she lost some of her lines. She grabbed Ralph's arm, right on the air, and said, "Just a minute, young man. I have a line here." Ralph just fell out. Later he said, "I don't know what impressed me more, the fact that she was so completely unconcerned about being on national television or that she called me 'young man.'"

I don't think Ralph had ever run into a family quite like mine, and I'm certain he never had a spouse on the show who responded the way Henry did.

That afternoon at rehearsal (where Henry had gone on the pretext of business), Ralph went over Henry's lines with him, then said, "Now, this is where you come in and kiss her," to which Henry replied, "I will *not*. I'm sick to death of her. She has given me a heart attack and high blood pressure this week, trying to keep her away from the phones and from guessing this secret. I don't want any part of her. I certainly won't kiss her." (They had told Henry that if I found out before the show they would run a film instead. They wanted the complete surprise element, even if it gave *me* a heart attack.)

Ralph thought Henry was kidding. What he didn't realize is that Henry has a strong aversion to public displays of affection. Besides, he meant every word he said. He hated being on television and was very uncomfortable. He was sick of the whole thing. So when Ralph said, ". . . and in 1947 you married a handsome pilot, Henry Cannon . . ." I *promise* you Henry walked out from behind the curtain, shook my hand and said, "Hi-de-doo." It didn't surprise me, but Ralph couldn't get over it. I laughed and hit Henry on the arm and said, "Oh, shut up," and we went on with the show.

They brought out many dear friends from my life, which really thrilled me. They had flown in Eddy Arnold and Pee Wee King. They even had Monnette there. She was living in Cuba at the time.

Afterward they gave a wonderful party for us at the Roosevelt

Hotel. It was a very exciting time for me and proved to be a milestone in my career. But Ralph Edwards never did do another country music star (with the exception of Tennessee Ernie Ford, who had his own network show). I think we cured Ralph's curiosity about "country" once and for all. He didn't want to take any more chances with those crazy folks.

That Christmas Henry gave me one of the nicest surprises of my life. It was Christmas Eve, actually, and I was standing in our bedroom talking on the phone when I felt something behind me. I turned around and there, lying on the white fur rug in front of the fireplace, was a tiny miniature French poodle puppy. He looked so precious and so frightened that I let out a scream of delight. He had been away from his mother for only a couple of hours and had never heard anything like that. I fell in love with him instantly.

Henry and I had looked at puppies that fall. Because we didn't have any children we'd decided to get a dog. But, after talking it over, we came to the conclusion that a pet would complicate our lives as we were on the go so much. I didn't know it then, but Henry was just setting me up for Christmas.

We named our new "baby" Faux Pas, which means mistake in French, but we spelled it Fo' Paw (pretty Southern, *n'est-ce pas?*). We took him down to the Opry with us later, and T. Tommy Cutrer, who was a performer from Louisiana, asked, "What kind of dog is *that?*" All you could see was a tiny ball of fluff, so it was hard to tell what it was. "It's a French poodle," Henry said.

"Oh, that ain't no *French* poodle," T. Tommy answered. "That's a Cajun. He's a Loose-e-anna dog. Looks just like an old uncle a'mine named Sam LeFleur. Lived down at Bayou Pom Pom."

We thought that was so funny we changed the dog's name to Sam right on the spot. And he became famous throughout country music as Sam LeFleur from Bayou Pom Pom.

Sam flew with us for 10 years and logged over 5,000 hours in the air. He took to the air like a born fly-boy, acted like a seasoned veteran from the beginning. He always flew backward, with his little front paws toward the back of the seat. Henry said he flew that way because he'd been so many places he wasn't interested in where he was going, just where he'd been. He got to know all the country music greats and stayed in some of the best hotels, always conducting himself like a perfect gentleman. He never snapped at anyone, and, when people would pet him and make a fuss over him backstage, he'd just turn his head and look bored. The little tombstone on his grave in our backyard reads: "Sam, A Gentleman." Someone has said, "A dog is a diary," and that certainly proved true of Sam. I think the reason we cried so when he died was that he was a part of all those happy, carefree days on the road.

We could never have found a Sam substitute, but we had to have another little friend to love and pet, so three months after we lost Sam we got a miniature schnauzer. She is jet black and her name is Heidi. She doesn't travel with us, but we're not gone much anymore, and she is a joy.

That New Year of 1958 began a wonderful period of my life. Henry and I moved into a beautiful home on a hilltop in Brentwood, about 10 miles from Nashville, and we loved entertaining our Opry buddies on Saturday nights after the show. That home was the scene of many unforgettable (and some I'd *like* to forget) parties. Henry never wanted our guests to go home. He'd stand at the door and say, "Now don't y'all go off and leave me by myself," just as though you-know-who wasn't standing right beside him!

We were traveling more than ever, but flying made it much easier, and flying with Henry made it very special. I look back on those years and seem to remember only the *fun*. I know it wasn't *all* fun, but that's how I remember it. We'd get into our little plane and take off, sharing a special kind of communion—just Henry, the little puppy and me. We never talked much. Henry would be checking the weather and his maps, while I read and Sam slept. But we seemed suspended in a safe, euphoric world, devoid of problems and pressures.

The fair tours I used to play were perfectly designed for the type of aircraft Henry flew. The majority of these fairs were in or near small towns with unpaved airstrips. I recall landing on hundreds of little fields where the airport consisted of one small hangar, sometimes with a tiny frame office attached. The wind sock would be blowing lazily above the building, and a lone attendant would walk out to meet us as Henry slowed the Beechcraft to a stop.

Even when these fields were listed as safe in the *Airman's Guide*, Henry always flew over low a few times to check them out. After we landed, getting into town often proved to be more difficult than flying in from Nashville.

Henry always radioed ahead to make arrangements for transportation into town, or the booker would promise to take care of it, but sometimes there was a mixup and on other occasions there simply wasn't any ride available. Many of these little places didn't even have a taxi service. I'll never forget the time we had to *hitchhike* to the date in town. There was no other way to get there. Some lovely people picked us up. There we were, standing on the side of the road out in the middle of nowhere, carrying a Valpac and a white French poodle. They accepted us as some crazy show people, and took us on in to the fair.

One summer we played 65 fair dates. That was our heaviest booking schedule, but we nearly always played 25 or 30 fairs a summer during that period. That's when I met some of the most interesting performers in country music when they were still on their way up.

One season a likable young man joined our troupe. He sang "Fraulein," a song made popular by Bobby Helms. The young man also played fiddle, and he was much more quiet and reserved than most of us crazy hillbillies. But when you got to know Roger Miller you discovered a marvelously spontaneous, dry, *dry* sense of humor. We didn't know his songwriting talent would carry him to fame, but we weren't the least bit surprised to see him become one of the top comedians in the business.

About the same time another young man came along to join The Minnie Pearl Show whose sense of humor had never been seen on stage. He had a stuttering problem and was so terribly self-conscious about it that he wouldn't talk at all on stage.

Mel Tillis could barely get out a thank-you after his act. But he sang beautifully, and was already writing hit songs. When Henry and I got to know him, and found out how hilarious he could be, I begged him to let go and be as funny on stage as he was with us. The rest, as they say, is history. Mel is now one of the superstars of country music and is also appearing in movies.

Mel tells a wonderful story about a movie he did for Burt Reynolds. With a little practice he got his lines down without a falter, and on the first take Burt looked at him dumbfounded. Mel beamed, thinking he'd done great. "You didn't stutter!" Burt exclaimed. "Yeah," Mel agreed. "But you *gotta* stutter," Burt said. "That's why I hired you." Mel had to do the scene over and over until he got the stuttering down right.

He laughs about the fact that he now has to *make* himself stutter to retain his image. Over the years, as his success and confidence increased, his stuttering decreased. Mel's story interests me because it points out something I've always believed—that we can make a handicap work *for* us instead of against us if we have a positive, determined attitude and a *sense of humor!* Henry and I still love to get together with Roger and Mel and talk about those old fair dates.

I've done my act many a time on an outdoor platform stage in the afternoon where the temperature was over 100 degrees and you could get a sunburn while you worked. But fair dates weren't the only place we had to contend with the heat. There was no air conditioning back in the old days, no matter where you were working, and they always seemed to schedule matinees at the hottest part of the afternoon, around 3 p.m. (I was doing a tent-show matinee one time with Rod Brasfield, and it must have been 120 degrees under that canvas. I said to Rod, "This heat is intense." He said, "Yeah, it's always hot in tents." He was so crazy!)

One of the problems with heat is that your temperature rises when you concentrate, and you're working really hard to project, which requires actual physical exertion, so you get doubly hot. The audience is sitting there fanning themselves while you're about to expire on stage. At the old Ryman Auditorium, the Opry's home for 33 years, they used to sell cardboard fans at the door in the summertime. When we moved to the new auditorium, a reporter asked me what I missed most about the Ryman. I said the fans (which he took to mean the audiences) which I used to see going back and forth, back and forth. The fans would move faster and faster with up-tempo songs, then slow back down for the ballads. We got such a kick out of it. The only good thing about heat is that an audience will come nearer to laughing when they're overheated than when they're cold.

My two pet peeves at outside shows like fair dates are high winds and bugs. At night the stage lights attract bugs in swarms. If a bug flew near my face I'd always do that silly old joke about pretending to swallow it. The band would pick up on it immediately, and one of them would offer to get me a drink of water. I'd say, "No, thank-you. I think I'll just let it walk down." The crowds thought it was funny, but it was too close to the truth for us to think it was all that hilarious. I've known singers who actually did swallow a bug on an outdoor stage, and they didn't think it was a bit funny!

I always had fun working with my old buddies on the fair circuit. Pee Wee King and Redd Stewart were often booked on the same date with me. Pee Wee and Redd had written the all-time great hit "Tennessee Waltz." Pee Wee had two adorable girls working with him then, the Collins Sisters, and Henry and I fell in love with them. We adopted them as our special daughters, and we still feel that way about them. You become "awful close awful soon" under road circumstances.

When Elvis Presley exploded on the music scene in 1956, the phenomenal effect he had on his fans was the talk of the industry. Girls had swooned over Sinatra in the forties and screamed for Eddie Fisher during the early fifties, but from all reports no one had ever seen a performer drive an audience absolutely wild the way Elvis did. It was said that he could produce hysteria simply by pointing his finger at someone in the audience. I had met him briefly but had never seen him work. Henry had flown Elvis many times during his early career and found him a quiet, polite young man who was always an easy passenger.

Then, in 1964, Col. Tom Parker, Elvis's manager, called and asked me and Henry to go to Hawaii with Elvis to do a benefit show. Elvis had already done his stint in the army, and now he was going to help the navy by putting on a benefit concert to raise the $50,000 they needed to complete the building fund for the U.S.S. *Arizona* Memorial at Pearl Harbor. After the concert, he was scheduled to stay on in the islands to film the movie *Blue Hawaii*.

Henry and I met Elvis and his group at the airport in Los Angeles, where we all boarded the commercial airliner that would take us to Honolulu.

Just as Henry had been earlier, I was impressed by Elvis's good manners and his quiet, almost shy, personality. He said "Yes, sir" and "Yes, ma'am" to everyone, even if they were only a few years older, and he treated me and Henry with the greatest respect. I remember marveling that his wealth and status as a worldwide superstar had not gone to his head. He was more polite than most young men his age, and certainly better looking, but other than that he appeared to be just a simple, down-to-earth, good-natured Southern boy. There was nothing in his off-stage personality to prepare me for what awaited us at the Honolulu airport.

When the plane rolled to a stop at the gate, the stewardess asked that all members of the Presley party remain on board until the other passengers had deplaned. I looked out the window and saw, to my horror, at least 5,000 jumping, yelling, screaming fans (mostly girls) pushing against the runway fence. Many of them were waving banners with messages of love for Elvis. A battery of policemen was stationed at the edge of the runway trying to calm the frenzied crowd, and to get them to move back from the fence so they wouldn't collapse it. The whole scene was bedlam, and distinctly frightening.

I looked back at Elvis, who was also staring at the crowd, a morose expression on his face. "How do you *stand* it?" I asked sympathetically. I couldn't help feeling sorry for him.

"Oh, I'm used to it now," he answered, trying to appear non-chalant.

I liked that, his refusal to complain about the restrictions imposed by superstardom. Because so many do complain. They work and struggle for years to win recognition, then moan and groan that they can't go anywhere without being recognized. If any star had the right to complain, it was certainly Elvis that day, and I'm sure it was equally bad no matter where he went. No wonder he became more and more reclusive as time went by. We had many stars in country music whose fans would crowd around and push and scream, but I had never seen such a demonstration in my life for anyone.

As we prepared to leave the plane, Colonel Parker said to me, "Stay close to Elvis. I want you in all the publicity shots."

So I got a taste of the real thing. The crowd exploded when they saw Elvis step off the plane, and by the time we got to the ground the policemen were struggling to hold the line. When Elvis raised his arm in greeting and flashed that famous crooked grin, I thought the fences would come tumbling down. I became more frightened by the minute. I knew that if a crowd that size broke loose we'd be trampled before anyone could do a thing. But I stuck as close to Elvis as possible.

Henry was fit to be tied. He wanted me out of that mess *right then*. But Colonel Parker had insisted I go with Elvis, and that was that. Henry followed in another limo.

Driving into town, we encountered scores more groups of screaming fans, and when we arrived at the Hawaiian Village Hotel, we were confronted by hundreds more, jammed together, awaiting Elvis's arrival. As our limo stopped, they surged, but the police held them back until we started through the crowd. Then they suddenly broke loose and we were literally swept off our feet. The screaming and yelling, pushing and shoving were horrible. At one point, Henry couldn't see whether I'd been knocked down or not. He was frantic, and so was I. We were engulfed, suffocating in a sea of people. I caught a glimpse of Elvis's face, and will never forget it. He had the look of a zombie—a resigned, deadpan, expressionless stare. All I could think of later was: "And he goes through this all the time. How could anyone live with it?"

Henry finally got me separated from Elvis and we hurried to our room, where I collapsed in relief.

Years later, as word filtered back to Nashville of Elvis's unhappiness and seeming withdrawal, I would think of that day in Hawaii. No wonder he lost touch with reality. The world he lived in had no resemblance to reality as the rest of us know it.

That night, for the first time, I saw the Presley charisma in action. We worked to a standing-room-only crowd at the auditorium at the Pearl Harbor naval base. Even the $100-a-seat section was sold out. The Jordonaires and Elvis's band went on first, then me, then Elvis. The rest of us might as well have stayed home. I've got a feeling that would have been true of any act opening a Presley show.

That night, I saw firsthand what was meant by Elvis driving an audience wild. The expression "holding the audience in the palm of his hand" doesn't begin to describe what Presley did to them. It was mass hysteria. The crowd would have stayed all night if Elvis had performed that long. The show raised $52,000, and it all went to the fund for building the beautiful memorial over the U.S.S. *Arizona*, sunk on that fateful Sunday morning in December 1941.

I saw Elvis only once after that, on a movie set in Hollywood when I was appearing on the Tennessee Ernie Ford TV show. As always, he was polite and courteous. Later, Henry and I grieved when we heard of his death. Elvis and Hank Williams had such similar fates—cut short in the very prime of life. They both seemed hounded by demons that kept them searching for a happiness that never was.

I have visited Hawaii on other occasions, but under very different circumstances. Henry and I first met Jim Nabors when he was working at a TV station in Chattanooga. He had big dreams then, but at that time they were only stars in his eyes. We thought he was one of the nicest and funniest young men we'd ever met. His enormous success since then has not changed those qualities. He is still cute and funny and *nice,* and he is also one of the most generous, unselfish men we've ever known. Jim gives of his time, his money and his love, not only to his family, but to his friends all over the world. Henry and I love him like the son we never had.

No one loves a good time more than Jim Nabors. And when he's having fun, he wants all his friends to have fun with him. He won't take no for an answer. If Jim wants you to go on a trip with him, he'll just call up and tell you all the arrangements have been made. He's taken Henry and me on some fabulous trips, including two to Hawaii. And, believe me, you haven't seen Hawaii until you've seen it with Jim Nabors.

One of those two occasions was a fantastic weekend hosted by the famous developer Del Webb when he opened the Kuilima Hotel, which is across the island from Honolulu. Del flew in 500 of his "closest friends" for a party before the formal opening, and Jim took Henry and me along as his personal guests. People who had been involved in building the hotel were invited, plus a star-studded cast of celebrities headed by Bob Hope. It was a feast— the incredible beauty of a tropical island, happy people wearing colorful Hawaiian clothes, the strains of haunting island music suspended in the balmy air, a continual parade of exotic foods and drinks. When the weekend was over and the plane circled the island and headed toward the mainland, I felt like Cinderella must have felt when the clock struck midnight.

Jim Nabors took us to another party once that beat anything I ever saw in my life. Henry and I had flown to Las Vegas to celebrate our twenty-fifth wedding anniversary as Jim's guests. (Jim was appearing at the Sahara Hotel.) We had a marvelous time. It was a real second honeymoon for Henry and me, and we were ready to go home when Jim said, "No, you've got to go with me to a party in Houston, first."

The party was held on the lawn of the Houston residence of a celebrated Texas couple. It was a very unusual party. The guest of honor was a bull. (Which is obviously why they held the party on the lawn.) Now, I've been to many kinds of parties in my time —from a presidential inaugural ball to hillbilly hoedowns—but I had *never* been to a party for a bull. Of course, this was no ordinary bull. This was Royal Saint, a very fine animal. The couple had purchased him in England, and the party was being held in celebration of that event. Refreshment stands and tables laden with food were set out on the lawn, and the guests were absolutely divine-looking—glamorous women in spectacular designer gowns, escorted by equally handsome men. And there, spotlighted right in the midst of it all, separated from the guests by a white picket fence, his massive neck garlanded with red roses, was Royal Saint. Only in Texas! Only with Jim!

Chapter Twenty-Five

ON a bright April morning in 1967, Henry and I boarded our single-engine Beech Bonanza in Baltimore to fly home to Nashville. We had no inkling that it would be our last flight in that little plane, or Henry's last flight as a pilot. We had no way of knowing that trip would bring an abrupt halt to our wonderful years of flying together in our own plane.

It was a perfect day—clear blue skies, visibility unlimited. The flight from Baltimore, where I'd done a show the night before, had been smooth and pleasant. As usual, I had stuff spread out all over the back seat—Henry always called it my turkey nest—and I was reading *Time* magazine. Normally, Sam would have been back there with me, but fortunately we had left him at home with Mary Cannon. Henry had his maps spread out over the copilot's seat. We had just passed Knoxville and were flying along peacefully at 8,700 feet, enjoying the wonderful euphoria that we always felt being up there alone. Then suddenly, in the blink of an eye, the euphoria vanished and I would have given a pretty penny to be on the ground. Without a sputter of warning our engine stopped dead.

I didn't say a word. Neither did Henry. He had been flying with some of his instruments on automatic, so he quickly but calmly began switching them over to manual, trying to bring the engine back to life. We had five hours of gasoline left, so he knew that wasn't the problem. He moved one control after another. Nothing. The silence was deafening.

No matter how you feel about your pilot—and I would rather have had Henry Cannon at the controls of a plane I was in than any other pilot in the world—it is nevertheless *very* disconcerting to look out the window of a single-engine plane and see the prop just *sitting there*. I personally like the reassurance of a propeller going around so fast it's invisible. This one was horrifyingly visible—as still as it could be.

Henry tried everything—switching gas tanks, doing whatever it is they do to controls under those circumstances—and nothing worked. We still hadn't spoken a word. For once I knew when to keep my mouth shut. I was determined not to say anything for fear I might distract Henry. It was as quiet as if we'd been in a glider.

Normally when we approached our destination Henry would reach back, pat my leg (I was usually asleep) and tell me to put on my seat belt and get ready to land. That gave me time to get out a piece of gum because our little cabin wasn't pressurized. This time when he spoke his voice was just as calm as it had been on those countless other landings. "Fasten your seat belt, honey. I'm going to set this thing down." I promise you he couldn't have sounded more casual if we'd been coming in for a routine landing, and the tone of his voice was enormously soothing.

I fastened my seat belt as tight as I could and looked out the window. What I saw below didn't look too promising as a landing strip. We were right above the interstate (I-40) that runs east and west from Knoxville to Nashville, and it appeared more crowded than I'd ever seen it.

Everything was happening so fast I really didn't have time to think, but I do remember that it never occurred to me to doubt whether Henry could land the plane. I just knew he would. What I didn't know was where. Then I saw he was headed for a short field next to the interstate (every time we drive past that strip of land it seems shorter). Later Henry said that for one split second he had considered landing on the interstate (he had only moments to make up his mind), but he knew he couldn't risk causing an accident there. In order to get us down safely, he had to keep our wings up because the gasoline was stored there and the plane would have exploded if those gas tanks had been ripped open. The tricycle landing gear we had caused the plane to buckle when we landed and the propeller went into the ground, but the wings never touched, so we were able to get out unharmed.

Afterward people asked me if I was praying while Henry was bringing the plane down. Since I believe strongly in prayer and have made it a part of my daily life for as long as I can remember, one would think I would have been praying frantically at that point. But I had complete confidence in Henry's ability to land the plane and I was concentrating so hard on keeping quiet so *he* could concentrate that I never consciously thought about praying. (I hope my religion is a daily thing rather than an "emergency call." When I was a child in the little church in Centerville I loved the song "God Will Take Care of You" and I believe that as firmly now as I did then.) Henry later told his Aunt Cynthia that if I had panicked and started telling him where to land he doesn't know what would have happened.

When news of the forced landing hit the papers we were asked if we'd had a copilot on the flight. Henry said he was the copilot and God had been the pilot. God had planned to let us live. And of course it was Henry's skill at the controls that made it possible for God's plan to be carried out. Later we discovered no mechanical defect had caused the problem. It was just a freak accident. A foreign object—a piece of metal or something—had gotten into the fuel line. A friend offered to loan us his plane to fly back to Nashville that afternoon, but Henry insisted I would be more comfortable on a commercial flight. If I'd known then what I realized later I would have put more pressure on him to pilot us back home, because as it turned out he hasn't flown a plane since.

By the time our Beech Bonanza was repaired a couple of months later, our lifestyle had changed so drastically that there was no longer any reason for us to keep a private aircraft.

Franchise food chains had become prominent, and Henry and I had gone into the fried-chicken business. For the next couple of years my road work was cut to a bare minimum and long tours of one-nighters became a thing of the past. I even cut down my Opry appearances. (The show had gone off the network in 1962, so I no longer had a contract that required me to work every Saturday night.) If we did have to go out of town on business, we used the company plane and pilot, so there has just never been an occasion for Henry to fly me again. Henry may yet pilot planes again, but we can never go back to those nostalgic days of the long tours in our little Beechcraft. Our flying in a single-engine plane on the long trips we made would be impractical now in the jet age.

When I left the one-nighters behind after 27 years, my life became more normal and slowly evolved into what I have now, which my friends say is the best of both worlds. I agree. I don't think my life would be so happy were I not able to enjoy friendships outside of show business as well as retain ties with my fellow performers. I think the two perspectives make my life much more interesting.

Some of my "civilian" friends are girls who date back to my Ward-Belmont days, and we get together weekly to play bridge and tennis. I cherish these friendships from my youth and love the close ties of having shared with them the unique experience of life as a WB girl.

Most of my social life these days focuses on tennis. I took the game up again in 1967—after a 33-year absence—when I came off the road, and I haven't tired of it yet. I play frequently when I'm home, and my tennis friends are among my very favorite people. One of them, Charlotte Beasley, got together with me to form a group called the Charlotte-Pearl Tennis Group. These girls, who range in age from their twenties to their sixties, are from various clubs around town. We hold tournaments each year, and we've even gotten the husbands involved. Our get-togethers have brought me untold pleasure. Thank goodness, Henry likes the game and the crowd as much as I do because our home has become a tennis hangout in the summertime. The girls refer to it as fun city. I luxuriate in the laughter that rings from the court and the poolhouse, with young people running in and out. Being a part of this world helps make up for the fact that I don't have children and grandchildren around to liven things up. (We moved from the house on the hill in Brentwood in 1970, mainly because we wanted a tennis court. Also, we had discovered that a house on a hill is fine for young folks but winter snows complicated matters for us older folks. Walking up that steep hill every time it iced over was too much.)

In the wintertime, Henry and I play mixed doubles every Monday night at the Racquet Club, but never as partners. I know he loves being across the net from me so he can tease me unmercifully when I miss a point.

Henry and I never got caught up in the cocktail party circuit after we left the road. At night we're old homebodies. We have an early dinner, then read or watch television unless there's some function we are absolutely obligated to attend. We prefer a social life that revolves around tennis because it's not only the healthiest at our age, it's also the most fun. It has also been my pleasure to be involved in various civic and charity events now that I have the time. We kid about the fact that I have periodic pet charities —the Humane Shelter, the Heart Association, the Cancer Society —but the one I'm constant with is the Vanderbilt Children's Hospital. I not only work to help it raise funds, I also thoroughly enjoy my visits there to walk the wards and entertain the patients. The children are so precious, and so grateful for the attention.

At home I'm on the go constantly during the daytime, but it's not a pressured pace. The fact that I have the freedom to indulge in all the activities I enjoy is largely due to Mary Cannon's invaluable, irreplaceable position as my household manager. (Sometimes she manages me, too!) It's an interesting coincidence that her last name is the same as ours, because Mary's just like family, and goes back almost as far.

Mary has her own home and comes to ours five days a week, but she always house-sits and/or dog-sits for us when we go out of town, and the secure feeling it gives Henry and me to know she's there taking care of things makes it immeasurably easier for us to leave home.

One of the many important responsibilities Mary has handled for me over the years has been taking care of Minnie's costumes. I now have about 20 Minnie Pearl dresses—one even designed by Bob Mackie (for an Ann-Margret TV special)—and Mary sees to it that they are all kept clean and in repair. For the first 10 years of Minnie's career, I wore only yellow, because it's my favorite color. I was told that in the old vaudeville days yellow was considered an unlucky color for performers to wear, but it was certainly never that for me. When I began doing television the yellow washed out and looked white, so they asked me to wear brighter shades. I now have a rainbow of colors, but the dresses are all basically the same style—puffed sleeves, fitted bodice and a full gathered skirt. I'm still wearing the same one-strap, button Mary Jane shoes I bought at a secondhand store in 1940. The buttons are long gone, and the black leather is so worn I can easily fasten them with a safety pin, so Mary sees to it that I always have a couple of extra pins in my purse when I'm going to work. (I've arranged in my will to leave the shoes to Roy Acuff's museum at Opryland Park.)

In short, at home, I have a relaxed, pleasant life. And, professionally, I have the good fortune to be able to run off and play dates whenever I want to. I would *hate* it if I never got to stand in front of an audience again. That marvelous sound of laughter is like a drug, and I'm totally addicted. When I work now, it's for the sheer fun of it, or the challenge, or just because I want to see my old show biz buddies for a few hours.

One of the challenges I've faced in the past few years has been working in Las Vegas with Roy Clark. The first time I was nervous and apprehensive. I didn't know if the audiences would be my people or not. When I started in the forties and fifties no one in the country field ever thought of playing Las Vegas. It was set apart as a place where country music would not be accepted. Now, of course, country acts are top draws along the Strip. But I was still unsure about Minnie's appeal there. That first night in 1977, I walked through the casino before show time to check out the folks who were waiting in line to get into the show. I wanted to see if they looked like Minnie's kind of crowd. I was surprised to find that they appeared to be almost the same as the Opry fans who line up before each show in Nashville. I found that, contrary to popular opinion, Vegas audiences are not sophisticated. The people at our shows were largely country music fans with only a scattering of curious sophisticates. Tour buses from all over the country roll into Vegas every day carrying visitors like those who roll into Nashville every week to see the Opry. I'm very conscious of this when I do my act in front of a Las Vegas audience, and recognize a rapport with them similar to that I have with Opry audiences. It comes across the footlights in response to Minnie's moth-eaten stories about Grinder's Switch.

The only thing I don't like about working Las Vegas is the hours —going to bed at 3 a.m. and getting up at 10 or 11. I did that for so many years I've had enough of it. At home I'm usually in bed by 10 and up by 7:30. But working with Roy Clark is so much fun it compensates for the turned-around schedule. His performances are sold out during his Vegas engagements no matter who works with him. His charming mischievous-little-boy image combined with his staggering versatility and his sex appeal make him a monster talent. (He also has a sense of humor that absolutely cracks me up!) Roy completely disarms an audience in his first couple of minutes on stage, and keeps them in the palm of his hand until the final bow. He plays practically every instrument and is a virtuoso guitarist; he sings ballads as well as he does up-tempo numbers, and is an excellent stand-up comic. Roy has great timing and I love working with him on stage. I never know what he's going to come out with next, so he keeps me on my toes. It is always a revelation to me to stand in the wings when he's working Vegas and watch him excite the audience and make them fall helplessly in love with him. He should give lessons to other performers. I've learned that working Las Vegas regularly keeps my act alive. It's where big time show biz is at, and I'm delighted that country music is now there, too.

Another great professional pleasure I have is working Hee Haw. The show went into production for CBS-TV in 1969, but it lasted only one season on the network. It was a controversial show, then. Some folks said it was a caricature of country music, and they put it down as such. I didn't agree. I loved it from the first. After it was dropped by CBS (owing to a change in personnel at the network), a group of men who had originated the show got the money together to put it into syndication. It's still going strong, and I hope it will continue indefinitely.

Hee Haw has much the same atmosphere as the Opry shows. There is a free-swinging informality that catches you up in a "let's laugh and have fun" mood. I love the people who run the shows and the regulars who perform on them. (I especially love working with Grandpa Jones. We've been friends for more than 35 years and share a mutual sense of comedy. He is a true professional and a joy to work with.) Hee Haw is taped in Nashville (which is obviously convenient for me) for about two months twice a year, in the spring and fall. I like working on tape because if you mess up you immediately do it again. But sometimes on Hee Haw our "messups" are so good they keep them in the show. The production staff comes in from California to tape the shows, then they take the tapes back to Los Angeles to be edited. It's a highly professional operation done in a deceptively simple manner.

But for me, there's still no place as great to work as the stage at the Grand Ole Opry. We're in a different setting now (the magnificent new Opry House at Opryland Park opened in 1974), but they brought a circled section of the stage from the old Ryman and had it inlaid in the new stage floor to make us old-timers feel at home, and to remind every Opry performer of the ghosts from the past—the all-time country music greats who have stood on those boards.

Every time I work the Opry—which averages about eight times a year—I wonder why I don't visit it more often. It's pure laziness.

After an early dinner, Henry and I find it so much easier to stay at home rather than dress and drive 30 minutes to Opryland.

Of course, the minute I'm there I'm always delighted I made the effort. I cannot adequately express the feeling that washes over me when I stand on that stage. After 40 years it is still just as much a thrill as it was when my whole life revolved around the Opry. It's Minnie's home, and every appearance is steeped in nostalgia and that wonderful, comfortable, *safe* feeling of being with family.

Many performers have said that Opry audiences are hard to play to, and perhaps they are. I've analyzed it over the years and think I know why. These people have usually come a long distance. They've spent the weekend sightseeing and they're already tired when they get to the Opry to line up for the show. Some of them have had reservations for more than a year so their anticipation is running high. Then, when they get inside and are seated, they find all sorts of distractions during the acts. So it takes the audiences a while to focus on what's happening. And this means the performer has to work a little harder. You have to be up and ready to rise above the conditions.

For me there's an added attraction to working the Opry that goes beyond even the overwhelming response the fans give Minnie. It's the joy of being there with Roy Acuff. When Roy introduces me and I walk out into the spotlight, it's as if I were back in the beginning days when every Saturday night was a momentous thrill and a challenge. Roy's introduction in itself moves me beyond words. Henry and I speak of it every time he does it. I get an instant flashback to the days when he was hosting the Prince Albert network portion of the Opry and his final "Cousin Minnie P-E-A-R-L" could shake the rafters! Now he is inclined to get a little sentimental and talk at length about our long years of friendship. I love it. He'll say, "This next little act I'm about to introduce is one of my dearest friends," and I get the same goose bumps every time.

When Roy is on stage with Minnie she can say anything she wants and get away with it. Roy plays the gently reprimanding parent and Minnie, the bad child. If she starts to say something slightly risqué, Roy will say, "Now, Minnie, you be careful." Of course, the audience is immediately pulling for Minnie to tell it. They think they are going to hear something titillating. They urge me on while Roy is shaking his head no. Then I go ahead and tell it and he makes a gesture like he's given up on Minnie. She's so *bad.*

Professionally, I have learned more from Roy Acuff than from any other human being. But he's taught me by doing, not telling. Take, for example, his attitude toward the audiences. He has such respect and love for them. He is always polite and considerate, always willing to talk to them and sign autographs.

In my opinion, Roy is the single most important exponent of country music in the world. The Opry is Roy, and Roy is the Opry. It is not only his career, it's his life. He takes it very seriously. A few years back he had a serious illness. Afterward he told me, "If my doctor had said I couldn't work the Opry anymore, I would have just gotten in my car and started driving south. I couldn't stay around and be near it and not be a part of it." Roy loves the work as much as he loves the fans. During the summertime, when Opryland Park is spilling over with visitors from all over the world, Roy often walks around mixing with the people, signing autographs, just talking. If I had to use one word to describe Roy it would be *dignity.* He brought a certain dignity to the Opry that has nothing to do with his charisma or his talent as a performer. It has to do with his integrity as a man. As Henry says, "He is the King, and there will never be another one."

Roy is a gentleman. He is also modest and unassuming, not an egomaniac like many of us in show business. I remember years ago when I was on the road with him hearing him tell his men, "Now, when we get back to town, if anyone asks you how the shows went, say 'pretty good.' Don't brag about having big houses." You don't brag if you're Roy Acuff. He comes from a good background and his breeding shows. Back in the forties he and his wife, Mildred, who is as charming and delightful a lady as I've ever met, decided to buy their first home. They found one they liked in a lovely section on Hillsboro Road. At that time most of the hillbilly pickers were still living in trailers or small apartments on the other side of town, and they weren't known for their financial stability. The house Roy and Mildred wanted cost $13,500. The real estate man said, "Well, Mr. Acuff, how do you plan to take care of this?" Roy answered modestly, "Would cash be alright?" And that's exactly how he paid for it.

Roy would never admit this, but he's helped more people out of financial difficulty than he can count. If an Opry member needed $5 or $500, Roy Acuff would come to the rescue and never tell a soul about it. I'm sure he never expected to get the money back, either. Roy is the father figure of the Grand Ole Opry and very protective of his "family." I believe it is largely due to his poise as a man, his ethics and the example he has set for us all that the Opry is still thriving after all these years. I'll never forget once walking out of the theater with him when I was still with his act and we passed a beggar sitting by the building. Roy dropped something in the man's upturned hat, so I put in some change, too. Roy said, "Minnie, always remember to share. I know people say some of these beggars can buy and sell you, but I'm superstitious about these things. I feel if you don't share what you've got the Lord will stop it from coming in."

Henry loves Roy and Mildred very much. Roy and Henry are alike in many ways, especially in their attitudes toward women. They both believe in that old code of the hills that a woman is a lady until she proves herself otherwise. I can't imagine either one of them being ungentlemanly around a lady. Not that I want to make Roy sound *too* dignified. He's great fun. He loves a good joke and loves to tell them, but he would never do so if it meant offending a lady. My friendship with him means more to me than words can convey.

A while back I was doing the Opry one Saturday night and I decided to search through my old files for some jokes I haven't done in 25 years. I wanted to find some things to tic in with the Fourth of July. Normally I rely on memory for my Opry routines, but this time I scratched the jokes down on a piece of paper because I hadn't done them in so long I was afraid I'd forget them. I was right! I even forgot the piece of paper and left it in my office. When Roy put me on that night I flubbed the first joke. He and his boys, most of whom had been with him since the early days, just *loved* it. Roy said, "Say that again!" So I tried another gag and goofed that up. Roy really got tickled, then. "Minnie, I never heard you tell that one before," he laughed. And then when I tried a *third* joke and messed it up, I lost it. We all got so tickled I just gave up and went on back to my regular, familiar stuff. The next morning I found the piece of paper with the jokes scribbled on it lying on my desk. I wrote across the bottom: "Just to prove to you I *did* prepare, here are the gags I studied." And I signed it, "I love you very much, Minnie." A few weeks later, I did the Opry again, and when Roy called me back for an encore he took the piece of paper out of his pocket. "I guess you all are wondering what this is," he said to the audience. Then he explained about the gags I had goofed up and the note I sent him as proof of my preparation. "This is the only letter I ever got from Minnie Pearl," he told them. Then he turned to me, "And, Minnie, I intend to keep it the longest day I live." The crowd applauded and just loved it. I said, "Roy, did you notice how I signed the letter?" Then I told the audience what I'd written. "And I mean every word of it," I said. And I do. We carry on a public love affair.

In the past few years I've noticed a difference in the way the fans respond to Minnie. They've always been good to her, laughed at her silly old jokes and made her feel loved, but now I've noticed they want to touch her, kiss her cheek, tell her they love her. One night not long ago I was doing some old routine at a show—really *old* gags—and the audience was just falling out. I stopped and looked at them and said, "Aren't we all silly?" A woman in the audience yelled out, "But we love you, Minnie." I was touched by that. It was so *personal*, and things like that happen frequently when I work. It always takes me right back to those early years when I fought accepting God's plan for me, still holding out for the dream of being a dramatic actress. I didn't appreciate Minnie. She was just a stopgap until I could get what I wanted, something I would settle for until my *real* destiny came to pass. It took me a long time to realize that my real destiny *was* Minnie, and that God had been leading me in the right direction all along, as He always does. I've run into many people over the years who felt they had failed because they had never reached a certain goal they had set for themselves. What I've come to see is that many of us were never intended to reach the goals *we* set, because God has another plan. I've learned that when we stop thinking that what we've got is second best and make it the *best*, our "failure" turns into success. For me, it evolved as Minnie Pearl being the very goal I had wanted to achieve. At 28, I thought I was a failure only because I wouldn't accept what I was. I would never have been a great dramatic actress. I was always Minnie Pearl, a plain, country girl comic poking fun at herself and sharing it with others. When I learned to accept that role, the one God had given me, He turned my failure into success.

I know many people scoff at the idea of God having some divine plan for our lives, but I believe it. There have been so many times in my life when things could have turned out differently that I can't accept any other explanation. Like the time in 1947 when I had the opportunity to leave the Opry to become a regular on Vaughn Monroe's popular radio show the Camel Caravan. The William Esty Agency handled this show as well as the Opry network show because both were sponsored by the R. J. Reynolds Tobacco Company. They put me on the show for several weeks, then offered me a permanent spot. By that time I was married to Henry and I certainly wasn't interested in leaving Nashville and moving to New York. They hired Irene Ryan instead, who later became Granny on the Beverly Hillbillies. If I hadn't been married to Henry I don't know whether I would have taken that job or not. New York was, after all, the big time (*Broadway*, and all that) and Vaughn Monroe's show one of the most popular on radio. At the time, the offer represented a prestigious step upward. Yet I know Minnie Pearl could never have become the institution they claim she is in country music had I left the Opry, and Sarah Ophelia Colley Cannon would have missed the best time of her life! I used to say I stood beside Minnie. But she has become like my child, and I'm able to look over her shoulder and see her more clearly, more objectively, and to love her.

This faith in destiny goes back to my Christian upbringing, my "pot-bellied stove" religion. Our little Methodist church in Centerville was heated by a pot-bellied stove, and you were either very hot or very cold, depending on where you sat. Life then was just that simple, and my beliefs are simple. I don't try to analyze the Bible or philosophize about religion. I believe in the golden rule and try to live my life as best I can. I don't know what sins the Lord is going to hold me accountable for, but I agree with a preacher friend here in Nashville, Jeff Fryer, who says too many people live with the theory of preparing for death when we should be living preparing for life. (Henry and I are active members of the Brentwood United Methodist Church in our area and we love it.) I believe in Heaven, but I'm no longer sure what it is. There's a beautiful passage by Anne Tyler in *Searching for Caleb* that says, "I used to think Heaven was palatial. I was told it had pearly gates and the streets were paved with gold. But now I hope they are wrong about that. I would prefer to find that Heaven is a small town with a bandstand in the park and a great many trees, and I would know everybody in it and none of them would ever die or move away or age or alter." I can't think of a Heaven more appealing than that.

I remember going through a phase when I became concerned about whether or not I was saved. There was a nice lady who walked around Centerville when I was a child asking people if they were saved. She meant well but she always wore black and talked doom, about how we were all going to hell if we didn't live right. One day I asked Mama why this lady was so unhappy if she was sure she was going to Heaven. I was too young to understand, then, that there are people who are just hyped on the subject of doom and because of it they don't find joy in their religion. I wasn't raised that way. When I asked Mama, "At what point in our lives do we feel we are saved?" she said, "There is no one point. It's a day-to-day proposition. You work at it every day." Before she died, when she was up in her eighties, I said, "Mama, have you changed your idea about reaching a point where you feel saved?" She said, "Never. Each day is a challenge and we are tested each day."

Mama's death in 1963 was easier for me to bear because I knew the strength of her faith, and I knew she was ready. When I lost her it was like losing two people—a mother and a child. She had been my responsibility for so long that I felt our relationship had been reversed. The time had come when she was going to have to leave her little house in Centerville that she loved so dearly and move up to Nashville. She could no longer be allowed to live alone because of her blindness and her age. She didn't want to make the move and I knew it, but we had no alternative. I was in Gaithersburg, Maryland, working a fair date when my sister called to say they had put Mama in the Centerville Hospital and she thought I'd better come. Henry and I flew home at once.

I don't know if Mama knew us when we got there. I hope so. She had suffered fibrillations of the heart, and the doctor said she might have had others from time to time and not told us. She never mentioned any illness for fear we'd start talking about moving her. She lived only a few days after we got there, and she was in and out of a coma. When she finally died on August 27, 1963, it was still a blow even though we were expecting it. She was 89 and seemed so indomitable, so indestructible. We always said she'd outlive us all. After her death we took her back to her hometown Franklin to lie beside Daddy. They're both happy together in Heaven, where I like to think of them as young and in love, as they were when Daddy brought her to Centerville as a bride.

Dixie's death in 1967 was more difficult for me to accept, because she was still so young and she had two sons and a husband who needed her. I felt a great deal of anger when she died, but my anger was directed at the cancer that killed her, not at God. We had remained close and I absolutely adored her. But I wanted her gone if I couldn't have her back the way she was when she was well, and I didn't want to see her suffer. She was never really strong in her later years, but she worked hard on their farm and loved it. She became ill in the winter of 1966 and the cancer moved with horrifying rapidity. It was my first experience of seeing the ravages of that disease close at hand, and it is a devastating monster. It was one of the saddest times of my life to see her go as she did. I wanted to cling to her, to try to hold her back. I depended on her so much. Even in all her pain toward the end, her eyes would light up when we talked of the old days and our idyllic childhood. It was such a comfort to me to know that a similar idyllic life had extended on for her through adulthood. The love affair between her and her husband, Wash, was an inspiration to all who knew them. Their love seemed eternally fresh. He died in the summer of 1979 and I know they had a joyous reunion. We are sustained by that thought.

Since religion was so much a part of my life as a child, and since my childhood was so happy and so full of laughter and joy, I associate the two. Even my concept of Jesus goes along with this association of happiness and religion. I don't agree with the image many Christians have of Christ as the sad, tragic man depicted in most religious paintings. You can't tell me He didn't laugh, or that He wasn't happy. I think He had a great sense of humor. I even have a picture of a laughing Christ a fan sent me. If He had walked along the Sea of Galilee with a look of doom on His face I don't believe for a minute all those people would have followed Him. I think they found such joy in His presence they were willing to leave everything behind to go with Him. I'm certain He knew the value of humor and the power of a smile.

The importance of smiling was brought home to me not long ago at my local supermarket. I had something on my mind and was lost in thought while going through the motions of putting things in my basket. A woman I know casually, passed me, then turned around again and did a double take. "Oh, Minnie Pearl," she said, "I didn't recognize you. You weren't smiling." It struck me that I have an obligation to smile. Everyone's obligation is different, but mine has to do with humor and smiling. God wouldn't have given me Minnie Pearl if He hadn't intended me to use her to make people smile or laugh. From time to time when I'm sitting at my desk, my eyes fall on this framed quotation:

> I expect to pass through this world but once. Any good there-fore, that I can do, or any kindness that I can show to any fellow creature, let me do it now. Let me not defer nor neglect it, for I shall not pass this way again.

What a wonderful world this would be if all of us could live by this philosophy!

Chapter Twenty-Six

Broadway has its Tony, the movies have Oscar, the television has Emmy, but to those of us associated with country music a CMA award is the most coveted, most prestigious honor of all.

The Country Music Association was founded in 1958 by a group of music industry leaders and executives for the purpose of gaining international recognition for country music. Under the inspired leadership of executive director Jo Walker, CMA quickly received enthusiastic support from the people in our business, and it has done an impressive job of promoting country music worldwide, as well as helping it to attain general acceptance that was often missing in the early days.

In 1961, CMA began naming certain performers to the Country Music Hall of Fame, the highest honor in our business. Since the candidates for this very special recognition are nominated by an anonymous panel of 200 electors (all of whom have been in the business at least 15 years and have made some noteworthy contribution of their own to country music), it represents the epitome of peer recognition, and is obviously coveted by all who love and perform in our field. I was no exception. From the time the honor was first given, I wanted very much to be in that select group. It wasn't just the promise of a bronze plaque with my picture and name engraved on it hanging for posterity in a special room at the Country Music Hall of Fame on Music Row; it wasn't even the thrill of receiving such heartwarming recognition from my peers that made me want it so much. Both those reasons played a part, but there was more. It was somehow tied up in my mind with a validation of my career, of giving public sanction to this silly ole country girl, Minnie Pearl, whom Sarah Ophelia Colley had rejected for so many years while she clung to her dream of dramatic greatness. Perhaps it was Minnie's sweet revenge—"Showed *you*, didn't I, Sarah?"—or just her desire to be up there with the best in her business, but whatever vague, yet deeply felt, motivations prompted the desire, I *wanted* that honor.

From the beginning, I was always in the top 20 nominees named by the committee, but I somehow couldn't make it to the finals. Jimmie Rodgers was the first to be named to the Hall of Fame. Hank Williams, Roy Acuff, Eddy Arnold, Judge George D. Hay, Uncle Dave Macon, Bob Wills, Bill Monroe, Pee Wee King —so many of my contemporaries followed. But Minnie's name was never called. By 1967 they had begun giving annual CMA awards in various categories—Male and Female Vocalist of the Year, Best Single, Best Album, etc.—and in 1968 they began televising the show. By this time the voting system had become more sophisticated, so they ended up each year with five finalists for the Hall of Fame honor. Each year when it came time to announce the winner the camera would pan the faces of all the hopefuls, and it was sheer torture to sit there knowing several million people were watching while you tried not to appear as eager as you were, and later, when you tried not to show your disappointment in losing.

For five years, every CMA award show brought Minnie the same anticipation, the same disappointment. Each time I would sit there in full camera view in the first few rows of the auditorium as the announcement was about to be made, hoping to hear my name called. Henry hated it. Because they requested that nominees be accompanied by their spouses, he had to sit through it, too. I don't know which he hated worse—the fact that I never won and he shared my disappointment, or the fact that he never knew when the television cameras might zoom in on us. Henry despises the limelight and will go to almost any length to avoid putting himself there.

Even Roy Acuff became disgusted with my annual also-ran position. He finally said, "Minnie, it's not right for you to sit out there every year and go through all that. I'm not gonna let you do it again. Next year I'll sit out there for you."

The next year, in 1975, I was nominated again, and again I knew I'd have to sit out there and go through it all. By this time, however, I had convinced myself that I hadn't been put into the Hall of Fame because Minnie is a *comic*, not a singer, and it is, after all, the Country *Music* Hall of Fame. I had accepted this reasoning and resigned myself to the fact that it would undoubtedly be many years down the road before they decided to recognize comedy in such an outstanding way. Henry had no doubt that I would eventually go into the Hall of Fame. His concern was whether it was going to be during my lifetime, and that prompted him to declare he wanted no part of it.

That afternoon when he took me out to the Opry House for rehearsals he was dressed casually and told me he wasn't going to sit out front with me, I was so certain I wasn't going to win that I didn't even try to change his mind. I was a presenter that year, so I had to be there early for rehearsal. Normally Henry would drop me off backstage, then go home and change into his tuxedo and come back in time for the show. But this time he came on in with me. I was waiting for my rehearsal call when Jo Walker approached me backstage. She had already seen Henry, and immediately noticed how he was dressed. She told me later that she was absolutely panic-stricken and had had to force herself to slow down when she approached me. (Jo is the only person outside the accounting firm that counts votes who knows the winners ahead of time.)

"Henry brought his tux with him for tonight, didn't he?" she asked me.

I said, "No, he didn't. He says he's not going to sit out there again this year."

We went on and talked about something else for a minute before they called me for rehearsal. I didn't realize that Jo was in a panic. As soon as she got away from me she ran looking for Henry. I had already accepted that he wasn't going to be there. He's like a bull when he takes a notion to do or not to do something, and I wouldn't even have attempted to change his mind. But Jo was shrewd. She got to him by saying how bad it would look for me on national television if the cameras panned me and I was sitting there alone. (With the marital situation as tenuous as it is in show business, I guess she was afraid the fans would think Henry and I had split.)

Rehearsals took all afternoon. Then we had a break before the show. Henry said, "I'm going on home to feed Heidi and then I'll be back later."

I was sitting in Roy's dressing room when he and Mildred came in dressed formally for the show. Roy said, "Where's Henry?" I said, "He's not going to sit out there tonight. He doesn't want to go through it again." Roy said, "Well, I don't blame him a bit." About that time Henry walked in wearing his tux, so it was obvious he had changed his mind. Roy said, "I don't blame you for feeling the way you do. It's embarrassing." Then he turned to me. "Now, truthfully, Minnie, I don't think you're going to get it this year, either. They've got Ernie Ford here as the Hall of Fame presenter, and Merle Travis is one of the nominees, and he wrote Ernie's biggest hit 'Sixteen Tons.' I believe Merle will get it this year." I was certain Roy was right.

I was copresenting the Single of the Year Award with Billy "Crash" Craddock. We kidded a little bit—Minnie told him she wanted to get him alone backstage—before we read off the nominees. The winner was Freddie Fender for "Before the Next Teardrop Falls," and the audience gave him a warm response. With that over, I went out front to sit with Henry. Finally it came time for the high point of the night—the moment when the Hall of Fame winner would be announced. Tennessee Ernie Ford came on stage to make the presentation. The bronze plaque, draped in blue velvet, had been placed on an easel beside the podium. Expectation and anticipation was running high in the audience, but I promise you I was not among the anxious. I just wanted it to be over. Like Roy, I was certain Merle Travis would receive the 1975 Hall of Fame honor.

Ernie first said that he was thrilled to be making this particular presentation. Then he said, "This performer joined the Opry in 1940 . . ." and I knew that it had to be me. No one else had been around that long except Roy and Bill, and they were both already in the Hall of Fame.

After all those years of disappointment it had finally happened! On the night when I least expected it, the honor was mine.

It's hard to describe how I felt in that brief time as Ernie continued the presentation. As a drowning man is said to review his life in the seconds before he dies, so I seemed, in these few seconds, to review my struggles to reach that point.

I saw the fine-drawn young girl—so desperately anxious to please—when I worked for Mr. Sewell; the frantic efforts to survive in a man's world those early years on the Opry before Henry; the long, hard years on the road; and then that surge of joy hit me —it was *all* worth it!

Tears sprang to my eyes and I turned quickly to kiss Henry. For an instant, as I stood up, I tried to pull him on stage with me, but he held back. I had so wanted to be cool and gracious when I won, to give a clever, inspiring acceptance speech like the one Shirley Booth gave when she won her Oscar for *Come Back, Little Sheba*. She said, "The road upward has been steep and hard at times, but the view has been lovely all the way!"

I had written several speeches over the years, but moths had eaten them by this time. Even if I'd had one with me, I would have been too shaken to say it. All I could think of was getting off quickly so we wouldn't run overtime on live television. I was so emotionally undone all I could say was, "Thank you . . . to all the people who made this possible, thank you, and God bless you all."

For the next few weeks the outpouring of love and happiness from my fans and friends was overwhelming. Everyone seemed to want me to know they were happy, too, and that made the honor all the more meaningful. Henry was so happy for me he even allowed himself to be interviewed on local television that night. Then, believe it or not, he turned to the camera and said, "I want to say hello to all my friends and neighbors in television land." We've always kidded about that line because the oldtimers used to say it whenever the camera turned to them, but, coming from Henry, it was completely unexpected and very funny—typical of the way he continues to surprise me.

When they talked to me for the local TV news that night, I told them, "The Lord has been good to me. He gave me 28 years with Henry and 35 years in country music," and I meant every word.

The Lord gave me something else, too, and I'll never take it lightly—the knack for making people laugh. Being a clown hasn't always been easy, and it certainly wasn't the role I saw myself playing when I was a girl all full of grandiose dreams and ambitions, but it is the most satisfying role of all.

There is no way to close a book like this. As my life goes on, so do my experiences, which I trust help me continue to grow. I think of this, then, as a pause for reflection, not as the end of a story.

People always ask me, "Where is Grinder's Switch?"

As I grow older the place is no longer a little, abandoned loading switch on a railroad in Hickman County. Grinder's Switch is a state of mind—a place where there is no illness, no war, no unhappiness, no political unrest, no tears. It's a place where there's only happiness—where all you worry about is what you're going to wear to the church social, and if your feller is going to kiss you in the moonlight on the way home.

I wish for all of you a Grinder's Switch.